Studies in American Popular History and Culture

Edited by
Jerome Nadelhaft
University of Maine

A Routledge Series

Studies in American Popular History and Culture

Jerome Nadelhaft, *General Editor*

Studies in the Land
The Northeast Corner
David C. Smith

First Do No Harm
Empathy and the Writing of Medical Journal Articles
Mary E. Knatterud

Piety and Power
Gender and Religious Culture in the American Colonies, 1630-1700
Leslie Lindenauer

Race-ing Masculinity
Identity in Contemporary U.S. Men's Writing
John Christopher Cunningham

Crime and the Nation
Prison Reform and Popular Fiction in Philadelphia, 1786-1800
Peter Okun

Food in Film
A Culinary Performance of Communication
Jane Ferry

Deconstructing Post-WWII New York City
The Literature, Art, Jazz, and Architecture of an Emerging Global Capital
Robert Bennett

Rethinking the Red Scare
The Lusk Committee and New York's Crusade against Radicalism, 1919-1923
Todd J. Pfannestiel

Hollywood and the Rise of Physical Culture
Heather Addison

Homelessness in American Literature
Romanticism, Realism, and Testimony
John Allen

No Way of Knowing
Crime, Urban Legends, and the Internet
Pamela Donovan

The Making of the Primitive Baptists
A Cultural and Intellectual History of the Antimission Movement, 1800-1840
James R. Mathis

Women and Comedy in Solo Performance
Phillis Diller, Lily Tomlin, and Roseanne
Suzanne Lavin

The Literature of Immigration and Racial Formation
Becoming White, Becoming Other, Becoming American in the Late Progressive Era
Linda Joyce Brown

Popular Culture and the Enduring Myth of Chicago, 1871–1968
Lisa Krissoff Boehm

America's Fight over Water
The Environmental and Political Effects of Large-Scale Water Systems
Kevin Wehr

Daughters of Eve
Pregnant Brides and Unwed Mothers in Seventeenth Century Massachusetts
Else L. Hambleton

Narrative, Political Unconscious, and Racial Violence in Wilmington, North Carolina
Leslie H. Hossfeld

Children and the Criminal Law in Connecticut, 1635–1855
Changing Perceptions of Childhood
Nancy Hathaway Steenburg

Children and the Criminal Law in Connecticut, 1635–1855

Changing Perceptions of Childhood

Nancy Hathaway Steenburg

Routledge
New York & London

Published in 2005 by
Routledge
270 Madison Avenue
New York, NY 10016
www.routledge-ny.com

Published in Great Britain by
Routledge
2 Park Square
Milton Park, Abingdon
Oxon OX14 4RN
www.routledge.co.uk

10 9 8 7 6 5 4 3 2 1

Library of Congress Cataloging-in-Publication Data

Steenburg, Nancy Hathaway.
Children and the criminal law in Connecticut, 1635-1855 : changing perceptions of childhood / by Nancy Hathaway Steenburg.
p. cm. -- (Studies in American popular history and culture)
Includes bibliographical references and index.
ISBN: 978-0-4159-7180-5

1. Juvenile delinquents--Legal status, laws, etc.--Connecticut--History. 2. Juvenile courts--Connecticut--History. 3. Juvenile justice, Administration of--Connecticut--History. 4. Children--Legal status, laws, etc.--Connecticut--History. 5. Criminal law--Connecticut--History. I. Title. II. Series: American popular history and culture (Routledge (Firm)

KFC4195.S74 2005
345.746'08--dc22 2005018103

Contents

Acknowledgments

In completing this book, I have had the advantage of the generous support and wisdom of many people. R. Kent Newmyer, my doctoral dissertation advisor, has been invaluable all along the way, offering his insights into the complexities of American Law, his skillful suggestions to help me strengthen and clarify my arguments, and his sense of humor to help me through. Irene Q. Brown, Richard D. Brown, and Cornelia Hughes Dayton all provided generously of their time and insights.

I owe Glenn Weaver, late of Trinity College, a tremendous thank you for introducing me to the fascination of original court records as a source for understanding American history and for encouraging me to pursue my goals.

I am indebted to the University of Connecticut Department of History for its support of my research with the Harry Marks Fellowship, the Albert E. and Wilda E. Van Dusen Scholarship, the Edward Victor Gant Scholarship, the History Department Graduate Student Teaching Award, and a doctoral dissertation fellowship. I am also indebted to Robert Asher and the Association for the Study of Connecticut History for the opportunity to present papers that emerged from my research.

Because I practically lived in the archives of the Connecticut State Library while researching state court records, I am grateful for the service and support provided by the staff members, especially Kevin Johnson who retrieved hundreds of boxes of files and papers with never a complaint. I am also grateful for insights offered by Dr. Mark H. Jones, State of Connecticut Archivist.

Since this book concerns the legal rights of children, I am perhaps most indebted to my two sons for their love and support as I worked on it. To their encouragement and understanding, I owe my persistence.

Introduction

> New claims will arise: . . . lads from twelve to twenty-one will think their rights not enough attended to.
>
> —John Adams, *Correspondence,* 1776

> It is an anomalous and incredible fact that there is almost no case or statutory law setting forth the rights of children.
>
> —Lois G. Forer, *The Rights of Children,* 1973

In the early stages of my research and writing on the legal rights of children, both fellow historians and curious friends asked an obvious question: "Why study children?" Children lack property, power, and political influence. They have always been at the periphery of society and, at least in the past, have had little impact on public policy. Nevertheless, I was interested in discovering how the American legal system, justly renowned for abiding by the rule of law and providing legal protection to adults, had dealt with the majority of its populace because, in truth, all United States citizens were once children.[1] After exhaustive research in the archives of the State of Connecticut, covering the period from Connecticut's settlement until just prior to the outbreak of the Civil War, I have concluded that understanding how society treated its most powerless members is critically important to understanding American society as a whole. Furthermore, as David J. Rothman has asserted in his studies of both reform and childhood in America, the understanding of children and childhood is central to understanding the social transformation of America.[2]

Even among historians who have investigated the history of childhood, few initially looked beneath the surface to ascertain the actual experience of children. Broad sweeping generalizations that lumped the lives of children in with the lives of the adults who controlled them were common. For a long time the idea persisted that children had no distinct identity, that adults treated them like little men and women. Those writers who admitted that some differentiation did occur nevertheless said that the modern "cult of the child" did not begin until the middle of the eighteenth century, under the influence of new ideas advanced by Jean Jacques Rousseau. In his landmark study of childhood, Philippe Aries provided a once widely accepted but flawed view of childhood, asserting that Europeans in the middle ages and early modern period had no concept of a separate period of childhood. Aries' major error was that he reached many of his conclusions by examining how Europeans viewed children but used the life course and experiences of the future Louis XIII of France as his source of evidence. Few of Aries' contemporaries questioned whether the life of a future king resembled the lives of ordinary children.[3]

When historians began to examine the experience of children on the American scene, many initially supported Aries' questionable analysis. John Demos, who had cogently challenged the Aries thesis by saying it did not accurately reflect the life experience of ordinary children, nevertheless assumed that adults in Plymouth, Massachusetts did not view children as a distinct segment of society, having special capacities or needs. Bernard Faber continued Demos' argument, asserting that once children reached the age of six or seven, parents expected them to behave "like little adults." Other historians accepted Aries' evidence from portraiture and asserted that since seventeenth and eighteenth-century artists painted American children dressed in adult clothing to appear as little adults, society had no separate conception of childhood. Michael Zuckerman even went so far as to claim that children in colonial-era Massachusetts "were part of a single undifferentiated community." With this rather wide rejection of the idea of a distinct identity for children, few historians saw the need to investigate the legal status of children because children had no separate legal identity. In this narrow interpretation, legally a child was but a "servant to whose services a father had an absolute right;" thus the best interests of adults were also the best interests of the children. Furthermore, this interpretation of the legal position of children assumed, "the legal identity of children (like that of women) had been wholly subsumed within a strictly patriarchal logic, under the male heads of the families."[4]

By the early 1980s, a number of historians began a new examination of societal attitudes toward American childhood and children; most acknowledged that from the beginning of American settlement, adults did recognize several distinct periods of childhood. Moreover, that recognition meant that adults did not treat children uniformly from birth to the age of twenty-one. Nevertheless, some scholars continued to claim that as treatment of children changed over time, the most dramatic changes took place after the American Revolution. Others perceived that in many areas, including the courts and the law, gradual changes in colony and state laws and legal procedures were a result of the changing perception of children. Still other historians of childhood such as Linda Pollack have argued against what she called evolutionary change, asserting that, at least in the area of child-rearing practices, there was little dramatic shift because the "method of child care was an enduring one."[5]

With this new approach toward adult attitudes concerning children, historians began to look for the authentic experience of childhood, reworking old sources and searching for new ones. In this effort Ray Hiner advocated extending research into four new areas: the attitudes of adults toward children, the conditions that contributed to child development, the subjective experience of children themselves, and finally the impact that children have had on adult lives and attitudes.[6] While Hiner's new approach would certainly be more helpful in discovering the reality of children's lives than studying iconography or adult descriptions of childhood, implementing it meant finding sources that provided an authentic record of children's voices and their lives.

The legal records of the seventeenth, eighteenth, and nineteenth centuries comprise one such potential source. Not only do legal statutes and court cases illuminate the changes in the perceptions of children; they also reveal actual alterations in the way society dealt with its most helpless members. Furthermore, court documents often provide the authentic voices of children themselves in depositions, pleas, and petitions. Therefore, a close exploration of the statutes, trials, and appeals, especially the details of case law with its procedures, judgments, and responses, will show examples of how adults viewed children and how they dealt with them across the range of human activity. An analysis of contracts, inheritance, torts, and the criminal law can be a benchmark for determining the authenticity of other sources on children.

This focus varies from that taken by historians who have looked for the meaning of childhood through the lens of the law. Some have taken only a cursory look at case law and have concluded, basing their conclusions almost entirely on statutes, that children in the colonial period did not have a distinct legal identity independent of their parents, and that the colonial and early national legal cultures provided few rights or protections to those under the age of twenty-one. Under this interpretation, parents, especially fathers, were the chief agents of social control, so that children themselves rarely faced criminal prosecution. Courts were there to back families up when they could not maintain order or fulfill their designated responsibilities.[7] According to Michael Grossberg, pre-Revolutionary custody law considered children as "dependent, subordinate beings" and provided fathers vested rights over those children. While Grossberg's study illuminated many areas of law as they affected the relationship between children and the adults, he apparently accepted without question that American law followed the British common law tradition. He claimed that in the eighteenth-century Blackstone's *Commentaries*, nowhere was there "a hint that the common law regarded the child as an individual with distinctive legal status." Nevertheless, Grossberg did suggest that seventeenth-century colonial court systems had begun to assume jurisdiction over the estates and persons of minors, apparently when the parents failed to fulfill the duties owed to children. This interference took place under the doctrine of *parens patriae*, the concept that the state was the ultimate parent of all children and could interfere with parental custody "when the morals, safety or interests of the children require it."[8]

While George Lee Haskins has viewed this intervention as an important measure of social control, backed by the courts, he denied that such intervention by the authorities actually recognized the need to protect the children from economic or social harm caused by parental actions or neglect.[9] In contrast, Everett Goodwin claimed that in Connecticut the rapid changes in laws on inheritance, guardianship, and apprenticeship forced the legal system to establish a special status for children under the law to protect them.[10] Yet despite the evidence of some statutes that designated such a special status, any protection such laws provided to children was largely academic according to Howard Cohen, who has claimed that children, ostensibly the focus of adult protection for over three hundred years, faced courts that rarely protected the rights of minors.[11]

Looking at the disagreement over the significance of statutes in establishing legal status and protection for children, little is clear beyond the fact of that disagreement. Certainly previous legal historians have noted the gradual maturation and formalization of the law from the colonial period into the nineteenth century that might lead to consistency in legal practices.[12] As a result I expected to find a shift in the way the courts treated children and anticipated that by the nineteenth century, there would be regularity in the way the state dealt with children who broke the law. Instead, case law revealed that adults continued to struggle with what to do about children, vacillating from a strict law-and-order approach to a concern for the impact of punishment on children's potential as upstanding citizens of the republic. The lack of a consistent attitude toward children who transgressed the standards of their communities appeared to reflect an ongoing social and racial bias, perhaps, as Cornelia Dayton has suggested, a change in the focus on private life amongst the rising middle class.[13]

Indeed, the sources for this study revealed that children of prominent or affluent white families often received lenient treatment from judges and juries. At the same time they obtained procedural protections of their legal rights that the court system appeared to neglect when trying black, Native American, Irish, or poor children. The bias may not have always been intentional. Adults in poorer families had fewer interactions with the laws, courts, and the legal system. Cases involving real estate, contracts, and challenges to wills comprised the majority of litigation in both the colonial and early national period in Connecticut. Because less affluent people had little property to protect and fewer opportunities to enter into contracts or to initiate lawsuits over inheritance, they were probably far less familiar with the procedures and protections inherent in the law. This inexperience could easily have extended to their knowledge of the rights or protections provided minors by the courts.

This study of children and the law differs from previous overviews of the legal rights of children by starting with the case law. I have examined all the legal documents available in a single venue. Because of the nature of the task, I initially limited my study to the legal records of New London County, Connecticut from the beginning of Connecticut's legal system in 1639 until 1855, the date of the first year of the Connecticut Reform School for Boys. This entailed reading an extensive collection of justice of the peace records, and trial dockets, case documents, and files from the New London County Superior and County courts. When Bruce Mann investigated the legal culture of early Connecticut, he was able to skim the majority of the cases and read about ten percent in detail.[14] Since children appeared in fewer than three percent of all cases recorded in the various court dockets, any type of sampling might literally have missed the evidence of children's interaction with the legal culture. Thus I had to read every case to determine if either the plaintiffs or the defendants were under the age of twenty-one.

A further problem is the fragmentary nature of vital statistics records, especially from the seventeenth century. I have omitted many promising cases because there was no way to confirm the age of the miscreant. A prime example is the lawless career of Alexander Pygan, who arrived in New London in 1666 from Norwich, England. In her *History of New London,* Frances Caulkins called him a "lawless young man" who had "left his country for his country's good." In 1667 his name appeared on the New London County Court docket for "enticing away the affections of Robera Redfin's daughter" and for fathering Elizabeth Walker's child, both crimes against public order typical of young men who were under the age of twenty-one. The court sent him to jail, apparently because he was unable to pay the fines and court costs. A few years later Pygan paid a five-pound fine for selling liquor to the Indians and a one-pound fine for recklessly shooting Ann Latimer's horse. Pygan might have been a minor when he committed these crimes, because the town did not grant him a license to practice his trade of tanning until 1669; usually apprentices who had not completed their terms would not have been able to obtain permission to practice independently. However, New London town records indicate that he married in 1667 and had achieved respectability of sorts when he became a town grand juror in 1674. (To be a grand juror he would have to have been an admitted freeman, over the age of twenty-one.) When he died in 1700, no one recorded his age. From his career from lawlessness to respectability, it is clear the community did not hold his early transgressions against him, but it was not clear whether he was a minor when he first upset the public order.[15] Perusing the minutiae of all the cases provides insight into the multiple ways in which children came into contact with the law and the legal culture in Connecticut, and convinced me that children had a distinct legal status in both the colony and the state. Finally, early court documents provided a vital record of adult voices and attitudes toward children.[16] Similarly, they provided the voices and direct experience of children as they went into apprenticeships, as they sought protection from abuse, or as they faced the majesty and power of the criminal law.

Having verified the presence of minors in the county legal records, I turned to the records of the Connecticut General Assembly to ascertain what part colonial and state laws played a part in creating and modifying the legal status of children. What I hoped to find was an understanding of the source of legal changes in the status of children, namely: was court-made law the most important in determining the change in the way the legal culture treated children, or did the black-letter law of the legislators create policy concerning children that the courts implemented as they saw fit? Was the law open to change, permitting magistrates and judges discretion to deal with new situations as they arose in the courts, or did legal precedent direct decisions? Did judicial law merely reflect changes already initiated by society as claimed by Christine Stansell and Constance Schulz?[17] What was the role of Connecticut's legislature in "interfering," after the fact with both statute and court-made law when children petitioned the Assembly for clemency or mercy?

In 1795 Connecticut legal commentator Zephaniah Swift wrote that in no state outside Connecticut was "it more arduous and difficult to obtain a systematic understanding of the law." Even so the cases and statutes showed clearly that children did indeed have a distinct status before the law from the beginning of Connecticut's legal system. Some of the earliest laws mandated education for all children, prohibited minors from using tobacco without a doctor's order, prohibited youths from entering into contracts, mandated the death sentence for boys of sixteen or older if they struck or disobeyed their parents, and exempted youths under fifteen from the consequences of committing either sodomy or arson. Together the cases and statutes revealed a legal system that had not one but many ways of dealing with children who broke the laws or needed the protection of the courts. Yet, ironically, in thousands of cases the Connecticut legal system stood ready to protect the property of minors, but it did not protect children from physical or sexual abuse. The only early law concerning protection against cruelty prohibited cruelty "towards any brute creature . . . usually kept for the use of man."[18]

My investigation treats primarily the criminal law, both cases where children themselves transgressed against community standards by breaking the Sabbath, stealing, lying, rioting, murdering, fornicating, raping, or other crimes and cases in which children themselves were the victims of crime, especially of the crimes of physical and sexual abuse. Chapter one examines crimes against property such as theft, burglary, or arson. Chapter two investigates crimes against persons ranging from assault to manslaughter and murder, and chapter three looks at crimes against public order such as Sabbath breaking, disturbing the peace, disobedience to parents, or fornication. Next, chapter four presents cases in which children sought remedies for physical abuse by masters, employers, or parents, revealing a legal culture that took a very long time to put the protection of minors above the right of parents to treat them as they wished. The fifth chapter examines the evidence concerning the sexual abuse of children and the development of the idea that children needed protection from sexual predators. Within each chapter, I have examined the changes in criminal procedures, the protections, or lack of protections, provided to children involved in criminal prosecutions, and the shift in attitude toward punishment for crime from restitution, to retribution, and, in the nineteenth century, to the concept of rehabilitation. I have also investigated the changing attitudes toward child abuse and the gradual development of the idea that *parens patriae* encompassed protecting children not merely from parental failure to mold them into moral citizens but also involved protecting them from parental abuse.

The final chapter concerns changing attitudes about the nature of children and society's responsibilities toward them that became evident in an active reform movement that gradually saw child law-breakers as patients to be cured, not as desperate criminals to be punished severely. This changing attitude reflected not only the reform impulse that influenced much of America's middle class in the nineteenth century; it also revealed the impact of ideas from the Enlightenment on the nature of children and the importance of the belief in the value of education to mold young citizens for the Republic.

Puritan religious ideals originally played an important role in the way the legal system in Connecticut initially treated children. Changes in the influence of religion on Connecticut's residents gradually appeared in the transformation of the attitude toward the criminal responsibility of children. Charles Andrews and other historians of the colony's early history have pointed out Connecticut was a Puritan commonwealth in which the Congregational Church had an important impact on society and law. As Everett Goodwin put it, Connecticut's founders intended "to promote and encourage the Puritan vision of future social and political development" with the result that the early courts were "a marriage of church and magistrate."[19] As a result of that vision, law and order took on important overtones of religion, starting with a belief in the innate sinfulness of human beings. Indeed, most of Connecticut's early capital laws came directly from Biblical authority with citations to the appropriate Old Testament sources. For example, the law against sodomy derived from Leviticus, while the regulation of stubborn children came down from Deuteronomy.[20] Furthermore, the formulaic language of indictments often labeled accused criminals of being in league with the devil. When Connecticut made the transition from a Puritan society to a more secular community in the eighteenth and nineteenth centuries, a transformation that took place in much of New England,[21] the sharp edges of the criminal law system softened, and gradually laws began to differentiate between children and adults, especially with respect to legal responsibility for criminal actions.

In the late eighteenth century Enlightenment ideas mixed with religious ones to shape Connecticut law as it dealt with minors. John Locke and Jean Jacques Rousseau both provided new ways of viewing innate human nature. While historians disagree about the availability and influence of Enlightenment ideas such as Locke's concept of *tabula rasa* and Rousseau's vision of children as naturally good but corrupted by contact with society, these new attitudes were particularly relevant to the issue of crime and punishment.[22] Most important of all were the new views of the inherent innocence of children and the critical importance of education in forming moral citizens, important factors behind the late eighteenth and early nineteenth-century changes in Connecticut's laws and legal procedures that attempted to soften the criminal law's sanctions against children, especially those under the age of sixteen. As the cases, appeals, and petitions of the late eighteenth and early nineteenth centuries revealed, Connecticut judges, juries, and lawmakers struggled to reconcile respect for the law and protection for property with this new conception of children. The difference of opinion over the nature of children and the importance of nurturing and education informed the debate over how to deal with children who broke the law, not only in sentencing for crimes, but in the very definition of those crimes.

More important in shaping children's law than either religion or Enlightenment ideas were English legal traditions of the seventeenth century as transmitted by Massachusetts and Plymouth colony. For the first few years after settlers from both Massachusetts and Plymouth started new settlements along the Connecticut River near present-day Hartford, the Massachusetts General Court mediated some of the land controversies in Connecticut because the colonists had not yet formed their own distinct legal system. Connecticut's law was derivative in those early years because in March of 1635/36 the Massachusetts General Court created the first legal structures in Connecticut by authorizing eight residents of the new colony to perform legal duties and make laws. The grant of power from Massachusetts also gave the eight men the power to create a Connecticut general court to implement this authority, giving the colony its own governing body. This temporary system was, according to Albert Van Dusen, a "logical antecedent to Connecticut's Fundamental Orders," adopted in early 1639.[23]

Following the lead of the temporary General Court, Connecticut's residents supported the creation of the Fundamental Orders in 1638/39 that granted law-making authority to the male residents of the towns, via their elected deputies. The framework of government also set up the first formal court system to administer justice, staffed by the governor, lieutenant governor, and six elected magistrates. This court, known as the Particular Court, functioned as the chief court for the colony. Connecticut's English Charter of 1662 altered this arrangement by directing a sharing of the judicial authority between either the colony's legislature or "the governor or deputy and any six assistants." The new Charter also confirmed the legislature as the lawmaking body for the colony, but ordered that legislators could not pass laws contrary to the laws of England.[24]

Connecticut's Particular Court from 1639 until 1663 was the primary place where children had direct contact with the legal system. This was because the court system not only resolved disputes between adults but also intruded into the lives of Connecticut residents in order to maintain order in the community. Because most residents shared the ideology of the Puritan religion, it was not unusual for the civil laws of society to reinforce the Puritan vision of an orderly society, and that order included regulating the behavior of minors. In examining the operation of the early Connecticut legal system, Everett Goodwin made a strong argument that a chief function of the newly created courts was to determine orderly relationships, for example minister-congregation, master-servant, or parent-child. The nature of the relationship rather than the specific age of the citizens seemed to be the determining factor in many of the prosecutions. Men could not physically assault strangers, but they could physically chastise their children. Married young men had more freedom of action than single young men. Even if they were under twenty-one, they could enter into contracts to provide for their families. The early decisions indicated that people often disagreed with just what constituted order, and the magistrates used fines and corporal punishment to keep both children and adults in line. In 1640 the Court fined Mary Brunson, Olmsted Rudd, and Jonathan Peerce for "wanton dalliance and self pollution." Samuel Gardner paid 10 shillings in 1641 for his disrespect for the watch. Dallying with another man's maid resulted in fines for Walter Gray and Thomas Walston in 1644, and drinking to excess brought a forty-shilling fine against Jacob Waterhouse in 1651. Any one of these defendants could have been under the age of twenty-one, but age appeared irrelevant to their treatment by the court. Only when the Particular Court put children into apprenticeships or had to deal with specific issues of inheritance was age an influence on most of the early legal decisions that the court handed down.[25]

Concern for children was not apparent in the laws Connecticut settlers wrote for themselves. In 1650 the colony's legislators drafted laws to provide for nearly every social and legal contingency; yet of interest to scholars and students of the family and children, the new laws made little mention of any rights, obligations, or protections specifically granted to children. Ironically, creation of a formal law code for the new colony followed rather than preceded the creation of its court system, and not surprising was the similarity between the new laws and Massachusetts *General Laws and Liberties of 1647*. Connecticut's law code was comprehensive, providing for nearly every possibility that might arise in both civil and criminal law, but it mentioned little about children as independent beings. Instead the laws defined the relationship of children to both their parents and to the colony in terms of the responsibilities the children owed to adults. Only in a few of the early statutes did the code specify any duties that parents or society owed to children. For example, the law said that parents had to "catechise their children and servants in the grounds and principles of religion," educate them to be able to read and to know the capital laws of the colony, and bring them up in some respectable calling. The statutes also granted children fourteen and older the right to choose their own legal guardians when necessary, for example when both parents had died. Strikingly, in only a few categories did those early laws recognize any legal difference between the criminal capacity of children and adults. The laws held children and adults to the same standard of behavior.[26]

Nevertheless, this new legal code, part of Connecticut's emerging formal judicial system, would have an impact on the way the courts dealt with children charged with crimes. *The Code of 1650* established the various levels of a system of courts and created the legal procedures governing both civil and criminal cases. Under the *Code* magistrates heard all cases involving sums less than 40 shillings. Furthermore, it directed the magistrates to impanel juries in all other cases, creating a multi-layered legal system for the entire colony. This organization created a community-based administration of justice in which magistrates and jurymen policed their neighbors. This had important implications for children in the Puritan community, which believed an important part of its Christian duty was to regulate the lives and actions of its members. As Edmund Morgan put it, "a zealous enforcement of morality on others was another way of proving to yourself you might have faith."[27] A number of seventeenth-century laws such as the law on Sabbath breaking encouraged such community policing by awarding part of the fine to the person who reported the crime.

Because the magistrates could overturn jury verdicts or even alter a jury's award of damages when they disagreed with the jury, this hierarchy of justice created a potential source of conflict and disagreement within the community. Yet it also provided some leeway in dealing with children who broke the colony's criminal laws. In addition, the new system of laws for the colony directed that a Grand Jury of either twelve or fourteen men convene annually "to make presentment of the breaches of any laws or orders, or any other misdemeanors." This meant that if parents did not properly educate or discipline their children or allowed them to break the laws of the colony, the rest of the community, usually through a magistrate or the town selectmen, had the right to take over the parental role. A prime example of this was the law that said that if parents neglected their duty to raise their children properly, "whereby children and servants become rude, stubborn, and unruly," the town selectmen could remove the children from their families and place them in apprenticeships "to force them to submit unto government."[28] How authorities applied such a statute might depend on the social and economic standing of the parents as well as the actual misbehavior of the children.

Notably the division of jurisdiction based on the amount of money at issue in a case virtually guaranteed that many cases involving minors who broke the civil and criminal laws of the colony were not jury trials. Furthermore, the officials hearing those cases were not necessarily trained as lawyers or judges. Initially magistrates and, after 1697, justices of the peace heard most of the cases that involved charges against children. Justices of the peace were, in effect, the police officers of the community, the spokesmen for law and order. They were residents in the various towns in which they served and were thus probably aware of the activities of their neighbors. These officers of the judicial system presided over cases involving breach of the peace, minor theft, assault, cursing, profanity, and Sabbath-breaking. They were also the original hearing officers for evidence of more serious crimes including manslaughter and murder. Unfortunately, because justices of the peace usually held hearings in their own homes, record keeping on such cases was often incomplete, leaving a very fragmentary record of the majority of children's contacts with the early courts in Connecticut. Only when a magistrate or justice of the peace referred a case to a higher jurisdiction, first to the Particular Court, and after 1665, to the county courts, did more serious lawbreaking by children receive a wider forum with more regular requirements of record keeping.[29]

The justices of the peace often had no legal training, a fact that contributed to the inconsistency of treatment of children who broke the law. Moreover, many justices did not note when the defendants were minors. The 1697 law creating the office of justice of the peace directed that the Court should appoint "three or four of the most able and judicious freemen" to serve in each county as justices of the peace. The Assembly did not set any other requirement. One consequence of the lack of criteria was that few of those appointed had prior legal training or experience. The fact that justices of the peace collected fees for a wide variety of legal actions may have meant the office attracted those more interested in augmenting their income than in administering justice. Moreover, in 1702 when the Connecticut's General Assembly began the practice of appointing justices of the peace for the various counties, the justices named were often the same men appointed as deputies from the towns of the county. Deputies were usually men of higher than average wealth, judging from the records of civil litigation in the colony. That was no guarantee of their legal acumen since most residents had no formal legal education, especially in the early years of the colony.[30]

Moreover, another factor influencing children's rights was that the General Assembly acted to prevent the informal practice of law, which previously might have given laymen extra experience with the legal culture. In 1708 the Assembly made it illegal for any person "except in his own case, to make any plea at the bar, without first being approved by the court before whom the plea is to be made." Furthermore, relatively few men met the standards of the County Courts for admission to the practice of law. In the two years following passage of this law, the New London County Court approved only eleven men as lawyers. Interestingly, not until the middle of the 1700s did applications for admission to the Connecticut bar make references to a candidate's education or legal training. For example in 1774 the New London County Court admitted Norwich resident Jonathan Bellamy to the bar, noting he was "a young gentleman of good moral character, of a liberal education, with considerable acquirements in the knowledge of the law" because he had served a "regular clerkship."[31] Prior to this limitation, the initial informality within the legal system meant individual justices could handle cases before them with great flexibility and that individual citizens could represent themselves or their neighbors. This could have translated into better protection for the rights of children, protection which might have diminished with restrictions on the practice of law.

Adding to the difficulty of discovering those cases involving children who broke the laws of the colony and later those who transgressed state laws was the fact that Connecticut was an extremely litigious society, one whose citizens frequently sued each other. Dockets of trials in the various county courts recorded five or six hundred cases per session of the court; some counties had two or three such sessions a year. Another factor made it difficult to identify cases involving children. Especially in the seventeenth century, those who recorded documents for the county courts did not always identify the age of either the plaintiff or defendant, and the surviving records of vital statistics preserve no record of many of those who appeared before the magistrates, justices, and judges. Sometimes only a handwritten note on a court file or the specific reason for the lawsuit permitted identification of children in the court records.

What was clear in the early years of Connecticut's legal system was the wide variety in the way in which magistrates, justices of the peace, judges, and juries handed down decisions. The practice of requiring plaintiffs in litigation to pay fees in advance to protect the authorities against the cost of litigation operated as an informal "gatekeeper" against lawsuits by the indigent or by minors without the assistance of a responsible adult. Connecticut's prohibition against minors entering into contracts helped guarantee that children who became involved in civil lawsuits would have the advice and assistance of a responsible adult, but a similar protection apparently did not apply in all criminal cases against minors. As a result a two-tiered system gradually developed in the seventeenth century and continued into the nineteenth. In civil lawsuits, nearly every case that involved minors included notification from the magistrate, justice of the peace, or court to the child's parent or guardian to appear to represent the child. In contrast, for cases involving criminal charges against children, that formal notification to parents was often lacking. As the following analysis of criminal cases illustrates, the formal requirement for legal representation of children developed slowly and unevenly. Poor children and children of color were consistently less likely to receive the full protection of the reforms in criminal procedure. Justices had broad discretion to impose widely varying sentences and were more than likely to impose harsher sanctions on those they viewed as greater threats to public order. Certainly, the evidence of both civil and criminal cases provided ample proof that justices of the peace and judges of the county courts were at times more lenient to offenders who confessed and showed remorse. Cases involving both children and adults often resulted in lower fines and shorter sentences, or even dismissal of the charges, when the offender confessed and sought mercy from the court.[32]

In numerous revisions of Connecticut's criminal laws in the nineteenth century, legislators attempted to maintain respect for the law even as they tried to reduce the penalties for children who broke the law. The most notable of those attempts was the creation of discretionary sentencing in the 1840s. That reform did not solve the problem, as the rising support for alternatives made clear. Finally, with the opening of the Connecticut Reform School for Boys in 1853, it was apparent that many people in Connecticut had come to blame shortcomings in society itself for lawbreaking by youths, and they sought ways to reform children and transform them into upstanding citizens. Ironically, despite the fact that some of the reasons for interfering in family life or trying children under the criminal law had changed by the 1850s, the ultimate goal of the legal system actually altered little from what George Haskins had identified as the principal function of the early colonial courts: the maintenance of good order.[33]

Chapter One

Protecting Property, Correcting Children: Prosecuting Theft and Arson

> If any person, whether children, servants or others, shall bee taken or known to robb any orchard or garden . . . or any other goods left out in orchards, gardens, backsides, or other place . . . or other goods from mens dores or yards, he shall forfeit treble damages to the owner thereof, and such severe punishment as the Court shall think meet.
>
> —The Code of 1650

> Law is the rule of human conduct in a state of society.
>
> —Zephaniah Swift *A System of the Laws of the State of Connecticut* 1795

Inconsistency in Connecticut's treatment of minors under its laws in the seventeenth and eighteenth centuries was perhaps most obvious in prosecutions of children charged with theft, burglary, and arson. The clear legal distinctions between children and adults in some statutes and the lack of similar differentiation in others reflected the colonists' conflicting interests in protecting property and in providing any sort of special status for children who transgressed the laws. In most early cases laws that protected property did not provide special treatment for minors. For example, the first law in the *Code of 1650* set forth the age of adulthood. "All persons of the age of twenty-one years, and of right understanding and memory" had the power to pass real estate by wills, enter into contracts, and act as plaintiffs in civil law suits. Those males who were twenty-one also could become freemen, vote, and serve on juries. Yet the directive that "no person under the government of parent, master or guardian" could make a valid contract complicated the question of the age of majority. Some young adults over the age of twenty-one were still clearly under at least the informal control of their fathers. Were they adults or not? When Zephaniah Swift examined the laws of Connecticut in 1795, he tried to clarify the definition of the age of adulthood by saying that "full age is twenty-one for males and females, when children are capable of acting for themselves and are liberated from the government of their parents." Yet his definition still did not take into account the dependent status of some who were over the age of twenty-one.[1]

Adding to the confusion over the age of majority was that over the first two hundred years Connecticut laws had differing definitions of the age of responsibility under different laws. Seventeenth-century Connecticut had one age as the age of responsibility in its tax policy, requiring payment of the full rate of two shillings sixpence per head on all males of sixteen years of age or older. Children who earned their own wages were responsible for their own taxes, a seemingly adult responsibility; for those who did not work, their parents had to pay the rates. By the late eighteenth century the age for full liability for personal taxes had changed; the rate due for boys from sixteen to twenty-one was nine pounds, half the rate assessed on those twenty-one and older, yet teens who worked were still responsible for making their own tax payments. In the 1850s, only white males over the age of twenty-one were responsible for such taxes.[2] Several other laws designated differing ages of responsibility for males in the colony. In the seventeenth century all males above the age of sixteen had to take an oath of fidelity to the colony and bear arms in the town militias. Surprisingly, by the 1740s the colony's law not only directed that all males of sixteen years of age or older must serve in the militia, but it also mandated that "all who bear arms will have the liberty to vote in the choice of commission officers," giving teens a limited right to vote. After the American Revolution, the state raised the age for military service to eighteen, perhaps to parallel the age requirement for service in the American army, yet still permitted all to vote for company officers. Differing ages led to differing demands for labor from minors. By the early eighteenth century, the colony directed that every male from fourteen years of age had to labor one day a year to clear underbrush on town commons, but only males of sixteen or older owed the towns an additional two days of work per year for mending and repairing highways. This reflected, perhaps, recognition of the differing physical abilities of teens of different ages. In another example of inconsistency, the law against lying recognized gradations in the capacities of children, directing one form of punishment for those over fourteen, "the age of discretion," and a milder punishment for those under fourteen.[3] Such laws revealed that those who wrote the laws had some understanding that children of differing ages had different capacities and responsibilities.

Another problem complicated the differentiation between childhood and adulthood. In Connecticut, people under twenty-one had few legal rights or protections, yet when the colony did recognize the need to protect them, the requisite age varied depending on the legal issue at stake. One early right specifically allotted to minors was the right to choose a guardian if a child had no living parent to manage his or her property or provide for his or her education. The colony originally set the age for selecting a guardian at fourteen. For younger children, the magistrate or selectmen could designate a guardian. By 1702, the General Assembly lowered the age for choosing a guardian to twelve for girls but kept it at fourteen for boys. Did girls have better "understanding" than boys of a similar age? Inheritance practice also differentiated between the age of adulthood for boys and girls. Most wills directed that sons would inherit when they reached twenty-one but that daughters would inherit at the age of eighteen. Another of the seventeenth-century laws supported a different definition of the age of maturity, identifying twenty as the age of adulthood for smoking. The law directed that persons under that age could not take tobacco without a certificate from a physician and a license from the court. A law to restrict drinking passed in 1703 clouded the issue because it prohibited licensed innkeepers from selling alcohol to "either men's sons, apprentices, servants, or negroes" without a special order from the respective parent or guardian. With no specific age designated in the act, the law could easily apply to adult males who still lived at home with their fathers.[4] Nevertheless, where it counted most, under the criminal law, lawmakers in Connecticut designated those twenty-one and older as adults and those under twenty-one as minors or infants, a term used to indicate the person was under the age of twenty-one.

Despite this recognition of differing limitations and obligations of minors, the actual language of most of the criminal laws of the colony of Connecticut recognized little difference between adults who broke the laws and minors who broke the same laws. Especially in crimes dealing with the theft or the destruction of private property, the legal system was far more interested in protecting the rights of the property owners than in safeguarding the rights of the children accused. Only gradually did the laws provide procedural protections for children who committed crimes. Crimes against property comprised the majority of criminal charges involving children, though court cases involving known minors represented less than three percent of the cases tried in the county courts. Yet, in the statutes themselves and, more to the point, in the punishments imposed on children, the legal culture revealed a system that was not monolithic. The criminal code had similar, often paired goals for dealing with breaches of the law by both adults and children, directed at restitution when possible and retribution when necessary. Nevertheless, many criminal laws operated less stringently when applied to minors. This implied that adults recognized some differences in the capacity of children of different ages to understand the consequences of their acts.

Although the common law adopted from England maintained the presumption that a child under seven lacked the discretion necessary to commit a crime and that children between seven and fourteen generally lacked criminal capacities, most early Connecticut statutes concerning the criminal laws did not specifically differentiate between children and adults. As already mentioned, one notable exception was the law specifying fourteen as the age of discretion for lying. In its earliest form, this law directed that parents or masters of children under the age of fourteen convicted of lying had to correct the child for the crime in the presence of a colonial officer at the direction of the magistrate.[5] In contrast for most other crimes, especially those against property, the early legal code initially did not officially recognize a diminished legal capacity for children. Despite that early limitation, between the 1600s and the mid-nineteenth century the laws did register an eventual recognition that children, not just those between the ages of seven and fourteen, at some times did have less capacity than adults to understand the consequences of their actions. Writing in his *System of the Laws of the State of Connecticut* in 1796, Zephaniah Swift addressed the issue of the general criminal responsibility of children as well as the issue of their liability for specific thefts. He reasserted the common law idea that children under the age of seven were incapable of committing a crime and said that for the period between seven and fourteen, the presumption was that children were in the "doubtful period." The child's capacity to tell the difference between good and evil would be the determining factor in holding him or her fully responsible for criminal actions. The key, according to Swift, was not the specific age of the child but the strength of that understanding. In the case of petty theft, such as stealing fruit from a tree, Swift claimed that by the 1790s in Connecticut the courts treated the crime as a trespass rather than theft and prohibited the jailing of those under twenty-one.[6]

THEFT AND BURGLARY

Despite Swift's assertion that the authorities treated children convicted of theft with less severity, early prosecutions of children charged with crimes against property in Connecticut revealed colonists trying to reconcile their desire to protect their possessions with their changing view of the responsibility of minors for their actions. An important example of this transformation of the statutory treatment of children under Connecticut criminal law starting in the seventeenth century appeared in the various statutes against theft. In the colony's initial law prohibiting theft, the statute directed that anyone who broke into a house and stole goods or who stole from any person "shall be branded on the forehead with the letter B." For a second theft or burglary, the punishment included a second branding and a severe whipping; a third offense resulted in the death sentence. The law did not specifically exempt children of any age from the punishments. More to the point, for the prevention of pilfering and petty thefts, seventeenth-century Connecticut law directly named children as among those who might steal fruit or clothing from gardens or yards, or take wood or goods lying outside boatyards or houses. Perhaps because there was no threat to the lives or safety of the property owners in such minor thefts, valued at less than forty shillings, the punishment could be mild. The act directed that any person or child who committed this type of theft would have to pay triple damages to the owners of the pilfered goods. On the other hand the law did not order branding of the culprit. Nevertheless, the law allowed the magistrates to implement other punishments as they saw fit, such as sitting in the stocks, whipping, or even incarceration. This discretion could mitigate the punishment against a child who was merely mischievous or hungry or could increase the penalty against a child who stole property and then sold it. Nevertheless, as written, the law permitted and in fact potentially directed the incarceration of children as young as eight along with adult thieves from the community. That children did serve sentences in the houses of correction was clear from a 1737 amendment to the law against theft that specifically directed that when the earnings of a prisoner in the workhouse "will not pay the costs of his support or sickness in the house of correction" the prisoner's parents, master, or town of origin were responsible to make up the difference.[7]

Perhaps because most of the laws themselves rarely differentiated between the criminal capacity of adults and children, the actual cases involving theft in the seventeenth-century records reveal a society whose legal procedure initially dealt with children as though they were adults. At the same time magistrates apparently had considerable discretion in imposing sentences beyond the fines and could potentially shield children from the consequences of their actions and thus from the full power of the law. This potential protection was notable because in seventeenth-century Connecticut no colonial law specifically mandated legal representation for minors facing criminal prosecutions. Many of the criminal cases involving thefts by minors appeared at the hearings by local justices of the peace who certainly should have known the ages and identities of children in their communities. Yet rarely did the surviving court documents from the seventeenth century record the justice of the peace notifying a responsible adult of the proceedings or calling a parent or master into court to protect the child's interests. In an early example, in 1642 the Particular Court of the colony ordered the arrest of James Hallett of Windsor for theft and sentenced him to a coarse diet, hard work, and "sharp correction" as punishment for his crimes. After Hallet had spent a month in the house of correction, the Court then ordered the magistrate to release the youth to his master Bartlet. As further punishment, Hallet had to pay four times the value for the goods he had stolen, rather than the three mandated by the law. Yet perhaps in recognition that the thief was underage, the Court ordered that the branding for the theft be on Hallet's hand rather than on his forehead. Nothing in the court record indicated if the master Bartlet represented the youth in court or assumed responsibility for payment of the fine even though the law permitted extension of the term of apprenticeship to cover those costs. Similarly, when Joane Sipperance stole some lace in 1649, no adult represented her before the Court, but the justice imposed less than the maximum fine, only double the value of the stolen goods, and no physical punishment. This reduced punishment might have been in recognition that Joane was under twenty-one.[8]

By the 1660s, some cases reflected recognition that minors were not capable of appearing in Court without adult guidance, but the protection was not uniform. Noting in 1660 that Mary Holdridge had been sentenced to be whipped for her crime, the Particular Court granted the Governor the right to remit her sentence if her mother came into Court, although there was no specific court order directing the mother to appear before the magistrates. In contrast, when Thomas Dunke accused his apprentice, Thomas Johnson, of stealing from him, the Court did not mitigate the sentence or order either the master or the youth's parents to appear in Court to represent him. Though the sentence was only for restitution to the master, with no corporal punishment, this failure to ensure that an adult would assist the boy during his trial was notable because under Connecticut's civil law at this period, no one could directly sue a minor for a tort such as slander, trespass, or trouver and conversion (a form of theft). To bring a civil lawsuit against a minor, the plaintiff had to sue through the child's parent, master, or guardian.[9]

THE BEGINNINGS OF LEGAL REPRESENTATION FOR MINORS

Through the eighteenth century, cases of theft by persons under the age of twenty-one appeared both as criminal and civil matters. In some instances the colony or state brought the charges against individual children, often without specific notice to the child's parents. In others, the victim of the theft sued the thief for trespass and theft, usually giving careful notice of the litigation to the child's parent, guardian, or master. Cases handled in the criminal courts continued to result in fines, brandings, and at times incarceration. Those dealt with as civil matters usually resulted in orders for restitution, fines, and court costs. What was apparent was that failure to follow correct legal procedure when prosecuting theft under the civil law could at times result in dismissal of the case. In 1737 Samuel Ely of Lyme brought a suit of trespass against Joseph and Richard Ely, whom he identified as the minor sons of Captain Richard Ely, also of Lyme. Samuel Ely claimed the two boys had cut down and stolen over two-dozen trees on his land in Lyme, and he sought damages of thirteen pounds. At the trial the two defendants appeared by their father and pleaded that the writ should abate. The argument was that the writ did correctly identify Joseph and Richard as minors but it did not include the boys' father in the lawsuit, "which by the law ought to be done." The Superior Court at New London County agreed with the defendants and dismissed the case.[10]

Another Lyme case revealed the proper way to make a minor responsible for his actions. In 1741 Richard Smith of Lyme accused nineteen-year-old George Dorr of Lyme with the theft of hay worth 20 shillings from land along the Bridebrook River owned by Smith. However, Smith made sure that Edmund Dorr, George's father, received a summons on the charge, and at the hearing the New London County Court formally named Edmund as guardian to George. Though George claimed he had not stolen the hay because the land actually belonged to Mary Dorr, the wife of Edmund, the Court found in favor of the plaintiff and assessed damages against young George.[11]

A case of the theft of over seventy-eight pounds of gold and coin resulted in one of the earliest examples of the New London County Court formally naming a guardian for a minor defendant. In 1755 a justice of the peace indicted New London residents Anthony Frasier and James Smith, Jr. for the theft of one hundred and three Spanish dollars and fifteen pieces of gold coin along with eight silk handkerchiefs and six Holland shirts, all of which belonged to Patrick Thompson of New London. Authorities arrested and jailed both of the accused prior to the County Court hearing. Not until the hearing itself did the magistrate identify James as a "minor under twenty-one," and appoint Nathan Stedman as his guardian in the case. Stedman counseled the youth to plead not guilty. The Court agreed with the plea, actually finding both defendants not guilty but assessing court costs against them. Frasier, who appears to have been an adult, could not pay those costs and bound himself to serve Charles Jeffrey of New London for six months to pay the expense. James was also unable to pay the costs. Through his guardian he asked that he "be bound in service" to Samuel Bill to satisfy the costs. The Court granted the youth's request, directing the boy to serve Samuel Bill of New London for six months, to begin once he had completed his "indentures formerly given." James was obviously already in service to some other adult. In the case files Samuel Bill acknowledged on August 18, 1756 that the lad had fulfilled his required service. Though the case file did not identify Stedman as James current master, notice to a master to protect both the child's interests and his own was not uncommon. The fact that the Court named Stedman as an official guardian was a departure from prior practice.[12]

Perhaps because his father was one of the accused in the theft of twelve tons of hay, twenty-year-old Vashni Hall had informal rather than formal representation against the charge that he participated in the theft. In 1773 Samuel Reynolds, Esq. of Somers accused five Somers residents of stealing hay from his land; the accused were Josiah Hall, Josiah Hall, Jr., Vashni Hall, James Ward, and Lott Pease. Nowhere in the original case documents did Reynolds identify Vashni as underage, but the Court record noted that Vashni had pleaded not guilty by his father and guardian, Josiah Hall. The jury found all five guilty of the theft but apportioned the fine, assessing 40 shillings to Josiah Hall, Sr. and just twenty shillings to each of the remaining defendants. All five appealed. At the appeal the legal position of Vashni was more formal because in that appeal court documents did specifically identify him as a minor. Again all pleaded not guilty, but Josiah Hall, Sr. did not plead for an abatement based on the magistrate's failure to identify his son as underage in the original proceedings. On appeal the jury found the five not guilty of the theft but ordered that they pay the costs of prosecution.[13]

Through the end of the eighteenth century, appointment of guardians appears to have varied depending on the severity of the charges against a minor defendant. In 1786 Wheeler Coit of Preston sued Denison Geer, also of Preston, for trespass and theft, seeking fifty pounds in damages. At a hearing on the original charges that the boy stole five beaver hats, three and a half yards of broadcloth, fourteen pounds of sugar, fifty fishhooks, and thirty coppers, the justice of the peace appointed Elisha Geer as a guardian to defend the lad against the charges. This reflects a shift from the older, more informal system of merely notifying the parent or master of a person under twenty-one of pending legal charges against the minor. Upon the transfer of the case to the county court after the elder Geer pleaded for an abatement, the judge appointed Timothy Larraby, Esq. as guardian. The judge gave no reason for the change in guardian, but the inclusion of Esq. following Larraby's name indicated his higher status in the community. At both hearings young Denison pleaded not guilty; the county court agreed at the second that he was not guilty and assessed court costs against the plaintiff.[14] Though this case could have provided a usable precedent in appointing legal guardians, in 1793 a New London County justice of the peace did not provide a guardian for a child accusation of theft and destruction of watermelons. Timothy Mather, Jr. of Lyme charged that John Mitchell and John Simon, also of Lyme, had stolen and destroyed his watermelons on the night of August 2nd. Though the records of Lyme Justice of the Peace William Noyes noted that John Simon was a minor, Noyes did not indicate any legal notice to the boy's father. Both miscreants pleaded not guilty to the charge, but Noyes found them guilty. Not only did he order each to pay 3 shillings in damages to Mather; he also assessed court costs of 25 shillings. Despite these relatively high costs in comparison to the actual damages done by the theft, there was no record of a plea for abatement of the verdict based on the lack of notice to the parent or guardian.[15] Similarly in a 1798 case Noyes again failed to protect a child's legal interests. Joseph Bust of Lyme sued Daniel Rogers, identified in the warrant as the son of Ezekial Rogers of Lyme, for the theft of four bushels of corn. Without issuing any other formal notice to Daniel's father, Justice of the Peace Noyes of Lyme found the boy guilty of the theft. The elder Rogers did not dispute the verdict, paying the treble damages of $1.28, court costs of $10.58, and a $5 fine. Identifying him as the parent on the original writ may have served as sufficient legal notice of the proceedings.[16]

INCREASING USE OF GUARDIANS FOR MINORS CHARGED WITH THEFT

Several factors contributed to the increasing use of court-appointed guardians to protect the interests of children charged with theft and burglary. First, when Connecticut converted the old copper mine in Granby from a Revolutionary-era prison to the official State Prison at the end of the American Revolution, the General Assembly passed laws altering the punishments assigned for various types of crime, including theft and burglary. In the colonial period most punishments under criminal prosecutions for theft directed restitution, fines, and possibly physical punishments of branding or whipping. Only occasionally did theft result in imprisonment in the county jails. Now specific prison terms resulted for breaches of criminal laws. These changes in the statutes translated into harsh sentences at Newgate for relatively minor thefts, especially if the theft took place during a burglary or if the theft was a second or third offense. Judges gradually came to recognize a greater importance in protecting children when they faced incarceration at Newgate rather than in the local county jails. In addition, belying Swift's assertion that the courts treated petty theft as a trespass rather than a criminal act, by the opening of the nineteenth century the majority of cases of theft charged to minors came under the criminal law rather than as civil suits by the victims. The use of Newgate for imprisonment, the institution of fixed sentences, and the increasing number of cases against minors under the criminal law were probably the reasons that after 1800 Connecticut courts were becoming more consistent in identifying minors in criminal cases and appointing guardians *ad litem* to represent them and to protect their interests. Yet the protection was still uneven because at the initial hearings at the justice courts many justices of the peace were less likely to identify defendants as minors and appoint guardians to assist them. The failure to provide legal protection and advice for minors in the justice courts probably reflected the fact that justices of the peace were less likely to have formal legal training than the judges of the county courts since the only requirement for a justice was that he be one of the "most able or judicious freemen" in the county.[17]

Even the formal naming of guardians to protect the interests of children tried by the County and Superior Courts was not consistent or especially effective early in the nineteenth century. In April of 1810 the state charged two youthful black transients with theft and burglary: thirteen-year-old Jack Clark and seventeen-year-old George Williams. The arrest warrant asserted that the two youths had broken into the sloop *Juno* with the intent to steal and had also broken into the Norwich store of Augustus Perkins and stolen several pieces of pork and some brandy worth $6. In both cases the judge appointed Ulysses Selden, Esq. as guardian for the younger boy but did not provide a guardian for the elder. In each case both youths pleaded not guilty, but the juries found them guilty as charged. Despite Jack's being four years younger than George and despite his supposed representation by a guardian, he received an equal sentence on both charges: two three-year terms to be served consecutively at Newgate Prison, a harsh sentence for a child barely into his teens. Also notable was that George did not appeal his sentence, though he could have done so on the grounds that he had not received the assistance of a court-appointed guardian.[18]

Both the inconsistency in the use of court-appointed guardians and the harshness of the new sentencing guidelines were apparent in 1822 with the sentence meted out to a teen who stole goods worth just $16 dollars. When he was seventeen years old, Lyme resident George Wade broke into the Lyme store of Stephen J. Lord and Daniel R. Noyes and stole four handkerchiefs worth $2; he also took $10 in cents and $4 in silver money. Nothing in the legal file indicated that the justice of the peace identified George as a minor or appointed a guardian to represent him at the original hearing on the charges. In fact the justice jailed the teenager for his inability to provide a surety. At the Superior Court hearing, the judge finally did identify George as underage and appointed C. J. McGurdy, Esq. to be the boy's guardian specifically to defend him in the case. By the nineteenth century, such court-appointed guardians could serve informally as legal counsel for the duration of a trial, but the specific appointment was as a guardian, not as a court-appointed attorney. Despite McGurdy's assistance and a not-guilty plea, for a total take valued at $16, the youth received a sentence of two and a half years at Newgate. George's rights were not particularly well protected. Neither McGurdy nor anyone else challenged the legality of the original hearing without a guardian, nor did anyone protest the severity of the sentence.[19]

Similarly, in 1826 a Stonington justice of the peace failed to identify Samuel Ingraham of Stonington as a minor, though the youth faced a harsh penalty for a relatively minor theft under the new sentencing guidelines. In 1826 the twenty-year-old broke into the store of Jedidiah Huntington and "feloniously and burglariously" stole 40 copper cents. At the original hearing before a justice of the peace, the justice did not appoint a guardian for Samuel. With no one to advise him, the young man still pleaded not guilty. Samuel went to jail despite that plea because he could not provide a surety for his appearance before the New London County Court. At the County Court, the judge finally identified the twenty-year old as a minor and appointed Asa Child, Esq. to represent him. After the jury found Samuel guilty as charged, Child made a motion for an arrest of judgment. The file does not mention the grounds for the motion, but it could have been based on the initial failure to identify Samuel as a minor. Whatever the reason for the motion, the judge denied it and sentenced the youth to three years at Newgate. No one filed an appeal of the sentence so the young man served the entire three years, not gaining his freedom from the new prison in Wethersfield until March of 1829. Although there was no extant record of a prior conviction, the severity of the sentence for the burglary and theft of such a minor amount could have reflected that the youth had committed previous crimes and received a longer sentence as a repeat offender.[20]

The continuing inconsistency in the appointment of guardians appeared in a case in 1828 in which the justice of the peace identified a defendant as a minor and appointed a guardian for him while the Superior Court apparently did not provide the requisite protection for the youth. A justice of the peace had identified Henry P. Fagins as under age at the original justice court hearing on two charges of theft and burglary. The justice appointed Samuel M. Downes as his guardian to defend him. Because the youth faced two separate charges, the judge jailed him for trial before the Superior Court. When the New London County Superior Court heard the case, the judge identified Henry only as "a transient colored person." Though the files from the justice of the peace court were included in the Superior Court files, Henry's age was apparently irrelevant to the Superior Court judge. He did not appoint a new guardian, and it is not clear from the records if Downes was still involved with the case. Even if Downes had continued to assist the youth, the help was ineffective. On the first charge the boy pleaded guilty to breaking into the home of Julius S. Hammond and stealing clothing valued at $5.75 and a silver watch worth $25. Also accused of breaking into the Colchester shop of Abiel Bartholomew and stealing thirty cents in silver and copper coins, fifty herring worth fifty cents, twenty-four pounds of crackers valued at $2, and forty oranges worth $2, Henry repeated his guilty plea. The Superior Court sentenced Henry to two years for the first offense and an additional year for the second; the judge apparently having no qualms about sending a youth to the contaminating prison at Newgate.[21]

Even as more consistency in the use of court-appointed guardians was apparent by the 1830s, with most minors gaining the services of a guardian, an important change was that the courts also began to designate these guardians as formal legal counsel to many minors. This designation was in addition to affording children the nominal protection of a guardian. The change reflected the increasing maturation of the legal system in the state. Furthermore, by this time, most men assigned as guardians or legal counsel appear to have been trained as lawyers because court documents in a number of cases used the designation Esq. following the names of the guardians. One of the first examples of this more formal designation of a guardian *ad litem* actually provided a minor with two adults to assist him in his defense. In 1834 Milo Davis broke into the Bozrah store of Havalot Mony by prying open the shutters, but he was caught before he could steal anything. The court first appointed Asa Lee as the boy's guardian and later named John A. Rockwell as guardian and Thomas S. Perkins as counsel. Perhaps the extra assistance helped the child because his sentence for breaking and entering was for only two months in the common jail. An alternative explanation for the relatively mild sentence could be that jurors were already concerned about sending children to the new State Prison at Wethersfield. In contrast, the sentence for an adult convicted nine months later of a similar charge of breaking and entering a store was a two-year sentence at the state prison.[22]

Having a legal counsel in addition to a court-appointed guardian did not always help a child evade responsibility for his or her criminal acts. In 1837 Halsey Cooper, a transient youth, faced multiple charges of theft, and the New London County Court assigned four different guardians, designating three of them to serve as legal counsel as well. Despite the wide array of legal assistance the jury convicted the boy on all four counts of theft. For the first two convictions he received sentences at the county jail in New London. For the third, because the lad was a repeat offender, the New London County Superior Court sentenced him to a two-year term at the state prison. For the final case, with yet another guardian and legal counsel, Halsey received a three-year sentence to be served at the state prison after the completion of his prior term. The youth apparently was satisfied with his legal representation because he did not petition the General Assembly for clemency after his conviction[23]

Having a court-appointed guardian certainly did not guarantee clemency, even for the very young and heedless. When Sally Reeves, a poor widow from New York, sought clemency for her eleven year-old son Selah C. Reeves, she did not complain that his rights had not been protected by his guardian *ad litem*. In her petition to the Connecticut General Assembly, Mrs. Reeves said she was so poor that she bound her children out to masters as soon as they were young enough to work. She raised the issue of the boy's intent and agonized that he was too young to face "the dangers that might result in his ruin by being confined in prison with old offenders." Selah, she said, had been an apprentice to Abel M. Sherwood of New Fairfield. In the summer of 1834, "in rash moments of his unguarded mind," the boy left his master and stole a horse owned by Gorham Barnum valued at sixty dollars. She said that she believed her son was a good boy and had not had the necessary intent to commit the theft. Reeves also pleaded with the legislators to consider her agonizing feelings as a mother to have such a young son confined in the state prison. Both the boy's master Sherwood and Barnum, owner of the stolen horse, and sixteen other residents of New Fairfield supported her petition for her son's release from the State Prison. Nevertheless, apparently neither a question about the boy's criminal responsibility nor a worry about the contaminating dangers of the State Prison swayed the legislators who rejected the request to release the child from his prison term.[24]

By the end of the 1830s the representation of minors by either court-appointed guardians or legal counsel seemed nearly universal, certainly a reflection of the increasing sophistication of the legal system. In nearly all cases, justices of the peace successfully identified defendants who were minors and provided guardians and counsel to all the recorded defendants in the decade. Even in a minor case of receiving five dollars worth of stolen goods, Charles B. Noyes of Stonington obtained the mandated legal protection. Justice of the Peace Francis Sheffield, identifying Charles as a minor, "in compliance with the statute in such cases provided," appointed John Lanpher "to defend him in the prosecution and advise him how to plead." With Lanpher's advice, Charles pleaded guilty to the charge. Sheffield fined the lad seven dollars plus court costs and sentenced him to thirty days in the Norwich jail.[25] Clearly, even at the level of the lower courts, justices were now fully conversant with the laws protecting minors charged with crimes.

Despite the increasing sophistication of the justices and judges as the courts began to be more consistent in supplying procedural protections for minors, ironically the General Assembly seemed reluctant to apply the more accurate application of the law to prior cases under appeal. In a few cases the General Assembly was unwilling to grant pardons to adults who sought reversal of their convictions based on the argument that the court had not provided proper representation for them in the past when they were minors. In 1834 Smith H. Barlowe of Sheffield, Massachusetts sought a pardon and restoration of his rights based on his claim that Connecticut had failed to provide him with a legal guardian in a trial for theft. In 1823, Smith, who was just eighteen, took one dollar from Lewis German of Salisbury. When German, who owed the youth one dollar, told him that the money actually belonged to John Van Dusen, Smith offered to return it, but Van Dusen had him prosecuted for theft. At the trial Justice of the Peace Eliphalet Wittlesley did not identify the youth as under age and did not provide him with a guardian or counsel to instruct or advise him. He found the lad guilty, fining him one dollar and assessing court costs of five dollars. What Smith was claiming eleven years later was that the conviction was invalid because of the failure to identify him as a minor and provide a guardian *ad litem*. The Assembly refused to reverse the conviction and restore Smith's right to vote or serve on a jury. A number of other rejected appeals revealed this same unwillingness to overturn prior decisions of the courts.[26]

Even as the use of guardians *ad litem* became routine in Connecticut's courts, guardians did not always perform their appointed function to assist the children temporarily under their care. Heedlessness was at the heart of the 1836 charges against sixteen-year-old Oliver Hazard Perry Lewis of Montville, and it also was partly the basis for his petition for freedom from a two-year sentence for burglary. However, the failure of a duly appointed guardian to protect the interests of his client was the real problem at issue in the appeal. The original trial documents presented a straightforward case against Oliver, charging he had entered a mill and stolen a watch. Facing the justice of the peace, the youth, represented by neither his mother nor a court-appointed guardian, pleaded guilty. Bound over to the county court, he gained the assistance of a guardian appointed to help him manage his defense but again pleaded guilty. Only after serving ten months of the two-year sentence did Oliver present his version of the events as he pleaded for a reduction in his term. He asserted that his guardian *ad litem* had done nothing to assist in his defense.[27]

In his petition the boy identified himself as the son of a colored man who had faithfully served the late General Alexander Hamilton during the Revolution, a claim to respectability. Oliver wrote that in the daytime he had gone to a mill owned by the father of one of his playmates and, finding the door open, had gone in. There he had discovered his friend's watch lying on the floor and decided to play a prank on him. Oliver said he had taken the watch out of the mill and left it on a path where the other boy would be sure to find it. Instead, said the hapless youth, Mr. Chappel found the watch and accused Oliver of theft. The youth claimed enemies of his mother then obtained a warrant for his arrest and urged him to plead guilty to the theft. They told him that once he confessed, he could forget about the affair. Without the advice of his mother or a court-appointed guardian, the lad did plead guilty to what he believed were charges of simple theft. However, because Oliver had entered the mill, the justice of the peace found the boy guilty of burglary rather than merely theft and bound him over to the New London County Court for trial. In his clemency petition, Oliver admitted that at the county court he did finally gain a guardian appointed by the court to manage his defense. The assistance was useless. The boy asserted that because his mother could not afford to pay the guardian, the man busied himself with his paying clients and even left Oliver alone in court to face the charges. Without legal representation, Oliver again lodged a guilty plea. In asking for his release the boy claimed he had acted out of high spirits, not out of malice. A separate petition signed by forty-two Montville residents seconded the boy's request for mercy, asserting that he sustained a good character among white or black boys of his age and had been tricked into pleading guilty. The boy's supporters claimed he was not guilty of any offense and "by a strange course of management" had been "induced to plead guilty before his friends had an opportunity to interpose their assistance." The petitioners were clearly critical of the poor representation provided by the court-appointed guardian. In response to the petitions the General Assembly Committee on the State Prison voted to release the boy from the remainder of his sentence. What is not clear from the vote was whether committee members reached their decision based only on the child's age or also took into consideration the blatant failure of the court-appointed guardian to protect to child's interests.[28]

CHANGING ATTITUDES ON SENTENCING MINORS: DISCRETIONARY SENTENCING

Though magistrates and jurors did continue to send many children to the state prison, by the 1840s in a number of cases the state dropped the prosecution of some children accused of theft. While the number of cases dropped comprised less than ten percent of the cases heard at the New London County Court during the decade, in the prior decades only rarely did the State's Attorney dismiss charges against any defendant. The change was perhaps because of increasing adult reluctance to expose children to the harshness and corrupting influences of the state prison. In none of the examples did the State's Attorney appear to question the evidence against the child; he merely refused to continue prosecuting the cases. In November of 1842, the state charged Catherine Dailey with the theft of $42 worth of cloth and lace and a separate theft of $60 in cloth. After the court appointed Patrick Dailey as the girl's guardian for the trial, the State's Attorney refused to prosecute the action. A similar reluctance to pursue the full legal remedy took place in 1843. L. T. Foster, Esq. became guardian and counsel for William Cook of North Stonington to defend him against charges of breaking and entering and theft of goods valued at eleven dollars. After the boy entered a not-guilty plea, the State's Attorney again declined to prosecute. When the minor Joseph Babcock of Norwich pleaded not guilty through his court-appointed guardian to the theft of a box of oranges, five drums of figs, and eight silver dollars in 1844, the state dropped the prosecution. Similarly, in 1848 the State's Attorney refused to continue the case against Edward Murray of Bozrah, a minor charged with the theft of over fifty dollars of store goods such as vest patterns, ribbons, and collars. The justice of the peace had appointed Jebiel Johnson as guardian for Edward and found the lad guilty. At the New London County Superior Court, the judge appointed L. H. Huston as both guardian and attorney, but the State's Attorney, "having personally doubts as to the prisoner's guilt," dropped the prosecution and released the lad. At the same time the state also dropped charges against the boy for escaping from custody while under arrest for the alleged theft.[29]

Other evidence of the increasing leniency of the criminal justice system toward minors appeared in testimony before Connecticut's General Assembly by residents complaining that such refusals to hold children responsible for their criminal acts undermined respect for law and order. The ongoing criticism arose because lawmakers were considering reforms of the criminal justice system. One proposed reform was a discretionary sentencing law applicable to minors. The General Assembly heard reports that under-age criminals were aware that juries did not want to send them to the state prison and that the youths exploited that repugnance by committing crime with impunity. Reformers who supported creation of a system of discretionary sentencing for children who broke the law acted out of the belief that children would suffer unduly while in the state prison. Law-and-order advocates liked the proposal because it still provided suitable punishment to the youthful lawbreakers. Even the prison warden entered the fray, advocating imposition of long, certain terms of imprisonment for minors who broke the law because "if we are to keep the youth under proper restraint, we must feel a deep interest to have the penalty sure." The state's passage of a discretionary sentencing law in 1843 did provide an alternative to dismissal of charges in a number of cases of theft or burglary charged against children. This new law allowed specific discretion to justices who convicted children who were under the age of seventeen. Whenever the court convicted anyone under seventeen of an offense "the punishment of which in whole or in part is or may be imprisonment in the state prison," the justice or jury could "in lieu thereof sentence such convict to imprisonment for the same term in the county jail." Thus, the new law left it up to the courts to decide what was appropriate for the circumstances of each specific case. Many cases after passage of the new law clearly followed the new sentencing guidelines, with justices writing to justify the milder punishment provided at the county jails by referring directly to the new statute and specifically noting the age of the youthful lawbreakers. Nevertheless, the courts still handed down harsh sentences for repeat offenders, minors of seventeen and older, children of color, and Irish children. Furthermore, since the duration of sentences remained identical whether served at the State Prison in Wethersfield or in a county jail, imprisonment for children remained a preposterous punishment in the eyes of many, especially among those who petitioned for pardons for children in the 1840s.[30]

Discretionary sentencing was not the anticipated panacea for overly harsh treatment of minor criminals. Because state sentencing guidelines did not specifically allow consideration of mitigating circumstances, many children served what appeared to be excessively harsh sentences whether in county jails or the prison for crimes of youthful disobedience or heedlessness. Judges often had no choice in assigning jail or prison sentences because the General Assembly mandated specific sentences for many crimes. More judicial leeway was apparent in some crimes than in others. For example, in 1821 procuring a miscarriage of a quickened pregnancy by means of administering "any deadly poison or other noxious or destructive substance" brought a term of life in Newgate or "any other term set by the court," wide leeway indeed. In 1821 another change in the criminal law ordered that the minimum punishment for breaking and entering during the day and stealing goods valued at over one dollar was to be punishable by a term at Newgate Prison, but did not specify the length of the term. In 1823, in all cases of conviction of theft for any amount, if the defendant refused to pay the fine, a new law granted discretion to the justices to sentence the culprit to not more than thirty days in the workhouse for the first offense and not more than sixty days for the second. A more rigid law was the statute that allowed few options in the punishment for murder in 1845: the death sentence for first-degree murder and life in prison for second-degree murder. In another example an 1849 law directed that theft or destruction of gas pipes, burners, posts, or lanterns drew a mandated sentence of either a $250 fine or one year in the county jail or both. The most rigid approach to punishments was that the state mandated long terms of imprisonment for the commission of a third crime of theft or a theft combined with breaking and entering, whatever the value of the purloined items. This was one law that operated with extra harshness for minors because even with the more merciful approach of discretionary sentencing, it resulted in their serving long terms of imprisonment in the company of career criminals at either the county jails or the state prison.[31]

The folly and failure of discretionary sentencing was apparent almost immediately with the case of eleven-year-old Lorenzo Barber. In August of 1842, prior to the passage of the new law, Lorenzo had stolen a one-dollar bank note and a check for one hundred and fifty dollars from Simon Arnold of Hartford. Because of the value of the items stolen, the court sentenced the poor lad, described as "friendless and without proper parental guidance," to a two and a half year term at the State Prison. Although no state law permitted suspension of a prison sentence, the Hartford County Court "in view of the extreme youth of the lad and of its also being proved that he was peculiarly feeble and puny in mind and body" had suspended the sentence and confined the child at the Hartford County Jail for a year. With the passage of the discretionary sentencing law holding the boy in the jail was now legal, but N. H. Morgan, the Hartford jailer, petitioned the General Assembly to release the youth for his time already served. Morgan wrote persuasively that continued imprisonment of the boy would not serve the public good, "but would be harsh and cruel to a lad of his tender years and condition and totally destructive of all hope of his usefulness to society in after life." Morgan asked for a pardon for the boy. The Assembly granted the pardon despite the legal alternative provided by the discretionary sentencing act, revealing that members saw the danger of incarcerating children with hardened criminals at any location.[32]

Even with discretionary sentencing in place and public concern for harmful influences affecting children in local jails, a child who committed multiple minor offenses could still face long, potentially harmful imprisonment. Jonathan Lasier of Norwich went on a minor crime spree between 1839 and 1844. In 1839 a justice of the peace found the lad guilty of theft, fined him five dollars, and sent him to the New London County jail for thirty days. In 1841, the boy again committed a theft; again the justice fined him five dollars and imposed a thirty-day sentence. It was not clear from the record if the justice of the peace in either case provided a guardian to represent the lad. In 1844, the child, still under the age of seventeen, stole two dead partridges. This time the New London County Court presided over the trial. After appointing A. C. Lescott as the boy's guardian to defend him, the Court rejected the child's not-guilty plea and sent him to the county jail for a full two-year sentence because he was a repeat offender. In a similarly harsh response, the New London County Court sent a sixteen-year-old boy to jail for two years. 1845 New London resident George Gardiner broke into the New London store of Thomas Hodgson and Joseph Bowens. His take for the burglary and theft was a grand total of twenty copper and silver coins with a total value of $2.50. The justice of the peace noted that George was a minor, appointed William Harris "as his guardian to act for him in this case," and then found the boy guilty, holding him for County Court trial. At the County Court, the judge specifically identified George as a minor under the age of seventeen and named George Hill, Esq. as guardian and counsel to assist in the child's defense. Though George pleaded not guilty, the jury found him guilty and sentenced him to a two-year term at the county jail because he had compounded the crime of the theft of a small amount of cash with breaking into the store. Reflecting the discretion granted to the courts, the jury specifically directed the sentence was to be at the county jail, "Gardiner being under seventeen."[33]

Even under the discretionary sentencing law, the punishment for simple theft could result in jail terms for children who stole small amounts. In

1847 two minors, William Steward and Edmund Dodge of New London, stole coins worth two dollars from Joseph A. Smith. New London Justice of the Peace John Graves appointed Thomas Hurley as guardian for William but merely noted that Edmund had his father to act for him. After William pleaded guilty, Graves fined him ten dollars. Perhaps because Edmund pleaded not guilty and thus forced a formal trial, the justice fined him five dollars but also sent him to the county jail for a twenty-five-day term. Despite this relatively short term, the use of imprisonment of youthful lawbreakers not only revealed that state would exercise its authority to punish children for even minor violations of the law. Sending children to jail also meant they came into contact with hardened criminals even in the local jails. Putting children into jail with adults raised the problem of reforming the youthful lawbreakers.[34]

Both the question of the criminal responsibility of a child and the need for juvenile reform were evident in the 1847 plea for clemency by the parents of ten-year-old Thomas Harragan of New Haven. The boy had stolen a horse and pleaded guilty to the crime. Using the option provided by the discretionary sentencing act, the New Haven County Court sentenced the child to two years in the county jail in New Haven, but it had no option allowing reduction of the mandated minimum sentence for horse theft. After the child had spent a year in the New Haven County Jail, his parents, John and Ellen Harragan, petitioned the General Assembly for his release. Using language that emphasized the child's inability to commit a criminal act, the parents claimed Thomas had been too young to comprehend the full extent of his crimes. In case the claim of lack of responsibility failed to move the legislature and reflecting the language of rehabilitation prevalent in many such petitions in this period, the parents also asserted that they believed their son was capable of reformation and that they were anxious to reclaim him and make him a respectable member of society. The Assembly granted the petition for early release without comment; as in the case of poor Lorenzo Barber, they seemed to agree that an eleven-year-old child did not belong in jail.[35]

Increasing hesitancy to expose children to the corrupting influence of even the county jails must have been behind the surprisingly light sentence imposed on sixteen-year-old Henry Jordan, "a colored boy of the town of North Stonington" in 1849. The state charged that Henry had broken into the store of Jeremiah Potter of North Stonington and stolen merchandise and coins to the value of forty dollars. Identifying Henry as a minor, the court first appointed Rufus Wheeler guardian "to advise and assist him in the trial." The lad pleaded innocent. The court then named N. F. Dixon as the child's guardian *ad litem*. Though the boy could provide no witnesses to prove his version of the events, when the jury found him guilty, it sentenced him to only fifteen days at the county jail, a very light punishment considering the original charge of theft compounded by breaking and entering.[36]

By the 1850s the use of discretionary sentencing was clearly evident not only in the location but also in the duration of sentences. In a number of cases, the juries appear to have used their discretion not only in where they ordered culprits under seventeen to serve their time, but also in the length of the jail term they imposed. In March of 1850 the State charged Robert Connor and John Charles with breaking into the New London store of Stephen Prentice. Identifying Robert as a minor, the indictment against him carefully identified the six dollars worth of goods taken in the burglary, a shirt, a pair of pantaloons, and a jacket. The court named Hiram Wiley, Esq. as guardian to the lad. Wiley apparently advised a guilty plea. Taking note that the defendant was under seventeen, the jury then sentenced Robert to six months imprisonment in the New London County jail. For John Charles, the indictment merely gave a total value of the goods stolen. In contrast to Robert's six-month term, the court sentenced the adult criminal to four years at the State Prison on the identical charge.[37]

Although a spirit of clemency did influence juries faced with young criminals, records of trials made it obvious that minors who were seventeen or older continued to pay a higher penalty for their crimes, but still sometimes served less time than adults convicted of similar crimes. Seventeen-year-old John Post of Hebron broke into the store of Robert Beebe of Waterford in 1850 and stole one hundred silver coins and over six hundred copper coins. The total came to a value of twenty dollars. Even at this later date, justices of the peace were not always consistent. The original writ for John's arrest did identify him as seventeen years old, but it did not designate a guardian for the youth. At the Superior Court trial the court appointed George C. Goddard as guardian for John. With no explanation, the court dropped the charge of theft, and the teen pleaded guilty to a single charge of breaking and entering. His sentence was for one only year at the State Prison as compared to the four-year term adult John Charles had received.[38]

Though cases that sent minor females to the State Prison were rare, in 1853 the state showed no leniency nor any concern about the contaminating influence of the State Prison on a transient young woman named Abby Jane Wade or Abby Jane Wilcox. The charges were that Abby had broken into the house of Calvin Spencer of East Lyme and stolen a watch valued at $25, a $15 coat, and a pair of pantaloons worth $8. Because the court identified her as a minor, it appointed A. Converse, Esq. as her guardian. With Converse's advice Abby changed her plea to not guilty but still received a term of two years at the State Prison. The Superior Court also prosecuted the girl for horse theft of a horse valued at $100 and sentenced her to a consecutive term of two years. Neither her tender years nor her gender softened the jury, although by the time of her trial numerous petitions to the General Assembly had emphasized the negative impact of incarceration in the State Prison for young persons of either gender.[39]

THE SHORTCOMINGS OF DISCRETIONARY SENTENCING

What was obvious to many Connecticut citizens by the 1850s was that neither applying the full penalty of the law nor interposing the more lenient terms of the discretionary sentencing act was turning youngsters in Connecticut from the paths of crime. Reformers had continued to push for more radical ways of dealing with children who broke the law, seeking an entirely separate institution for the incarceration and reform of criminals under the age of sixteen. For much of the 1840s various reform groups besieged the Connecticut General Assembly with petitions seeking the creation of a State Reform School for Boys. Several studies by the Assembly's Committee on Prisons endorsed the need for a change in the way the state dealt with youthful lawbreakers. Even the prison warden came to be a supporter of a change in the way the state punished criminals under sixteen. Wardens of the various county jails provided statistics that increasingly stressed that the jails themselves were no better than the prisons in reforming young criminals. In most of the county jail reports, theft was the most common reason for the imprisonment of minors, and many of the thieves were quite young. At the Hartford County jail in 1843, sixty percent of arrests had been of youths under the age of twenty-one, including eight prisoners who were under the age of twelve. In 1845 at the same jail, fourteen of the seventy-seven inmates were fifteen or younger, including two eleven-year-olds. Theft and burglary accounted for over half of the crimes. By 1850, one third of those committed to the Hartford County Jail were under twenty-one. Apparently rural areas had less of a problem with youthful lawbreakers. Windham and Litchfield reported a lower incidence of youthful crime; only about ten percent of Windham inmates were under twenty-one while at Litchfield eight of thirty-eight new admissions were from age ten to twenty. Reports from 1851 noted another problem for the urban jails. Though it did not break down age and ethnicity together, for Hartford thirty-eight percent of new jail residents were Irish while twenty percent were under twenty-one. In the same year the New Haven County jail report did not provide a breakdown in the ages of those arrested but blamed the year's increase in arrests on drunkenness that was responsible for nearly half of all the crimes. The report also claimed crime had gone up because of an increasing "amount of immigrants into our land of liberty and freedom." In 1853, the year the new reform school finally opened, Hartford County reported that over twenty percent of new inmates at the county jail were twenty or younger.[40]

As the culmination of the reform movement to provide rehabilitation rather than merely punishment for children who broke the law, in 1851 Connecticut legislators finally authorized the creation of a state-funded reform school for boys under the age of sixteen. The arguments for the separation of children who broke the law from the adult population of criminals were the same reformers had been putting forth since their criticism of Newgate back in the 1790s. In proposing the new school, the report from the Committee on the state reform school noted that "the extent of the evil to be remedied is of sufficient magnitude" to warrant state action. It summarized statistics on youthful crime, saying about eighty boys a year ended up in the state's county jails, primarily for theft, and that the total number of juvenile offenders each year was not less than two hundred. The majority, according to the report, were either orphans or "their parents were grossly intemperate, or had absconded, or were culpably negligent of their education." Repeating the fears that had led to the passage of the discretionary sentencing act in the 1840s, the report declared there was "a very general reluctance of prosecuting officers to cause the laws as they now exist to be executed with all their force upon persons so young, so neglected, and so ignorant." The result, complained the committee members, was that failure to punish the youthful lawbreakers tended "to induce boldness and hardihood in guilt" yet the alternative was far worse, putting children in direct contact with seasoned criminals. A new institution would provide greater certainty of punishment (one of the reforms advocated by Beccaria nearly one hundred years earlier), and it "would secure to the offenders themselves when of tender years a course of moral training and instruction so combined with the necessary restraint as to induce and generally achieve a thorough reformation." With full support from the State Prison warden and reform-minded members, the General Assembly voted for the appropriation of funds for the creation of the State Reform School for Boys.[41]

Cases of theft continued to be the most common charge against minor criminals. When the State Reform School for Boys opened in Meriden in 1854, fully one third of the commitments were for theft. In his first annual report the school's chaplain identified the young thieves as "those who have unfortunately swerved from the path of rectitude." The goal of the reform school was to replace the pernicious example of intemperate or dishonest parents with a system of moral instruction. To illustrate the unfortunate background of his charges, the chaplain related the story of one fatherless child who told him that his mother would send him out in the morning to steal and if the child returned home empty-handed his mother would send him to bed without supper. With the opening of the new school, such children obtained a chance for an education and learned, as one child wrote home to his brothers, to "never take anything that does not belong to them."[42] The school thus protected the property of Connecticut taxpayers while trying to make law-abiding citizens out of hapless, youthful lawbreakers.

ARSON AND THE ISSUE OF CRIMINAL RESPONSIBILITY

Of all the crimes against property, arson was perhaps the one that provided the greatest problem in determining the criminal responsibility of a minor defendant. The motive for theft was usually strikingly clear; the culprit wanted someone else's property. What were the motives for arson? Without insurance, was vengefulness the only possible motive? Difficulty in assigning a motive might have been behind the fact that in the original laws of the colony, there was no differentiation in punishment for children or adults convicted of the crime of arson. However, by the early eighteenth century, the statute concerning arson clearly distinguished between those perpetrators under and over the age of sixteen, perhaps recognition of the different capacity for children of certain ages to understand the consequences of their actions. In 1715 a change in the colonial law mandated that if any person sixteen years or older willfully set a fire that endangered human life, the penalty was death. More notable was that the law did not specify any penalty at all for those under sixteen. Setting the age at under sixteen rather than under fifteen was somewhat of a departure from the common law assumption that a child from seven to fourteen was incapable of committing a crime unless prosecutors could prove the child able to discern right from wrong.[43] In addition, the relative paucity of prosecutions of anyone, children or adults, in arson cases might have reflected the inability of prosecutors to distinguish intent from carelessness or have been a result of the generally flammable nature of all buildings in the early years of the colony.

Though there were few criminal prosecutions for arson in the seventeenth century, it was clear from early Connecticut case law that even when the colonial authorities did not see cause to bring criminal charges of arson, property owners could instead institute civil suits for damages caused by arson. In 1744 Christopher Stubbins of New London brought suit against fellow New London residents Eleazer Bishop and seventeen-year-old Eleazer Bishop, Jr. in a plea of trespass, seeking seventy pounds in damages. Stubbins accused the youth of breaking into a mill owned by Stubbins and setting it on fire, with the result that all but the chimney was destroyed. Apparently Stubbins thought he could get more satisfaction from a civil prosecution because there was no record of a criminal prosecution for the arson, nor was the issue of putting human life at risk raised in the civil trial. Though the evidence makes it clear that Stubbins did not accuse the elder Bishop of the actual arson, under the civil law he had to sue both the father and the son. Eleazer, Jr. pleaded not guilty by his father, and the jury found him not guilty, awarding him court costs of over twelve pounds, costs that Stubbins had to pay.[44]

By the end of the eighteenth century, Connecticut laws on arson changed to include a lesser penalty for causing a fire that did not put people in danger, but for those under sixteen who set fire to a building without endangering human lives, the law still did not mandate any specific punishment. For arson that did not result in putting people in danger, males sixteen or over received a sentence of up to seven years at Newgate Prison. For a second such crime, those over sixteen could face a sentence of up to life in prison. The alteration in the statute was very specific, including a section concerning those over the age of sixteen who set fire to a shop but did not risk human life. Again the sentence was for seven years. The punishment of death for putting life in danger by arson also still applied only to those over sixteen. Maintenance of the immunity against prosecution for those under sixteen, at least under the criminal law, argued that Connecticut adults continued to see younger teens as less capable of recognizing the consequences of their actions, at least in the crime of arson.[45]

In the late eighteenth century one of the few arson cases that involved a minor was a grand jurors' complaint that Robert Crary, 2nd, of Preston, who was over sixteen years old, willfully set fire to the house of Samuel Tracey in Preston. The warrant alleged that Tracey and the family were living in the house at the time of the fire and that the fire partially consumed the structure. Certainly this made the charge a capital case. Nevertheless, the justice of the peace resolved the charges at the justice court level, finding Robert innocent but assessing him court costs of $21.21. Perhaps because the case did not go to a higher court, the justice did not deem it necessary to assign a guardian for the boy's defense, although as a child over the age of sixteen, he faced the death penalty if convicted.[46]

INCREASED RESPONSIBILITY OF MINORS FOR ARSON

By the early nineteenth century a change in the laws against arson ironically appeared to place greater responsibility on younger minors because it removed the immunity from prosecution for those under the age of sixteen, making them accountable for their actions. The irony lay in the fact that changing ideas about the nature of human beings arising from the ideas of John Locke and Jean Jacques Rousseau had been leading to a softening of the old Puritan belief in the innate sinfulness of human beings, including children. Despite this changing opinion, in 1801 the new law directed the death penalty for *any* person who burned a building leading to the endangering or loss of human life. Those who committed arson without creating a threat to life would go to Newgate Prison for a seven-year term. For a second such offense the sentence was life in prison at Newgate. In 1821 a different section of the law against arson specifically directed that anyone who willfully or maliciously burned any public building, including college, academy, or schoolhouse buildings, (without a specific mention of endangering human life) would go to prison at Newgate for seven years. The precise mention of buildings where young people congregated revealed that by the 1820s youths of any age were not automatically exempt from the penalty under the revised law.[47] The reason for the change was not clear, but the increasing congestion in towns and urban areas may have led legislators to worry more about the potential sweeping destruction of property from fires than about the clear intent of those accused of arson.

Arson crimes were an area where minors, especially those of color, often lacked the legal protection of court-appointed guardians. Despite Zephaniah Swift's formal assertion in 1795 that under the civil law the state must appoint a guardian to assist a minor in his or her defense and despite the existence of an established group of lawyers who practiced in the county courts and who stood to gain by their appointment as guardians *ad litem*, it took considerable time before magistrates were consistent in providing that protection for all minors charged under the criminal laws of the state. In 1801, Lizzie, a seventeen-year-old African-American girl from Norwich, faced charges of setting fire to Jackson Brown's house, burning it to the ground, and causing the death of seven-year-old Sophia Brown. As noted earlier, arson, when it resulted in the death of a person, was still a capital crime in the state. If convicted, Lizzie faced the death sentence. Nevertheless, the New London County Superior Court tried Lizzie without any parent present and without a court-appointed guardian to assist in her defense. Perhaps because the jury found her not guilty and dismissed the charges without costs, the issue of reversible error was moot. Nevertheless, at no time did the court accord Lizzie the protections due to her because of her age, an apparent violation of established procedures that might have been because she was African American. An alternative explanation could lie in the fact that neither Lizzie nor her family may have known of her legal right to a guardian and a form of legal representation and thus did not raise the issue at any point in the case.[48]

In another arson case three years later the procedural protection provided for a minor defendant by a court-appointed guardian eventually came into play, but only after the accused had pleaded guilty. Whatever minimal protection the guardian provided did not alter the outcome of the case. Nevertheless, the fact that the eventual sentence was to the county jail rather than to Newgate Prison may have reflected the Court's concern over sending a minor female to the state prison. In 1804 Colchester Justice of the Peace Ebeneezer Lathrop charged Colchester resident Lynda Doyle with two attempts to burn down the house of Caleb Gillet in the town. The justice court did not identify Lynda as a minor nor did it direct the notification of her parents or the appointment of a guardian. When Lynda pleaded guilty, Lathrop set a $200 bond to guarantee her appearance at the Superior Court for sentencing. As a result of her inability to pay the bond, the girl spent five months in the county jail. Despite the fact that Lynda was in jail awaiting formal sentencing, nothing in the justice court writ indicated that her parents had received notice of the charges against her. At the Superior Court hearing the judge finally identified the girl as a minor under the age of twenty-one and appointed Jeremiah G. Brainard as her guardian. Brainard was an ineffective guardian of the girl's legal rights. He did not enter any challenge to the legality of the original proceedings though he did counsel her to withdraw her guilty plea. Despite the presence of this court-appointed guardian to assist in her defense before the Superior Court, the Court found Lynda guilty and sentenced her to one year at hard labor at the county jail, a noticeably lower sentence than the maximum directed by the new law on arson. Brainard neither filed an appeal of the second conviction based on reversible error, a possible ploy since the girl had not received the mandated legal advice and protection at her original hearing, nor did he petition the General Assembly for further clemency for his client.[49]

Prison records from Newgate Prison and the new State Prison at Wethersfield made it clear that after 1800 prosecutions for arson were resulting in more convictions against minors as a result of the changes in the law. A number of minors convicted of arson in the early nineteenth century served their sentences first at Newgate, then at the new State Prison in Wethersfield. Milford youth Francis McCune served his sentence for arson at Newgate

Prison in 1803, despite a plea for clemency to the Connecticut General Assembly in which he cited his youth as a reason to lessen his punishment. Jeffrey Jeffers, a Lebanon youth of nineteen identified on prison records as black or mulatto, went to Newgate in 1810 to serve a three-year term for arson. Norwalk native David Canfield was only fourteen years old and five feet tall when the court sentenced him to a two-and-a-half-year term for arson in 1815. In one of the few instances that revealed an attitude of clemency toward an underage arsonist, the county released fourteen-year-old Samuel Hatch on bond paid by his mother after he set fire to an office building with a lighted cigar. Betraying both his mother's and the county's trust, the boy fled the state. In 1825 Edward Hall of Columbia was only eighteen when he served a nine-month term for arson. Based on a lighter than normal sentence of two years at the Wethersfield prison, Nathan Perkins of Norwich may have received a measure of clemency as a result of his age when the court convicted him in 1838 of setting fire to the barn of fellow Norwich resident, William H. Law. The magistrate identified Perkins as under the age of twenty-one and appointed Henry Strong, Esq. as his guardian to defend him against the charge. The case file indicated that the barn was close enough to the Law house to endanger the lives of Law and his family. Although the house also burned, the jury found Nathan guilty of just a single count of arson and sentenced him to less than the maximum term prescribed by law.[50]

LESSENED PENALTIES FOR UNDERAGE ARSONISTS

Though the change in the law now held minors of any age responsible for crimes of arson, both appeals and sentences in the 1840s revealed public support for milder treatment for underage arsonists. While being just thirteen did not protect George Cam from the consequences of his actions in burning down a barn in Fairfield in 1842, after serving four years of his five-year sentence, the boy filed a petition for early release, notably without the apparent assistance of a legal guardian. George asked that the General Assembly consider his youth at the time of the crime and his current feeble state of health after spending four years at the State Prison at Wethersfield. Whether the child's age at the time of the crime or his poor health was the deciding factor, the Assembly voted to release the seventeen-year-old. Age may also have been a factor in the 1845 exoneration of Ashley Otis York of Norwich after eighteen witnesses testified against him. The arrest warrant charged the boy with putting matches near the storehouse of the Norwich Falls Company and lighting combustible materials with the matches. Originally the justice court failed to identify the boy as a minor and jailed him because he was not able to provide a surety for his county court appearance. The New London

County Court assigned L. F. S. Foster, Esq. as his guardian to "direct and advise him *ad litem.*" Because the case occurred prior to the creation of the State Reform School for Boys, the not-guilty verdict could have reflected the jury's reluctance to send a child to the state prison, or it could have been the result of the jurors' understanding that children played with matches, often without thinking of the possible consequences. Age was almost certainly a factor when an eleven-year-old girl did not have to pay the maximum penalty for burning down a house in 1853. The original writ of the justice court called Ursula S. Babcock of Lyme "an evil disposed person" when she burned down the house of James M. Beebe of Lyme. This labeling of the girl made it clear that the justice of the peace believed the child had the necessary intent to turn her action into a crime. Nevertheless, the Superior Court ruled that because the girl was only eleven years old and had already received a sentence of a term of two months in the common jail and a fine of $300 for conspiracy to incite arson, it would not prosecute the actual charge of arson. Contrary to most cases against minors by the 1850s the justice court had not identified the child as a minor; only at the Superior Court did the state assign her two separate guardians to defend her. The mildness of her sentence in 1853 certainly reflected the unwillingness of adults to send young children, especially girls, to the State Prison.[51]

Several arson cases revealed the increasing reluctance to hold some male youths fully responsible for their actions in starting fires, perhaps reflecting the reform attitudes that contributed to the opening of the State Reform School for Boys in 1853. In 1851 Stonington Justice of the Peace Francis Sheffield brought arson charges against Joseph Lanpher, asserting that he had "wilfully and maliciously" set fire to and burned the Stonington schoolhouse and that he had also burned down a barn in Stonington owned by George W. Noyes. Sheffield, upon Joseph's stating that he was a minor, appointed Nathan A. Dixon, Esq. as the boy's guardian to "assist him in the management of his case." Sheffield then found the boy not guilty and discharged him from custody, perhaps from a reluctance to send the youth to the now notorious state prison. However, at the same session of his justice court Sheffield also charged Edwin A. Briggs of Stonington with the burning of Noyes' barn. Since Edwin too was a minor, the justice of the peace asked Dixon to serve as his guardian as well. In this case, though the teen pleaded not guilty, Sheffield found grounds for the complaint and bound the boy over to the County Court on a $300 bond. Nothing in the case file indicated why Sheffield came to different verdicts for the two boys. Because there was no record of a trial of the charges at the county court level, the state's attorney may have dismissed the case once it reached the higher court.[52]

The case of a twelve-year-old sent to the state prison for arson in 1852 revealed the dilemma faced by both the courts and the General Assembly in dealing with underage arsonists. The Superior Court in Fairfield convicted Benjamin Townsend of arson for the burning of a barn in Danbury in February of 1852. Although the boy had pleaded guilty to the charges at his trial, by 1853 the Court received new evidence exonerating the child. In a petition for release from his prison term, Benjamin claimed he had been coerced into his guilty plea and asserted his innocence. Though the legal system apparently recognized its mistake, the General Assembly members were unwilling simply to release the boy, since he had "no parent or guardian with whom he can be safely entrusted." The State Reform School was not yet open for inmates. Because the child had committed no crime, the General Assembly had to release the youth from prison. The debate made it clear that Assembly members wanted some way to influence the hapless child's future. Therefore the Assembly appointed Frances W. Cowles, Esq. as the boy's guardian with the power to place the young teen into an apprenticeship until he was twenty-one. The youth might have been better off had he served his sentence at the prison because he would have gained his freedom earlier.[53]

An 1853 clemency petition to the Connecticut General Assembly from Dennis Kelly illustrated that the pattern of milder treatment of under-age arsonists was not always consistent. After serving thirteen years of a fourteen-year sentence for arson, Dennis, now twenty-nine, pleaded for an early release from prison. The fact that he was Irish might have contributed to the harshness of the original sentence because in his petition he claimed that at the time of his conviction at the Litchfield County Superior Court, he had been under the age of seventeen and he had had no malicious intent. He also asserted that others had improperly influenced his actions, further clouding the question of whether he had had sufficient intent to commit the crime. He also claimed that the buildings he had burned had been old and uninhabited so that he had not endangered any people. In the face of the increasingly common reform rhetoric concerning the responsibility of children for their criminal actions, those factors ought to have resulted in a milder sentence in the 1840s. To support his plea to leave prison before the end of his term, Dennis also wrote that while in prison he had become a reformed man and felt he could now lead a Christian life. Since the General Assembly granted the young man's plea for immediate release without comment, it is not clear whether his youth at the time of conviction or the overly harsh sentence was most influential in winning clemency.[54]

Clearly by the 1850s Connecticut's legal system treated thieves and arsonists who were under twenty-one less harshly than had the judges and juries of earlier centuries. Nevertheless, Connecticut property owners still demanded protection for their possessions. Between the operation of the discretionary sentencing law and the new option of indeterminate sentences at the State Reform School for Boys, residents could be sure that punishments for breaking the laws of the State would be certain and swift to maintain respect for law and property. At the same time, both laws gave minor criminals a second chance, a chance for education and moral redemption that would eventually allow them to become upstanding citizens of the community. Control and redemption, two watchwords of middle-class reformers in the nineteenth century, culminated in the new institution of the reform school.

Chapter Two

Murderous Minors: The Treatment of Assault and Murder

> He assaulted him violently in a wanton, wicked, unfeeling manner and beat and bruised him by throwing at him and hitting him with a large club on the side of his head whereby the plaintiff was so stunned he was unable to help himself and is in great peril of his life.
>
> —*Mallory v. Moore,* Connecticut Justice Court Records, 1825

> As she sat with her face to the door, he took the ax and struck Mrs. Bolles on the hinder part of the head with the ax and she fell down and he struck her another blow with the ax and killed her.
>
> —Examination of Jonathan Stoddard, July 26, 1678

Court records from Connecticut's colonial period make it clear that the colony's society was far from peaceful. Even though Everett Goodwin has claimed that colonial inhabitants saw the law as an expression of God's will to produce a righteous order, the laws actually did not prevent both young and old residents from acting in a very violent fashion. Although cases of murder and manslaughter were relatively rare, the second most common type of criminal cases brought to the courts at both the justice of the peace level and at the county courts dealt with charges of assault or trespass, the catchall term from the civil law that included assault. *Black's Law Dictionary* defines assault as a "willful attempt or threat to inflict injury upon the person of another, coupled with the apparent present ability so to do." In practice this encompassed both the threat of an attack and an actual battery as defined by Zephaniah Swift:

> Battery is the actual commission of violence to the person. Any injury however small that is done to a person in a spiteful, revengeful, rude, or insolent manner, either by beating, striking, or pushing him, or by

> spitting in his face, treading on his toes, or in any way touching him in anger or violently jostling him out of the way. . . . For the law holds everyone's person to be sacred . . . and as it is difficult to draw a line of distinction between degrees of violence, it is necessary to prohibit it at every stage.[1]

Swift's definition made it clear that intent was an important part of determining whether either an assault or the resulting battery were either civil wrongs or criminal acts.

Judging from court records, Connecticut's society in both the seventeenth and eighteenth centuries differed from the "peaceable kingdoms" described by Michael Zuckerman. Residents committed violent assaults for what often appear to have been petty aggravations, and people under twenty-one were as likely to commit assaults as their elders. In both centuries the disposition of assault cases in Connecticut in which minors were defendants revealed the community's desire to maintain a peaceable society, and followed a pattern similar to the prosecutions for theft, because the majority of colonial-era cases came to the courts as civil actions rather than as criminal cases. Furthermore, few assault cases utilized language condemning the innate depravity of the child who committed the assault. Instead of using assault cases to bemoan the godlessness of society, the courts actually rarely used language that addressed the question of evil intent. Instead their goal appears to have been to restore and maintain order and compensate the victims of the assault. When the courts tried assault cases as civil actions, the civil procedures of the colony required that the plaintiff sue the child through his or her parent, guardian, or master. Because of a minor's age and inexperience, children were incapable, in the eyes of the law, to prosecute or defend against a lawsuit. Zephaniah Swift noted that when a plaintiff brought a lawsuit against a child who did not have a parent or guardian, the court would appoint a temporary guardian to assist in his or her defense. Swift even asserted that the court's failure to provide such assistance was grounds for reversal of the judgment. Not only did this practice insure that children would have a form of legal representation, it also meant that plaintiffs could collect damages from a child's more solvent parent or guardian. Courts could also require that adults pay the costs of prosecution of children under their care as well as making the adult post a bond to ensure the child's good behavior in the future. If an assault involved attacks on public officials or were part of a full-blown riot, or if colonial authorities believed assaults threatened public order, the courts heard the resulting charges under the criminal law. In those cases, the colony did not always follow its own practice of prosecuting minors through their guardians.[2]

ASSAULT

Many of the seventeenth-century assault cases in Connecticut against minors revealed that a child had attacked and beaten another person, often with no provocation at all. In a number of cases, one child assaulted another. Yet as mentioned, few cases raised the question of intent, examining why one person attacked another, unless the defendant pleaded self-defense. Because records of vital statistics, especially of age, are so incomplete for the seventeenth century, determining whether minors received different treatment compared to adults who committed assault is difficult. When Jonathan Stevens, Jr. faced charges for assaulting and threatening his uncle in 1680, the mention of the family relationship may have indicated that Jonathan was under the age of twenty-one, but his treatment by the New London County Court was no different than for adults. The magistrate fined him two pounds ten shillings for the assault and bound him for good behavior. In 1693 the New London County Court prosecuted Harvard student George Denison, the grandson of Captain G. Denison of New London, for assaulting the town constable. Though in the seventeenth century Harvard students generally were under the age of twenty-one, the file indicated nothing about George's age, treating him as it would any adult.[3]

The age of the accused apparently had little influence on the procedures of the New London County Court when it charged twenty-year-old David Tillotson of Lyme with breach of the peace and assault in 1714 for threatening Jasper Grissing of Lyme, and fined the youth twenty shillings plus five shillings in court costs. Notably, there was no written record that the court notified the young man's father of the charges. In 1715 fifteen-year-old Isaac Williams of Stonington answered civil charges that he had assaulted John Stoyls, the Stonington schoolmaster. This was a civil rather than a criminal case because Stoyls brought the action against Isaac, even though Stoyls was a representative of town officialdom as the schoolmaster. Though the files did not indicate that the boy's father, John Williams, received notice of the action against his son, the case did go to trial. Because Stoyls, himself a minor, did not appear to pursue his case, the court dismissed the charges against young Isaac. This dismissal came despite Stoyls' original claim that two Stonington adults, Eleazer Williams and Thomas Atwood, had hired the teen to assault the schoolmaster. Although the magistrate dismissed the case because of Stoyl's failure to appear, he assessed court costs of five pounds against Isaac rather than against the absent plaintiff. [4]

In 1721, a fourteen-year-old Killingworth boy, Nathaniel Williams, assaulted the town constable, Peter Ward, and the town collector, Samuel

Griswold, by throwing sticks at them and hitting Griswold with a club, breaking his arm. Perhaps because both men were town officials, the boy faced criminal charges for the assault rather than a civil lawsuit initiated by the men for damages. The writ for the case identified the youth as the son of Thomas Williams of Killingworth but provided no specific additional notice to the father. Though the child was just over the age of discretion, the court did not raise a question about the boy's intent. Perhaps the mere commission of the action was enough evidence of evil intent. Nevertheless, in a rare display of mercy, the court was lenient towards the child, recording that he had been under fourteen at the time of the assault and had confessed his fault saying that he was "very sorry for it and asking them please to forgive him, promising never to do it again, appearing to be very penitent by the shedding of many tears." The constable and collector, also moved by the boy's contrition, were willing to forgive the child and agreed to the dropping of the charges. The court charged the boy's father court costs of four pounds, but assessed no fines or damages against the youth himself.[5]

By the mid-eighteenth century, the formal notification of parents to defend children against legal proceedings for assault became more common. In 1756 Justice of the Peace Isaac Huntington charged Comfort and Nathaniel Fillamore of Norwich for their assault against the Norwich tax collector, Jacob Hazen. Using clubs to attack Hazen, the fourteen and sixteen-year-old boys then drove away some swine in Hazen's possession. Huntington identified the boys as minors in his original writ and named their father, Captain John Fillamore, to be their guardian for the defense against the charges. This change in the form of notifying a parent may have reflected the increasing sophistication of Connecticut's judicial system but could also have been the result of the elder Fillamore's standing in the community. When the father pleaded for an abatement, or dismissal of the charges, Huntington sent the case to the New London County Court. The County Court also named the boys' father to be their guardian. At the county level the boys pleaded guilty to the charges, and each paid fines of five shillings with court costs of over two pounds. Since the justice of the peace did not charge the youths with theft for taking away the swine, it is possible they were retrieving the animals at their father's direction.[6]

Some assault cases involving minors during the eighteenth century revealed a curious phenomenon. At times minors brought suit against other minors for assault, usually seeking payment for injuries suffered in the attack. The existence of such litigation may have reflected several aspects of colonial society. Parents who incurred the financial expense of treating an injured child would want redress, but since the child was the victim, the child had to be the plaintiff, and yet could only bring the lawsuit with the assistance of a parent or guardian. Such litigation might also have been an outgrowth of tensions or hostilities between different parents. Since children could not legally bring lawsuits in their own names, it was the parent or guardian who would decide when a childish fight turned into an intentional assault or when a petty disagreement became grounds for a lawsuit. This type of lawsuit may also have been a reflection of parental responsibility to protect children. Zephaniah Swift declared that parental obligation towards children not only required that they "aid, assist, and uphold" the child in lawsuits, but also that they could justify assault and battery in defense of the child. Litigation was clearly the less risky way to protect a child's interests. In most of such cases, the father or guardian of the plaintiff made the complaint on behalf of the child, but the courts were not always consistent in assuring legal representation for the minor defendants.[7]

A clear example of this use of the courts to seek redress for an assault on a child appeared in an assault case in Suffield. In June of 1772, five Suffield boys assaulted seventeen-year-old John Hathaway of Suffield. John Hathaway the elder filed a complaint against the five, Isaac, Jacob, and Moses Shelton, Diah Dewey, and Benjamin Sheldon, identifying all as minors "but of the age of discretion." Hathaway claimed the youths had attacked his son in the schoolhouse and had beaten him with clubs and staves, had flung fire on his head, and had burned his hair and clothes. All of the accused boys pleaded not guilty to the charges "by their fathers and natural guardians." The Court found all five guilty as charged and ordered each to pay two pounds six shillings to the town of Suffield as a fine and the same amount to the elder Hathaway. Benjamin Sheldon appealed the sentence through the agency of Phineas Sheldon, his father, but the Court found him still guilty on the appeal. Considering the odds of five to one, the elder Hathaway obviously chose to sue the boys rather than to defend his son physically.[8]

In an assault case in 1780 that may have been the precursor of a murder case six years later, the legal system provided only cursory protection to two African-American children charged with assaulting a seven-year-old child. The state accused Groton children Charles Aves and Hannah Sharper, also known as Hannah Occuish, with attacking Mary Fish, age seven, as she went home from school in Groton. The two hit the child in the head with a stone, beat and bruised her, and then stripped her and robbed her of her clothes. Though the writ in the case did not specifically identify either defendant as a minor, it directed that the magistrate read the writ at the house of Joseph Parker of Groton to notify Sarah Sharper, "the mother of the delinquents."

Because the magistrate could not locate Hannah after reading the notice, the state dropped the prosecution against the girl. Tragically, a few years later Hannah assaulted and murdered another seven-year-old, Eunice Bolles.[9]

During the Revolutionary War, Connecticut courts prosecuting breach of the peace or assaults by Tories were none too careful to protect the rights of minor defendants who were part of Tory families. In June of 1781, guards in the New London harbor apprehended a boat and two men on charges that the men were involved in illicit trade with the British on Long Island. When the guards attempted to deliver the boat and its contents to the proper authorities, a mob of men assaulted the guards using clubs, staves, and stones. The mob, including several minors, disarmed the officials, released the captives, and retrieved the boat and its contents. Charging all with a misdemeanor assault, the magistrate found all guilty. Perhaps because the fathers of the minors were also defendants in the case, the magistrate gave no special notice to the boys' fathers to defend them against the allegations and issued a guilty verdict, assessing each six pounds as a fine. All refused to pay and sought a review of the charges. Unsurprisingly, the verdict stood at that review.[10]

In a 1784 case that illustrated the disparity between civil and criminal laws on assault, John Stark of Stonington sued Steven Martin and Samuel Hawley, Jr., charging they had assaulted a Stonington minor, Frederick Denison. Stark's relationship to Denison was not clear in the court records, but no one questioned his right to bring a lawsuit in the child's name. At the original trial at the New London County Court, the Court awarded Stark a writ of attachment in Frederick's name against the two assailants to satisfy the ruling in his favor. The two appealed the ruling to the Connecticut Superior Court in New London County, and Stark failed to appear at the hearing. As a result, the original defendants obtained a dismissal of the original action. What created a problem was that the Superior Court also awarded a large bill of costs against Frederick rather than against Stark. Here the law requiring notification to parents or guardians of minors in lawsuits complicated the picture. Isaac Denison of Stonington, Frederick's father, brought suit against Martin and Hawley and Stark, claiming that Stark had brought the original lawsuit for assault and trespass "without his knowledge and consent and without any authority to do so." The judge agreed with his plea and dismissed the charges against him.[11]

In a civil suit in 1786, the assault charges against fourteen-year-old Joseph Herrington of Preston were part of a larger assault charge against Herrington's employer and two other adults. Joseph Baldwin of Lisbon charged that all four had attacked and beaten him and sued for five hundred pounds in damages. The files for the case revealed that the Court had immediately identified Herrington as a minor and cited Asel Adams, his master and guardian, to advise and defend the boy against the charges. Herrington played little role in the case; all the testimony was by the adults. Adams asserted that he and the other three defendants were on Adams' land and that Baldwin had actually attacked first. At the County Court the magistrate found in favor of the defendants. When Baldwin filed an appeal at the Superior Court on the basis that he had a right to be on Adams' land, he lost again, and the Court assessed costs against him. Because Herrington was in Adams' employ at the time of the incident, Adams would probably have defended the boy even without the legal notification from the court since he would have been liable for any fines or costs assessed against his apprentice.[12]

An assault case brought by a girl from Montville against another Montville youth raised the issue of the veracity of the plaintiff's testimony, but both the minor plaintiff and the minor defendant did secure the assistance of adults in the case. Mercy Maples originally brought suit in 1788 with the aid of her father, William Maples, against Joshua Vallet of Montville, a minor, and three Montville adults, Joshua and Sarah Monroe and Lydia Chappel, charging they had attacked and assaulted her by beating and bruising her and imprisoning her for four hours. Mercy claimed she had lost a lot of blood and still "languished" from her injuries. In her lawsuit she sought one thousand pounds in damages. After a justice of the peace heard the charges in August of 1788, he transferred the case to the New London County Court that without explanation dismissed William Maples as Mercy's guardian, naming instead her brother, William Maples, Jr. The County Court also clearly identified Joshua as a minor, the son of Jeremiah Vallet, 2nd, but instead of appointing the boy's father as his guardian, it named Jeremiah Gates Brainard to represent him in the case. Through his guardian, Joshua pleaded that he was not guilty, as did the three adults charged in the assault. Nevertheless, the Court found all four guilty. It awarded fifty pounds in damages directly to Mercy and assessed fines of twenty pounds against Vallet and ten pounds against each adult. Not content with the verdict both Joshua through his guardian and the adults applied to the Connecticut Superior Court at New London for a writ of error, but the Court refused to issue the writ. All four then launched an appeal in 1789. At the appeal hearing Mercy appeared by her guardian and pleaded for an abatement or dismissal of the appeal. The grounds for the appeal relied on the testimony of Vallet that on the night of the assault Mercy "had not behaved as she ought" with Joshua at his house and that Mercy's own mother had called her a "good for nothing dirty trollop." The Court granted the abatement requested by Mercy's guardian and awarded her costs. In a rare show of litigious persistence, the Monroes and Vallet continued to try to reopen the case on appeal until 1793, long after both Mercy and Joshua had achieved adulthood; each time the County Court found in favor of Mercy Maples.[13]

Notification to a parent or guardian did not always provide a minor defendant with assistance, leaving some minors to defend themselves. In 1789 Jonathan Brooks, Jr. of New London brought a civil suit for assault against William Chew, also of New London, identified in the original writ as a minor under age twenty-one. Brooks sought two hundred and fifty pounds in damages, claiming Chew had "struck, kicked, wounded, and bruised him," breaking his knee. Though the writ ordered that Joseph Chew, Esq. be notified of the action against William so that he could appear in court to advise and assist his son if he saw cause to do so, a note on the writ made it clear that the elder Chew was currently living in London and was wholly unable to assist the boy. The justice merely directed that notice be left at the Chew household. Notably, the official did not appoint any other adult to assist the youth with his defense. Unprotected and unassisted by adult support, the boy tried some legal maneuvering. First he pleaded for an abatement of the writ on the grounds that it was invalid because his full legal name was William Johnson Chew. One can imagine Brooks' indignation when he responded that the boy never used the name Johnson. The justice agreed that William was known as William Chew and awarded damages of two hundred and fifty pounds to the plaintiff. At no time at the original hearing was there any evidence that an adult assisted the minor defendant. Finally, at William's Superior Court appeal of the original judgment, the Court appointed Samuel Wheat as guardian to assist the boy in presenting his case. With this help, William succeeded in having the damages reduced to just forty pounds. Yet at no time did either the minor or his guardian plead for an abatement on the grounds that he had had no assistance at the original trial of the facts. Perhaps not everyone knew of the legal procedures in place to protect the interests of those under twenty-one.[14]

By the 1790s the New London Courts at all levels were becoming more careful to make a specific identification of minor defendants in assault cases and to notify the child's father or to provide a court-appointed guardian even in cases seeking relatively minor amounts for damages. Still, the question of intent rarely appeared in the records. In 1792 Lyme Justice of the Peace William Noyes heard a case in which Lyme resident Henry Denison, a minor, "appeared" by his father Samuel Denison and sued fellow minor Peter Peck Clark for assault seeking four pounds in damages. Roswell Clark,

Peter's father, represented his son at the hearing and entered a plea of not guilty. Whatever damages Henry had suffered must have been comparatively minor because Noyes found Peter guilty of the assault but only ordered that Henry, "under his guardian," was to recover ten shillings plus court costs. Furthermore, Peter's father had to pay a fine of six shillings to the court. Though the damages were not as high as the amount demanded by Henry and his father, apparently being a minor did not shield Peter from the expense of breaking the law. In the same session of his justice court when assessing a fine against an adult convicted of assault, Noyes again set the amount at six shillings.[15]

In the aftermath of what may have been a simple fight between two boys, William Huntley, 2nd, a minor from Lyme, brought a complaint and lawsuit with the assistance of his father against Lyme resident Ruel Beckwith for assault and battery and breach of the peace, seeking five dollars in damages. Ruel was also under the age of twenty-one. Justice of the Peace William Noyes reported that Ruel did have assistance by a guardian at the hearing and that the teen pleaded not guilty to the charges. Nevertheless, Noyes found the boy guilty but assessed damages of just one dollar and a fine for the same amount.[16] Clearly, the provision of legal representation for minors did not depend on the severity of the charges.

A notable feature of nearly all the assault cases in the late eighteenth and into the early nineteenth centuries was that they rarely resulted in prison terms at either the county jails or the state prison, even when the State itself brought charges of criminal assault. As a result, there were few defendants to appeal their sentences or seek clemency from the General Assembly. Thus there is little evidence in the records of prosecutions for assault of any softening in attitudes toward minors who broke the laws. Records from Newgate Prison dating from 1810 indicated that of forty-seven criminals, only two were serving sentences for assaults, both found guilty of attempted murder: a sixty-year-old Connecticut native and a twenty-four-year-old Irishman. Two years later fifty-three prisoners were at the prison, but only two additional inmates were in for assault. By 1825 Newgate Prison held 117 inmates, but the incidence of assault was still quite low. Only two prisoners were serving terms for assault; neither was a minor. When the State transferred inmates to the new State Prison in Wethersfield in 1827, only five of the 129 prisoners had been serving terms for assault, ranging from six years to life. All were adults at the time they committed their crimes. Violent assaults became more common by the 1830s, a change that the prison warden blamed on alcohol consumption. A State Prison report in 1834 revealed that thirteen percent of the 189 inmates were serving time for assault, but all but one had actually faced charges of attempted murder. Only two were under the age of twenty-one when convicted: fourteen-year-old Ephraim Treadwell, found guilty of an assault with an attempt to kill serving a four-year term, and seventeen-year-old Perry Dunn, convicted of assault with attempt to murder and sentenced to three years. Both of these were clearly cases where the intent of the assailant had figured in the punishment for the crime.[17] For assaults not aggravated by allegations of an attempt to murder, the State's prosecutions for assault apparently remained more intent on providing compensation to victims and maintaining order by fines or bonds for good behavior, rather than imposing long terms at the State Prison.

A new feature of assault trials of those under the age of twenty-one in the early part of the nineteenth century was a change in the way minors defended themselves. As in the 1790s, the courts provided notice to the parents or guardians of most minor defendants, but the majority of under-age defendants now officially entered pleas by those adults rather than doing the pleadings themselves. This was probably because an increasing number of parents who chose to represent and defend their children had more formal experience with the procedures of Connecticut's court system. For example, in 1800 William Huntley 2nd again sued Ruel Beckwith charging trespass, assault, and battery. The more formal language of the defendant's response was clear: "The defendant by his guardian Nehemiah Smith pleads and says he is not guilty." Ruel was Smith's apprentice; perhaps this had negated the need for a formal appointment of Smith by the court as the boy's guardian. Because the justice of the peace had not identified Ruel's guardian in the prior case, it is not clear whether Smith had represented Ruel in the earlier case. Certainly, in 1800 Smith was a more skillful assistant than the adult who had previously represented Ruel. Perhaps as the result of Smith's help in the rehearing of the case the Court reversed itself, finding the youth not guilty of assault and assessing court costs of $15.62 against the plaintiff.[18]

In all other cases during this decade at the County Court level involving white minors, similar language appeared in the documents. Only in one case, heard only before a justice of the peace in a justice court, was the legal role of the parent or guardian less explicit. In this 1809 criminal case the State of Connecticut charged Samuel Hoyt of Norwich and Thomas Higgins of New London with assaulting New London resident Solomon Roberts with their fists, sticks, and billets of wood and bruising his body, shoulders, and head. The assailants also broke down the door of Roberts' New London shop with stones and clubs. In his record of the justice court hearing Justice of the Peace Josiah Isham wrote, "Thomas Higgins a minor - his father William Higgins present." Furthermore the justice recorded that upon the guilty verdict, the boy paid the $5 fine and court costs of $5.07 with his father's note. There was no record of a formal notice to Thomas's father, nor was there a formal appointment of the father as guardian to defend the child, but he was clearly involved in the disposition of the case.[19]

This more formal type of legal assistance by way of notification of a responsible adult or appointment of a legal guardian did not appear in the few cases involving assaults by African-American minors. In 1801 John Smith 2nd of New London sought two hundred dollars when he sued Sawney Durfey, identified in the writ as the nineteen-year-old Negro servant of Richard Durfey of New London. Smith claimed the teen had hit him with a club and threatened to cut him with a scythe, leaving him wounded and in fear of his life. Despite civil procedures that directed that minors could not defend lawsuits alone, Smith did not notify any adult when he initiated his suit. To make up for that oversight, at the justice court, the magistrate served notice on Richard Durfey as Sawney's guardian and master so that he could assist with the defense if he saw cause. Although the master did provide surety for his servant, nothing in the case file indicated whether the master actually represented the youth in court. The court found Sawney guilty of the assault and assessed damages of $25 with additional court costs of $35.73. The court files contained no indication that Durfey challenged the conviction perhaps providing evidence to prove that he was not in court to protect the interests of his servant. However, his failure to challenge the legality of the original lawsuit may have been evidence that he was not familiar with the laws protecting the interests of minors.[20]

In the following two decades there continued to be a difference in the manner in which the justice courts dealt with minors as compared to the County Courts. In nearly every case at the justice court level, the justices of the peace did identify which of the defendants were minors and then either notified the appropriate parent or guardian or appointed a guardian to represent the child's interest. Yet in all the justice court cases, the writs merely said to summon the parent or guardian to defend "if he sees cause," and gave no indication if a responsible adult actually assisted in the child's defense. In several related cases, the state brought assault and other charges against the sons of two New London African Americans, but only in the subsequent trials did the justice appoint an independent guardian, perhaps because the boys' fathers had failed to assist in their defense in the prior case. In 1825 Richard Smith and George Jeffery of New London supposedly assaulted Daniel G. Alright. The legal charge said the two did "cruelly hit, beat, ill-treat, violently seize, and strike (him) on the forehead, face, and eyes with a big stone so that he was greatly injured and lost much blood and still languishes." Though the writ did not explicitly identify the two defendants as minors, a written note on the face of the document noted that Justice of the Peace Edward Learned had appointed the boys' fathers to represent them, designating Charles Jeffery as guardian to George and Parker H. Smith as guardian to Richard. However, the document did not record if either father actually appeared before the justice of the peace to defend his son. The justice found both youths guilty and fined each $7. In 1827 a different justice of the peace heard new charges against George, this time a breach of the peace rather than assault. George and three others had assembled on a night in April and created a five-hour uproar by setting off firecrackers and making "horrible oaths and imprecations." The justice, William P. Cleaveland, Jr., wrote that as George was a minor he had summoned his father Charles Jeffery to defend him. Clearly Jeffery did not appear because Cleaveland noted on the front of the writ that he had subsequently appointed Charles Bolles as guardian to George. Unfortunately, having an adult to represent his interests did not shield young George from the consequences of his actions; Cleaveland fined him five dollars. A few months later Cleaveland heard a new assault charge against Richard Smith, this time alleging Richard had attacked Henry Campbell of New London, hitting him with his fists. This time the justice did not even bother notifying the child's father; he appointed Benjamin Brown as his guardian. With Brown's advice the boy pleaded guilty, and Cleaveland collected a five-dollar fine. Two years later Samuel Jeffery of New London, a brother of Charles Jeffery, assaulted Thomas Sizer, also of New London, striking violent blows on the man's face, chest, and back. In this case Cleaveland identified the Jeffery boy as a minor and wrote that he was "required to notify Charles Jeffery the father and natural guardian to appear and defend said Samuel if he thinks proper." Apparently the father did not appear to defend his son because Cleaveland noted on the case file that he had subsequently appointed Nathan Haily as guardian to defend the youth. Even though the child clearly had a form of legal representation, Cleaveland found the boy guilty, fined him one dollar, and committed him to jail, apparently because he was unable to pay the fine.[21] Cleaveland's eventual recognition of the requirement to provide proper protection for the black youths' rights did not result in any lessening of their punishments.

In contrast to the continuation of somewhat casual treatment of minors in the assault trials at the justice courts, at the level of the County Court minor defendants often acquired more skillful legal assistance by court-appointed guardians. The language of the specific pleadings also became more formulaic and formal in the period from 1810 until 1830. On the complaint of Calvin Goddard, Esq., state's attorney, the state brought charges on June 19, 1814 against New London residents James Crocker, Henry Rogers, James Carrol, Reuben Davis, and Charles Young for assault and breach of the peace for invading the house of Edward Beebe and beating Beebe and his wife Betsey. The judge specifically identified the last three defendants as minors and wrote that they were "put to the bar to plead by the advice and direction of J. B. Gurley, Esq. who is by this court appointed their guardian." According to the case documents, the defendants had broken into Beebe's house at night, demanding brandy and ardent spirits. Since Beebe was not a licensed tavern keeper, he had refused to give them any liquor so the men and boys had attacked the hapless Beebe and his spouse and "did assault, beat, wound, and injure" them both. Despite the assistance of their court-appointed guardian, the three minors lost the case. The judge fined Reuben and James $15 each but charged Charles, who was only sixteen, just $5. Nothing in the case files indicated a reason for the youngest defendant's lesser fine, but it may have reflected the judge's opinion of which defendants bore the greatest responsibility for the attack. Although the formal sentence did not include a jail term, all three served six days in jail until June 25, not gaining their release until they paid their fines and court costs.[22]

By the 1830s the more formal proceedings against minors found their way into the justice of the peace courts. Both at this local level and at the county court, magistrates were becoming more careful to identify minors facing charges and to provide court-appointed guardians when parents were unable or unwilling to represent their children on court. A new feature appeared as well: court-appointed guardians at times charged a fee for their services in protecting the minors temporarily assigned to their care. In an 1830 case heard first at the justice court and then at the New London County Court, the State charged Horan and Austin Barber, Lewis Freeman, and Hesekiah Chesebrough, all of Hebron, with a vicious assault, saying they "did beat, pound, strike, drag about, throw down, bite, scratch, bruise, kick, and ill treat and threaten to kill" their victim. The justice identified the two Barbers and Freeman as minors. He summoned Lude Barber, parent and natural guardian to Horan and Austin, to see to their defense and appointed S. A. Peters as guardian *ad litem* for Lewis Freeman. The youths appeared at the county court by their respective guardians and obtained differing results. The court found Chesebrough, the one adult charged in the case, guilty and assessed a $3 fine plus costs. It also found Horan Barber and Lewis Freeman not guilty. Austin had pleaded not guilty at both the justice court and the county court, but both courts found him guilty and eventually sentenced the youth to one month at the county jail. It is not clear whether his punishment, much heavier than that of the adult convicted in the case, was the result of his greater responsibility for the assault or his inability to pay the fine and court costs.[23]

In an apparent recognition that the legal representation initially provided for a minor at the justice court could be insufficient, in an assault case later in 1830 the New London County Court appointed a lawyer to represent one of the youths after the case shifted to the New London County Court. Nevertheless, the change in guardian did not alter the outcome of the case. At the justice court William P. Cleaveland, Jr., Justice of the Peace, appointed Christopher Potts as guardian *ad litem* to New London youths Jeremiah Potts, Jr. and Henry Holmes to represent them against charges that the two boys in company with Jeremiah Slate and John Mapey had assaulted George Wilson of New London. Wilson claimed the four had grabbed him, shaken him, knocked him to the ground, and pounded him with their fists and feet. On the advice of the elder Potts, who was probably the father of Jeremiah, both boys pleaded not guilty. Cleaveland found both adults guilty, fining Slate $7 and Mapey just $5. The justice of the peace then declared Jeremiah was not guilty but found Henry guilty and bound him over for a hearing at the New London County Court, setting the bond at $40. After the boy spent a month in jail because of his inability to post the bond, at the County Court trial the magistrate appointed a new guardian for Henry, lawyer Jerale Isham, Esq. Set to the bar to plead to the charges against him, the boy pleaded through his new guardian that he was not guilty. Despite Isham's assistance to the youth, the court found the boy guilty as charged and assessed a $10 fine and court costs of $22.92. Since bill for the costs did not itemize the various charges, it was not clear whether the higher bill for costs was solely the result of having two hearings or was in part due to the costs of Isham's services.[24]

That representation by a court-appointed guardian was relatively expensive was apparent in the 1831 assault case against eighteen-year-old Henry Duncken of New London, even though the case was entirely at the justice court level. New London Justice of the Peace William F. Brainard heard charges that Henry had assaulted his master and employer, John Gard, also of New London. Gard alleged the youth attacked him by "quarreling, threatening, assaulting, and beating" him with his fists on his face and other parts of his body and knocking him down in the street. Though the writ did not specifically identify Henry as a minor, the face of the document noted that Henry Douglas had been appointed the youth's guardian. Though in many cases an apprentice's master could serve as the court-appointed guardian, clearly in this instance, Gard would not have provided disinterested advice or protection for the child. Found guilty by justice of the peace, Henry had to pay a $1 fine and court costs of $4.33. A note written on the file under the amount for the costs indicated that Douglas's fee for service as guardian for the boy accounted for $4.03 of the total, four times the fine charged.[25]

The reform attitudes of citizens trying to modify the treatment of children under the criminal law had little apparent impact on the sentencing of minors convicted of assault in the Connecticut court system in the 1840s and 1850s. The growing public perception of the necessity of mild correction for youths led astray by improper education and family influence did not result in milder sentences for youths convicted of assault at the county court level of state jurisdiction. The State dismissed few cases, and the sentences handed out to the guilty minors were usually the equivalent of those imposed on adults convicted of similar assaults. This lack of reform zeal may have been because jail sentences for assault were still comparatively short in comparison to the terms set by law for theft. Another reason for this uncompromising attitude might have been that, especially after the mid 1840s, a number of the youths charged with assault were Irish. A State Prison report of 1834 listed only 8 of 189 prisoners as Irish. Reports from the county jails and the State Prison in the 1840s cited the increasing number of Irish lawbreakers. By 1855 the Hartford County jail reported that 68 of 168 persons jailed that year were Irish; the next year 52 of 133 commitments were from Ireland. In his report on the State Prison for 1855, the warden claimed twenty-five percent of the prisoners were Irish. The perceived Irish threat to the Connecticut citizens and the public order may have outweighed any concern for their tender years if the criminals were underage. Yet even for those who were not clearly Irish, the penalties usually included fines and possibly a jail term. When a jury convicted Francis Remington of Norwich of assaulting Russell Johnson in 1841 by threatening to shoot him with a pistol on the streets of Norwich, the youth spent 12 days in jail and paid a $15 fine. In 1842 James H. Trumbull of Colchester assaulted Albert Otis, also of Colchester, by beating and bruising him and shooting at him with a fowling piece, loaded with lead shot. Otis suffered wounds to his head, neck, shoulders, and other parts of his body. Rather surprisingly, the court did not consider this an attempted murder and send Francis to the county jail or state prison but only assessed a sizable fifty-dollar fine against the youth. This was perhaps because the judge appointed Henry Strong, Esq. as guardian to represent the boy and Strong apparently negotiated a reduction of the charge from assault to discharging a gun, a lesser offense.[26]

Most youths charged with assault in the 1840s faced jail terms upon conviction, but judges were not consistent in assigning sentences. In 1843 merely threatening to "inflict great bodily harm" on Jacob Smith and to shoot him drew a conviction for assault for Frank Collins, a minor from New London. Justice of the Peace Henry Douglas used the less formal method of assuring the youth of legal representation, merely summoning Peter Collins, the boy's father, "to advise and assist in his defense." Douglas did note on his files that the father was present before him when Frank pleaded not guilty. Despite the fact that the youth apparently did not actually commit a battery on Smith, the justice of the peace rejected the not-guilty plea and sent the lad to jail for 10 days and fined him fifty cents. At the same session of his justice court, Douglas ordered an adult to serve only four days in jail for an assault, combined with a four-dollar fine. In 1849 the state accused Patrick Blake of Bozrah with an unprovoked attack on Phineas Ryan. The judge noted his appointment of David Young as guardian *ad litem* on the face of the writ. Blake pleaded guilty to the charges on Young's advice and received a fine of $40 plus court costs. He served no time in jail. Perhaps as a result of that guilty plea which saved the cost of a drawn-out trial, the court did dismiss additional charges of breach of the peace against the youth. In 1855, J. T. Wait, Esq. represented two Norwich youths, George Hosier and Jeremiah Sullivan, in their defense against assault charges. The State complained that the two boys had attacked Michael Elliot and Henry Carson of Norwich with a pistol and knife, with the intent to kill them. This was one of the rare assault cases in which the charge raised the question of intent. Though the two boys had pleaded not guilty at the justice court, at the New London County Court, Wait entered guilty pleas for both. Their punishment was a thirty-day sentence in the county jail and payment of court costs of $91.29. Though this sentence was longer than the typical term for assault, there was no record that anyone appeared in court to argue specifically against the length of the sentence.[27]

Because assault continued to draw relatively short sentences, few of those adults who lobbied in favor of opening a reform school for boys in the 1840s and 1850s spoke of it as a solution to ending the problem of assault by minors. That lack of concern was understandable in view of the statistics from the opening years of the school. Of the one hundred and fifty boys who were at the State Reform School for boys in 1855, only two were serving time for simple assault and another two had committed assault and battery.[28] Two possible solutions to the paucity of admissions for assault could be that Connecticut judges and juries still saw assault as a question of restitution or that assault sentences remained so mild that adults did not worry youngsters would suffer unduly during short terms in the county jails.

MURDERING MINORS

Clearly questions of the severity of the damage done by children affected the sentences imposed on minors who committed assaults from the seventeenth-century to the mid nineteenth century in Connecticut. Yet the question of evil intent had rarely been a factor. In contrast, those few cases in which a person under the age of twenty-one committed murder did deal with a determination of intent since nearly all the culprits were over fourteen years, the age of discretion. Prosecutions of murder charges against minors reveal a society committed to biblical retribution rather than concern for the rehabilitation of the youthful criminal. Until the nineteenth century rarely did arguments for clemency for minors or a chance for their reform appear in the legal records.

The colony's earliest statute on murder provided no loophole for those underage, ordering the death penalty if "any person shall commit any willful murder, which is manslaughter committed upon malice, hatred or cruelty."[29] Not only did the colony look to the *Bible* for this language; the law also clearly indicated the crime of murder required the intent to commit the crime. Early in the nineteenth century, on paper those under twenty-one faced the identical penalty as adults if they committed murder. Despite this blanket condemnation, the almost formulaic language used by the courts in adult murder indictments was at times absent when children committed heinous crimes, perhaps an indication that adults viewed child murderers through different eyes.

Even in the 1790s Connecticut legal authority Zephaniah Swift decried the unwillingness of the colony and then the state to consider the extenuating circumstances of age and criticized the state for continuing the practice of holding youths fully responsible for their actions, even when the crime was murder. Swift asserted that determination of guilt should not depend on age alone, insisting if a child between the age of eight and fourteen "appears to have a mischievous disposition and to have conducted himself in such a manner as to show himself possessed of discretion, he may be considered guilty of a crime."[30] Thus evaluating guilt depended on the strength of a young person's understanding and capacity to discern the difference between good and evil. Yet Swift was also arguing if a child between eight and fourteen lacked malice and understanding, authorities should not apply the *full* penalty of the law. As in other types of crime, by the middle of the nineteenth century citizens adapted some of Swift's analysis on the legal capacity of children. This new attitude, combined with gradual acceptance of Enlightenment ideas about the inherent goodness of children, led to increasing concern for the fate of under-age murderers. The members of Connecticut's General Assembly began to debate about society's responsibility toward children who broke the law. The murder cases found in Connecticut's colonial and state legal records provide insight into how adults viewed minors who committed murder. They also reveal how changes in the idea of the criminal responsibility of minors influenced the way the court system examined, tried, and convicted such children.

In 1678, in one of the earliest cases in which the colony charged a minor with murder, magistrates accused sixteen-year-old Jonathan Stoddard of committing four murders in the New London area of southeastern Connecticut. Just past sundown on June 6th in 1678, thirteen-year-old Deborah Stebings saw Jonathan Stoddard pass by her father's house in New London as her father and Jonathan Lockwood were standing there together. After the boy walked by, Stebings and Lockwood met Thomas Bolles by the bridge which, according the girl's testimony, made it appear that young Stoddard must have been at Mr. Bolles' house on his way home. Elizabeth Waterhouse also testified that she saw the boy pass by her house a little after sunset that same evening. These seemingly unimportant bits of observation were a key eventually linking Stoddard with a bloody slaughter at Bolles' house earlier that same evening.[31]

Not long after Stoddard had passed, Kerveebhunt, identified in the legal documents as an Indian, reported a vicious murder had taken place at the house of Thomas Bolles. An assailant had smashed Mrs. Bolles' head in with a hatchet, killing her, and had also murdered Mrs. Bolles daughter, Mary Bolles, and her nephew, Thomas Bolles, by chopping them in their faces with the same hatchet. The only survivor of the massacre was a month-old baby whom Mrs. Bolles had been nursing when she died. Kerveebhunt said he suspected an Indian named Resuekquinek had committed the crime because he had traded venison with Mrs. Bolles earlier in the day and had seen him trying to trade venison with the woman for rum. When the justice of the peace questioned the second Indian, he admitted that he had been at the Bolles' house but claimed he had been unsuccessful in completing a trade. In what seemed an incriminating statement, Resuekquinek asked the justice if Mrs. Bolles and the children were dead.[32] His question made Resuekquinek suspect in the eyes of the colonists and produced a great deal of unease in the New London area, especially because members of the community still had clear memories of King Philip's War that had ended only two years previously.

Because Deborah Stebing's testimony placed Jonathan Stoddard near the site of the murder, magistrates Edward Palmer and Daniel

Wetherall interviewed the boy to discover what he might know about the crime, yet they did not require that Jonathan's mother or stepfather be present during the examination. This failure to notify a responsible adult may have been because the boy himself was not yet a suspect in the case. (Had the magistrates been pursuing a civil action against the youth, they would have had to notify a parent or guardian to represent him because he was under the age of twenty-one.) The teen admitted that he had passed by the Bolles' house. He claimed that because it was late he had decided to ask to stay there for the night. The reason he gave for passing on was that when he came to the house, he had found the door open. He asserted that he had heard no noise nor seen anyone about the house or yard, circumstances that convinced him to continue home to his mother's house that evening. He further testified that he did pass by the Stebings' house but saw no one else going toward Mr. Bolles' house.[33]

As a result of the testimony of the two Indians, the boy himself, and the witnesses, the magistrates initially charged two Indians with the murder of the Bolles' family but did not charge the boy. The charges against Resuekquinek apparently resulted from his being in the wrong place at the wrong time; magistrates provided no additional evidence beyond what Kerveebhunt had testified. The charges against a second Indian named Sucquanch depended on additional testimony by Kerveebhunt and by Chachasymus, a "Moheag" Indian. Chachasymus claimed that Sucquanch had said before his arrest that he would spoil one family in New London before authorities transported him. The other witness testified that while they both were in jail Sucquanch had bragged to him that he had "helped to eat some English flesh." Though James Lathrop and John Latham, who acted as interpreters, and Sucquanch himself claimed that he had merely boasted he would do some mischief to the English in the future, the magistrates indicted him for the murder of the Bolles.[34]

Less than two months later, on July 25, 1678, Jonathan Stoddard himself went to the house of Daniel Wetherall to report another vicious crime by Indians. He said his stepfather, John Sampson, and his mother had gone over the river and left him for a few days to keep house and to look after his two young brothers, aged six or seven, and one. The teen's own father, who had also been named Jonathan Stoddard, had died about two years before, and his mother had married John Sampson, a man known to local authorities for his quarrelsome disposition. Young Jonathan had come to report the violent death of his baby brother, John Sampson, in circumstances that seemed to mirror the Bolles' murders. He told the magistrate that while he was outside and some distance from the house with the older of his two brothers, he saw some Indians go into the house and come out shortly after. The sixteen-year-old said that as soon as they had disappeared, he had gone into the house and found his young brother knocked on the head with a hatchet and lying on the floor. When the magistrate sent a constable to the house with the boy to investigate the crime, they found the baby gravely wounded but still alive. They took the infant away to try to care for it.[35]

When Wetherall questioned Jonathan again the next day about the assault, still without the presence of the boy's mother or stepfather, he found the boy's recollection differed from he had reported earlier. Apparently the magistrate had some suspicions about Jonathan, because he continued to question him, eventually confronting him with his dying brother who had been taken to Palmer's house. Wetherall, apparently unconcerned with the possibility the lad would incriminate himself, also displayed the bloody murder weapon to him. This triggered a confession by the boy who admitted he had knocked his half-brother on the head to stop him from crying. Not only did he admit to the crime; he rather callously asserted that he had no love for the child's father and none for the child himself. Both statements provided evidence of intent and malice, necessary to the crime of murder. Jonathan killed the child to stop the noise and perhaps also killed him because he disliked both the child and his father. Nothing in Wetherall's report of the boy's confession indicated that either parent was present to protect the boy's interests or that he had even informed them of his intent to interrogate the youth.[36]

Not content with this confession, Wetherall, remembering that several witnesses had seen the youth near the Bolles' house on the night of the axe murders of Mrs. Bolles and her family, taxed the boy again about his possible involvement in the prior "horrid murder." Initially Jonathan stuck to his earlier story that he had never been inside the house, but he eventually broke down and confessed to those crimes as well. He said he had gone to the Bolles' house on the night of June 6th and had asked Mrs. Bolles if he could stay the night. Not only had the woman refused him shelter, Jonathan complained, but she had shoved him out the door and struck him as he left, angering him. The youth then related that he went around to the back of the house and entered, taking up an axe inside the house and striking Mrs. Bolles in the head as she sat nursing an infant. After she fell to the floor, he struck her again to make sure she was dead. Certainly, acting out of anger indicated malice while his inflicting several blows was evidence of intent not merely to injure the woman but to kill her. Stoddard also admitted killing the young girl and boy who were in the house with Mrs. Bolles because he was afraid they would go into town and tell of the crime. Again, this was evidence of either intent or motive. He asserted that he had not thought it necessary to kill the baby because there was no danger of it telling on him. Jonathan next told the magistrate that after committing the crimes, he had calmly gone back to his mother's house. As a further trial of the boy's guilt to reinforce the confession, the other magistrate, Palmer, displayed the murder weapon along with several other axes to Jonathan. The teen correctly identified the weapon and again admitted he had done the murders.[37]

In the face of the boy's confession, Palmer and Wetherall formally charged Jonathan Stoddard with the murder of Mrs. Bolles, her daughter Mary Bolles, and her nephew Thomas Bolles. Unlike many contemporary murder indictments, this initial indictment did not use the formulaic language that the teen had been in league with the devil; it merely said he had wickedly risen up against his neighbors and taken their lives. In contrast, the previous indictments of the two Indians had charged the men with "rising up against Mrs. Bolles and smiting her and two of her children with an ax." Surprisingly, the word "wickedly" was absent from both of their indictments. The New London grand jury found a true bill of charges against the sixteen-year-old boy and bound him over for trial in Hartford before the Governor's Assistants who functioned as a court for the entire colony. Because of the youth's confession and lacking any factual evidence linking either Indian to the crimes, the grand jury dismissed the indictments against the Indians.[38]

While much of the original investigation had taken place in the homes of magistrates Daniel Wetherall and Ebenezer Palmer in New London, the murder trial itself took place in Hartford. Authorities carried the boy to Hartford where William Lester and John Allyn, two of the Governor's Assistants, repeated an examination of the facts of the case on July 27, 1678. Jonathan reiterated his confession, again admitting he had hit Mrs. Bolles two blows on "the hinder part of her head" and that he had killed the two children for fear they would go down to the town and tell on him. He also repeated that he had murdered his baby brother because of the child's crying. In the written record of the boy's testimony, there was no notation that his parents or any other adult had accompanied him to Hartford to look out for his defense. He was alone. The Assistants lodged a formal indictment against the boy that made it clear they considered that he had the requisite intent to commit murder. The document asserted that Jonathan "not having the feare of God before thine eyes (had) most wickedly and maliciously" taken the lives of Zipporah Bolles and the two children. The indictment continued by saying that the boy's actions were against both the law of God and the law of the colony, for which he deserved to die.[39]

At the actual trial before the Governor's Assistants in Hartford in October of 1678, the evidence of witnesses that placed the boy near the murder scene and Jonathan's own confessions provided a clear-cut case of the boy's guilt. Noticeably lacking was the standard phrase found in the murder indictments of many adults that the youth was influenced by the devil, a surprising omission, considering the biblical basis for much of the colony's criminal code. Yet the colonial officials did hear testimony that the boy had always been "a terrible wicked boy (who) would cuss and swear bitter oaths and lie and steal." He was, according to a witness, a "very vile, stubborn, and rebellious child." No one provided any defense for the youth. Despite colonial law that required that in any civil lawsuit against a minor the plaintiff had to prosecute the child through his or her parent or guardian, at no time in the proceedings against Jonathan was there any evidence that his mother or stepfather assisted in his defense or that any other adult served as his legal guardian or advisor. No one raised the defense that the boy's parents had not properly raised or educated him; no one mentioned that his mother and father, and later his stepfather, had previously been guilty of theft, assault, and of several breaches of the peace. No one argued for a stay in the teen's execution. On October 9th, 1678, the Connecticut authorities executed Jonathan Stoddard.[40]

While no one argued that Jonathan Stoddard's family or even colonial society as a whole bore any responsibility for his crime, one hundred years later the question of adult responsibility for the moral education of children did play a part in the 1786 murder case against Hannah Occuish, a twelve-year-old, half-Black, half-Pequot-Indian girl from New London. By the 1780s the ideas of John Locke and Jean Jacques Rousseau had influenced many people to think that education was essential in raising moral, responsible adults. Nevertheless, as in some earlier cases concerning assault and theft, race as much as age may have played an important role in determining Hannah's guilt for the murder of seven-year-old Eunice Bolles, the daughter of a neighbor. The issue of Hannah's race aside, adults responsible for her did face their share of criticism for their failure to teach Hannah Occuish proper morals and standards. Moreover, at age twelve, Hannah was under the age of discretion, age fourteen, the age at which adults presumed children were capable of having evil intent.

According to the inquest following the discovery of the body of Eunice in July of 1786, some unknown person had "willfully and barbarously" murdered the girl. After an investigation the magistrate charged that Hannah, a child of mixed Pequot and African-American heritage, had lured the younger girl away from her home and crushed her skull with a rock, acting out of revenge because the younger girl had previously stolen some strawberries from her. A newspaper report later claimed that Hannah "had been heard to threaten" the victim and had followed Eunice, waylaying the girl on her way to school. Perhaps adding to the suspicion against Hannah was that authorities had charged her with a prior assault on seven-year-old Mary Fish when she was coming home from school. In that assault young Hannah allegedly had beaten Mary on the head with a rock, and then stripped the child, stealing her clothes. Because Hannah's mother had concealed her, the state had dropped that earlier prosecution. Yet the prior case was evidence of Hannah's evil tendencies and of her criminal methods. In the murder case, the court said that Hannah's actions after she killed Eunice showed she understood the wrongful nature of her act because she had supposedly hidden the body under some rocks on a stone wall to conceal the crime by making it appear to be an accident. The indictment claimed that Hannah acted with malice aforethought and great violence, striking many mortal blows on Eunice's head and body, so the intent to kill was clear. As in many other eighteenth-century cases against children, especially when the children were Black, Native American, or poor, the court did not notify either Hannah's mother or her mistress, the widow of Ichabod Rogers of New London, of the charges against her. Neither did it provide a court-appointed guardian to assist in her defense at the time of the original hearing. Taken to the site where the authorities had found the body concealed, Hannah supposedly showed that she recognized the location and burst into tears when shown the body, displaying what onlookers decided was a guilty reaction. The magistrate and jury viewed both facts as proof not only of her responsibility for Eunice's death, but also, more importantly, her understanding of the evil nature of her actions. The court found grounds to charge Hannah with murder and jailed her for trial in September.[41]

At the New London County Superior Court trial, Judge Law did finally recognize Hannah's youth and appointed Timothy Larrabe as counsel to advise the girl. When Law summarized the evidence to the jury, he pointed out the depravity of the murderous act, saying Hannah had revealed "such evidence of premeditated malice, and marks of such a mischievous and guileful discretion" in her concealment of the body to make the crime appear to be an accident that the "circumstances have supplied the want of age." She was therefore fully responsible for her evil actions. Law added that to spare Hannah from hanging would be a dangerous precedent, "holding up an idea, that children might commit such atrocious crimes with impunity." Yet Law did take note of Hannah's youth and ignorance. He said that if the "unhappy prisoner" had been properly taught she would not have been "so abandoned as to have committed the fatal deed." The trial documents did not record how Larrabe assisted the girl with her defense, but whatever he said was useless to shield Hannah. After hearing the evidence, the jury took only one day of deliberation to convict Hannah of willful murder and sentence her to death.[42]

In October, Hannah petitioned the Connecticut General Assembly for a "reprieve from the sentence of death." The petition, written by Larrabe, tried to play on the sympathies of Assembly members. He claimed that Hannah was actually only eleven and a half years old and had descended from "low parents." The girl, wrote Larrabe, had "been totally deprived of a Christian education" and did not even know the difference between her right hand and her left. In the petition, he presented a slightly different version of the crime, to support his contention that Hannah had lacked murderous intent. He claimed that Hannah had only intended to whip the younger child for an earlier theft of strawberries, but when Eunice cried out, the older girl had hit her on the head to silence her. She had not intended murder. Larrabe further claimed that the ineffective hiding of the body displayed the girl's lack of understanding of right and wrong. Nevertheless, he could not offer any other evidence to demonstrate that Hannah lacked an understanding that deadly assault was wrong. Larrabe's petition asked the Assembly to find some other suitable punishment for the child. The request evoked no sympathy from the Assembly. On October 26, 1786 members rejected Hannah's plea for clemency and reaffirmed the death sentence.[43]

Newspapers noted that Hannah did not seem conscious of her fate until about two weeks before the date scheduled for her execution. The Reverend Mr. Channing "was indefatigable in his attention to her during her confinement" and finally brought the wretched child to an awareness of her impending death. The *Connecticut Courant* reported the girl was in tears the day before the execution and appeared "in distress for her soul." In reporting the execution, the paper picked up on Larrabe's plea, noting the girl's inadequate education: "The unhappy fate of this young girl is particularly to be lamented, as it is to be charged principally to a want of early instruction and government."[44]

In an execution sermon delivered after the girl's hanging, the Reverend Channing developed a similar theme. Channing, a young Yale tutor who had Unitarian sympathies, put some of the blame for the crime on innate depravity, an old Puritan concept, saying that the girl's actions were "striking evidence of the depravity of human nature; that we are indeed transgressors from the womb." Yet as Daniel Cohen points out, the young minister focused more attention on "the critical role of upbringing" in creating a moral adult. Thus the real point of Channing's sermon was not to castigate Hannah for her sins but to admonish not just the adults in Hannah's life but the entire community for failing in their responsibility towards her. In Lockean terms he explained that if responsible adults did not provide the example of "virtuous principles" it would lead instead to the development of "those which are vicious." He blamed the girl's master and mistress for their failure to teach her proper moral standards, noting that her religious education had been neglected. Because Hannah lacked such guidance, Channing said authorities could not hold the girl responsible for her actions, despite her being within the questionable area of having legal discretion. Failure to provide Hannah with a moral upbringing, Channing claimed, had resulted in her "ignominious end." Instead of blaming evil results on original sin, Channing was saying what later reformers would emphasize: that failure by parents or guardians to set their children's feet on the paths of moral rectitude was the cause of criminal behavior by children.[45] Connecticut would not enact legislation that reflected these ideas for another sixty years.

Writing of the child's execution in 1850, New London historian Frances M. Caulkins lamented that the only alleviating circumstances of the case were Hannah's extreme youth and ignorance. Though Caulkins wrote that those were forcible arguments in her opinion, neither consideration had swayed the jury that sentenced the girl to death. The child died on December 20, 1786, on a gallows erected behind New London's old meetinghouse.[46]

Nineteenth-century cases involving children accused of manslaughter or murder illuminate the influence of racial prejudice on the functioning of the Connecticut legal system. These cases also indicate the way the spreading influence of Enlightenment ideas gradually changed the attitudes of judges and juries, and led to the transformation of statute law in the state.

Though there was no question that eleven-year-old Edward Perkins, a white boy of Norwich, shot Prudence Maples of Norwich to death in 1808, the white males who made up the jury of inquest found the death was by "misadventure or casualty." They accepted the "young lad's" explanation that he had snapped the gun once "without discharging it" so that he assumed the gun was not loaded and then had fired it. Unfortunately, the records of this case are very sparse, making it difficult to determine if the shooting was, in fact, an accident.[47]

Eight years later the Connecticut Superior Court found twenty-year-old Minor Babcock guilty of murdering his stepfather, London Babcock, by stabbing him with a knife. Despite Minor's being underage, the original indictment identified him as a black man rather than as a youth and charged that he acted feloniously with malice aforethought. Though witnesses testified that Minor was protecting his mother from a murderous assault by London Babcock and acting only to stop the attack, the Court did not examine the question of motive or make any effort to determine whether Minor acted with the requisite malice. The jury found the youth guilty of murder and sentenced him to die on the gallows on June 6, 1815. Fairly late in the legal proceedings, the Superior Court had appointed William Cleaveland, Esq. as a guardian *ad litem* for Minor. Twenty-three witnesses testified in the case, including Thisbe and Olive Babcock who were Minor's sisters, but his claim of defending his mother was not sufficient to gain him clemency from the jury. Unable to forestall the guilty verdict, Cleaveland filed a motion in arrest of the judgment, not on the grounds of his client's age but on the claim that one of the jurors had not been a freeholder in New London County and that the jurors had not remained together to deliberate a verdict but had gone to their own homes. The Court found the matters alleged to support the abatement were insufficient. The State executed young Minor on June 6, 1816. In awarding fees for the case, the court allowed $21 for Cleaveland and Josiah Isham for pleading for the prisoner and an additional $21 for their application for a new trial. Allowing fees to Isham was the only mention of his participation in the case.[48] Both the belated appointment of a guardian and the guilty verdict suggesting that the jury ignored significant evidence to support Minor's claim of justifiable homicide may indicate that the jury treated a black youth more harshly than white defendants. Thirteen years later, a white youth, in a somewhat comparable case, convinced a jury to reduce a murder charge to manslaughter.

In 1828, Dexter Adams, a transient mariner, assaulted a Stonington resident. At the justice court level, Josiah Isham, now serving as a justice of the peace, charged Dexter with assault with intent to commit murder for his knife attack on William Sewall of Stonington. The indictment asserted that Dexter had attacked Sewall with a four-inch Spanish jack-knife, inflicting diverse serious wounds on the left side, giving Sewall a four-inch-deep wound on the left side between the fifth and sixth ribs. Sewall lingered from September 9th, the day of the assault, until September 12th, when he died of his wounds. Although the indictment drawn up by Isham included a minute description of the specific injuries and even the murder weapon, including its cost at thirty cents, it did not identify Dexter as a minor. On the exterior of the writ, in a different handwriting, someone entered "David C. Smith is appointed guardian to Dexter a minor." Apparently the appointment of a guardian was nearly an afterthought although Isham, from his earlier experience representing Minor Babcock, ought to have been familiar with state standards for providing representation for underage defendants. Isham summoned Thomas Cogseller and John George as material witnesses in the case but noted on the file that they could not be found because they had put to sea on the schooner *Harriet* on September 11th to avoid testifying. Because the witnesses were inaccessible, Connecticut State's Attorney J. B. Gurley dropped the charges against Dexter.[49]

The state reopened the case against Dexter Adams as a murder charge at the end of September 1828 because authorities had located and detained the witnesses Thomas R. Cogseller, George Armour, and Matthew Toole of Stonington, who had previously fled to avoid giving evidence. At this new hearing Isham took formal note that Dexter was under age and appointed Coddington Billings as his new guardian for the reopened case. Under Coddington's advice, the youth pleaded not guilty to the charge, but the justice of the peace found sufficient cause to arrest Dexter and commit him to the New London County jail to be held for a hearing before the Superior Court in October of 1828. At the Superior Court hearing, the judge clearly identified Dexter as a minor and continued Billings' guardianship of the boy. Again Dexter pleaded not guilty. The jury found him guilty of manslaughter rather than murder, but since the witnesses appeared in person, there is no record of their testimony that may have partially exonerated the defendant. Furthermore, rather than sentencing the youth to the maximum term for manslaughter, the court sent Dexter to the new Connecticut State Prison in Wethersfield to serve a three-year sentence. Neither of Dexter's guardians appealed the sentence, though the late appointment of a guardian at the initial hearing could have been grounds for an appeal.[50]

One of the most critical issues in the criminal prosecution of minors was the question of whether or not they had sufficient understanding of the crime as well as the requisite intent and malice. Thus, the 1833 murder trial of John Barnum was important because it raised the question of whether a minor over the age of discretion always had sufficient understanding of his or her actions to be executed for murder. In 1833 the state charged that eighteen-year-old John, a resident of Danbury, had murdered his own father, Noah Barnum. The case for the prosecution claimed that the boy had ambushed his father through an open window of the house, shooting him with a musket filled with stones and gravel. At the trial the teen's mother testified that John had been eating dinner with his parents "in harmony" when his father sent him on an errand to his sister. Minutes later, the shot through the window killed the elder Barnum. Though no one witnessed the actual shooting, authorities charged John with murder.[51]

At the trial John himself maintained his innocence, saying he had had no grudge against his father and no recollection of committing the crime. Reflecting this claim, evidence at the trial raised the question of David's mental competence. His teacher testified that the teen was "not an idiot" but added that the boy was "much below mankind in general understanding." The teacher pointed out that eighteen-year-old John was far behind his peers at the school. When the jury found the lad guilty and imposed a death sentence, even the presiding judge, David Daggett, was surprised because of evidence that the boy lacked sufficient understanding of the crime. Daggett was so convinced of the incorrectness of the verdict that he later supported the petitions that pleaded for commutation of the youth's death sentence. John's own petition for clemency revealed that he viewed his impending death by hanging with terror, but that he felt no guilt because he could not remember shooting his father.[52]

Friends and neighbors petitioned the General Assembly for clemency for the youth, seeking commutation of the death sentence to internment in an asylum or to life in prison. John also filed a clemency petition in his own behalf, pleading for mercy because he had previously been visited by insanity. All of the petitioners stressed the boy's reduced mental capacity, repeating the teacher's claim and adding that the teacher had noted on the day of the murder the teen's eyes had "a wild and unusual appearance." A separate memorial from the grand jury that had indicted the boy commended the boy to the mercy of the General Assembly, saying that John had been insane eighteen months before the crime but had seemed to recover. They said that they had not anticipated the youth would receive the death sentence because they believed his disease had returned by the time of the crime. Though adults had previously used pleas of insanity to escape the death sentence, in this case the combination of pleas concerning the defendant's youth and his questionable mental capacity may have capitalized on the reluctance of Connecticut citizens to execute children. The General Assembly Committee considering John's plea for mercy reviewed the facts of the case and interviewed Judge Daggett and other witnesses. It ruled that John had indeed killed his father. Nevertheless, the committee members also agreed that John's insanity had returned at the time he killed his father and commuted the teen's sentence to life in prison.[53]

Whether John Barnum was indeed insane or if insanity rather than his youth had been the reason for clemency became an issue again in 1846 when John, now age thirty-one, petitioned for release from the State Prison. In his petition, John reviewed the facts of his case but asserted that he was but eighteen when convicted and had acted "without consideration or knowledge." Thus he seemed to allege he had lacked the necessary motive to commit the crime. Moreover, he claimed that he acted through excitement caused by the abuses of his father against him and that his father had repeatedly threatened to kill him and had once thrown an ax at him, actually endangering his life. As a result, he seemed to be arguing self-defense as justification of his actions. Notably, he did not raise the claim that he had been insane at the time of the crime. More striking was that the petition lacked any sense of remorse. John seemed to be asking the General Assembly to take into consideration his youth and heedlessness, without his accepting any responsibility for his actions. The language of repentance and reformation was missing, and perhaps in consequence the General Assembly refused to consider the petition.[54]

Five years later John Barnum again sought release from his life sentence. He wrote in his petition to the General Assembly that he had been but eighteen at the time of the crime, "young, ignorant, and very inconsiderate." He once more claimed that his father had often threatened his life and had actually made a dangerous assault on him not long before the time of the crime. Differing from the prior plea, this time John admitted that he had killed his father in a fit of fear and anger. In this petition, using the language of rehabilitation, he claimed that he had reformed and been born again. Six prison officials co-signed John's petition, supporting his claim of reformation and seeking his release. Despite John's admission of guilt and his change of language, the General Assembly again refused to agree to a commutation of the life sentence. Apparently neither heedlessness nor self-preservation could work as a defense of the crime of murder.[55]

By the 1840s reform attitudes had led many in Connecticut to question whether society should treat children who broke the law with the same severity as they treated adult criminals. Some laws attempted to soften the action of the criminal justice system on minors. The General Assembly had finally passed a discretionary sentencing law, which allowed children to avoid incarceration with adults in the State Prison at Wethersfield. While the discretionary sentencing act most certainly would not have resulted in imprisoning a child convicted of murder at the county jail rather than at the prison, many reformers now stressed that lack of education and poor moral upbringing rather than innate depravity were responsible for most of the crimes committed by children. This new attitude, reflecting the beliefs expressed by both Judge Law and The Reverend Channing in the Hannah Occuish case, had been behind the effort to create for an alternative to making children serve their sentences with adults where they had no chance for an education or proper role models. This campaign to treat child criminals as patients in need of care rather than as felons in need of punishment had ultimately led to the creation of the State Reform School for Boys in Meriden in 1853. Even murder cases illustrated the transformation of public attitudes about youthful responsibility for crime. A murder case from 1854 revealed how those currents of reform influenced public attitudes toward minors who committed murder.

A crime nearly as horrific as the 1678 murder of Zipporah Bolles and the children shocked and horrified New Haven County in 1853. Returning from church in North Haven on July 24th, 1853, Barzilla Bradley, "one of the most respectable citizens of North Haven" according to newspaper reports, had found his wife Esther brutally stabbed to death, "horribly mutilated and weltering in blood." Though Mrs. Bradley had been ill and had been too weak to attend church, she had "fought desperately with the fiend who had attacked her." Blood soaked her apron, and defensive wounds covered her hands as she had tried to shield her face from the knife. The inquest determined that the cause of death was loss of blood from over 50 stab wounds. Making the crime seem even more vicious, after Mrs. Bradley had fallen to the floor under the rain of blows, her murderous assailant had slit her throat from ear to ear, cutting to the back of the windpipe and sawing back and forth to enlarge the wound. Barzilla Bradley also found that the murderer had ransacked the house and stolen thirty dollars, leaving bloody hand and footprints to mark his passage.[56]

As reported in the local newspapers, Bradley immediately directed suspicion on "an Irishman" who had worked for the Bradleys a few weeks previously. The grieving widower said the man had left his job without settling for his wages but that his son had seen him in town just the day before the murder though the two had not spoken. More damning was an eyewitness report from a neighbor who claimed to have seen "a man answering the description of this Irishman" wearing a straw hat, brown pants, a checked shirt, and a coat going up the road towards Bradley's house only three quarters of an hour prior to the estimated time of the murder. The same witness testified that he had seen the same man return between 1 and 2 P.M., but that the man no longer was wearing the coat. Only belatedly did the newspaper reveal that the Irishman was, in fact, just a teenager, a seventeen-year-old Irish youth named Michael Jennings.[57]

Michael Jennings was an Irish boy who had worked for Bradley in his brickyard for a few weeks earlier in the summer. He had hired himself to Mr. Bradley for a period of time but, according to Bradley, had stayed only fifteen days, including three Sabbaths, supposedly long enough to learn the family's habits. Michael then left without giving notice or any reason for leaving his job other than to claim he had found another job at higher wages. Bradley refused to pay him for his work for the short time he had stayed, but Michael considered that Bradley owed him for his time. Bradley later testified that he had, indeed, not paid the youth, assuming they would settle accounts at a later time. Michael had then hired himself to Amos Harrison of Northford who lived about six miles from the Bradleys, agreeing to work for a period of one and a half months. In what seemed to the suspicious investigators part of a premeditated plan, the boy had lied to Mr. Harrison by telling him he had just arrived in the area directly from New York, concealing that he had been working for Mr. Bradley. Just a few days later, Michael left Mr. Harrison's employ saying he was returning to New York City.[58]

More circumstantial evidence mounted against the youth. On July 20th, Enos Camp of Durham had given Michael a ride into New Haven, where the youth stayed until Sunday the 24th. Witnesses claimed that Michael knew the Bradleys' practice of weekly church attendance but that he also knew Mrs. Bradley was a small, weak woman who was too ill to attend church. In the chain of damaging evidence, as reported by the newspapers, Augustus Munson testified he saw Jennings going toward the Bradleys' house on foot the morning of the crime and spotted him returning from the house an hour and a half later. Both Mrs. Patty Barnes and Mrs. Adeline Brockett seconded Munson's evidence. After learning of the crime and seeing the bloody footprints in the house, Bethuel and George Brockett followed the bloody trail from the house to the railroad tracks.[59]

When authorities arrested Michael the next day near the train station in New Haven on the suspicion that he had committed the murder, the teen's clothes were wet, as though recently washed, and blood had soaked into his boots and sprinkled his hat. Michael's explanation of the blood and newly washed clothes was that he had helped some friends slaughter a pig. More incriminating was the discovery of a bloody jackknife in the youth's pocket, a knife with a broken edge and snapped point that matched pieces of a knife taken from Mrs. Bradley's body. The *Hartford Courant* noted the fact that the broken point of the knife matched the point of a knife found in Mrs. Bradley's breast proved the knife had killed the woman and fixed the blame on the youth "unless he can show otherwise." Perhaps more damaging to the youth's claim of innocence was that his boot matched a bloody footprint found outside the house, placing him at the site of the murder. Though the arresting officer found no valuables upon the boy, witnesses claimed he had disposed of the loot with Richard Connor and Connor's wife and brother, fellow Irish immigrants. The police found the three had some of the stolen money and arrested them as well. When confronted with the supposed evidence of his involvement, Michael denied his guilt and asserted that he had spent the previous afternoon at the Catholic church in New Haven, but the fact that no one could testify to his being there seemed damning evidence, adding hypocrisy to the murder. In fairly short order the court found Michael guilty of murdering Mrs. Bradley and sentenced him to death.[60]

The reaction amongst the Irish community was prompt, but Irishmen were not the only people who protested the death penalty for the boy. Nine different petitions for clemency arrived at the Connecticut General Assembly, all seeking a commutation of the lad's death sentence to one of life imprisonment. Many of the signers did bear Irish surnames, but the majority did not. Most shared the attitudes and pleas found in a separate petition from the boy's father, James Jennings, writing from Brooklyn, New York. Jennings wrote that Michael, just turned eighteen according to his father, had always been of good character and was a kind, affectionate brother and a mild, peaceable, and affectionate companion. He mentioned the lad's industrious and steady habits and vowed that he had never committed a crime, having spent nearly all his life "in the country, surrounded by healthy moral influences." Mr. Jennings was adamant that "no felon's blood flowed in his veins." He described the situation between his son and the Bradleys, saying that no unkind feeling existed between them and the boy, and that though Bradley did owe his son money, Michael had had no complaint against Mrs. Bradley. Though Jennings asserted that all the evidence was circumstantial, he also claimed that if his son had indeed killed Mrs. Bradley, he had not done so with malice or premeditation; he was afraid of getting caught. Michael's case, the father said, differed "very widely from that of old and hardened offenders who wind up a long life of crime and infamy with a deliberate murder in cold blood." Yet, complained Jennings, the law made no distinction between such career criminals and his son and punished them equally. Speaking the same language as those who sought to reform the criminal justice system for minors, Jennings concluded that reformation was one of the principal objects of punishment and could not be achieved by executing his son.[61]

Clearly influenced by the reform impulse, a majority of the General Assembly members on the Committee on Capital Punishment initially supported the pleas for clemency and recommended commutation of the death sentence to one of life in prison. Reviewing the trial evidence and the various petitions, the members agreed with Mr. Jennings that the evidence was entirely circumstantial. They said there had been no evidence of quarrels between the boy and the Bradleys, nor had there been any problems between Michael and the Harrisons. The Irish youth had even gotten along well with the children of both the Bradleys and the Harrisons. The committee members clearly accepted the idea that Michael's youth and lack of understanding of the consequences of his actions had been important factors in the events leading up to the crime, if he had actually killed Mrs. Bradley. They said the prosecution claimed that the boy had returned to the Bradleys' home to collect money owed to him for his work for Mr. Bradley. "To a youth of seventeen, this might not appear criminal." They viewed the fact that the boy carried only a pocketknife as evidence of lack of premeditation. They explained the killing of Mrs. Bradley as the reaction of a frightened, trapped youth who saw in her unexpected presence a bar to "reputation, safety, and liberty." Therefore he had no intent to murder, just to escape. Michael Jennings, they said, was very unlike the old and hardened offenders who normally received the death sentence, and the majority of the committee recommended that a life sentence would better serve the ends of public justice. Testimony from Michael's jailers in the New Haven County Jail supported the idea that the boy could be reformed because they said that his behavior had improved in the months he had been in jail awaiting trial and sentencing. In a final plea for mercy, the committee added that it would be more conversant with Christianity not to hurry Michael into "the presence of his Maker" while he was still in his boyhood.[62]

In response to this recommendation of clemency, the indignation of the minority report from the Committee on Capital Punishment was palpable. This opposing report built up a damning case against the boy. The hostility was apparent in the opening sentence of the document that called Michael an Irishman, rather than an Irish youth or boy. There was no sympathy evident for the boy's youth or inexperience. The first strike against Michael was apparently that he had but lately arrived from Ireland. Second were the alleged lies he told when obtaining work first from the Bradleys and then from the Harrisons. The members said the fact that the attack took place on a Sunday when the boy knew the "small, feeble woman" would be home alone supposedly proved premeditation. The report provided as proof of malicious intent the fact that he had ransacked the house and taken all the valuables he could carry. These facts proved that the youth had intended robbery rather than merely collecting what was owed to him. The committee members disposed of the claim that Michael was of good character, saying it was unreliable because the source of that claim was the boy's own father. Furthermore, they rejected the claim that imprisonment could reform the teen. Instead they asserted that, rather than his deportment improving while in jail, the boy's behavior had been worse than that of any other prisoner since he was sullen, uncooperative, obscene, and profane. The minority, which did not cite any specific evidence to contradict the report of the jailors, recommended that the state carry out the death sentence.[63]

Although the recent opening of the State Reform School for Boys in Wethersfield was ample evidence of strong support for more lenient treatment of underage criminals, the minority report calling for Michael's execution was more influential on the members of the General Assembly as a whole. After first postponing its decision, the Assembly then rejected the petitions for clemency and refused to commute Michael's sentence. Though an editorial in the *Hartford Courant* had revealed wide public support in favor of the reform school because prisons lacked any" reformatory or educational" influences, the Assembly's refusal to mitigate Michael's punishment clearly showed the vast gap between the crimes committed by ""idle and vicious boys" and the premeditated murder of a weak and helpless woman by. The state executed Michael on July 11, 1854 on a gallows in the yard of the New Haven County jail.[64] In this case, the desire to maintain law and order and to provide swift and sure punishment was stronger than any desire to redeem an unfortunate youth who might have lacked an understanding of the consequences of his actions.

Chapter Three

Public Order and Private Rights: Keeping Children in Line

> Any persons young or old that are under a parent's or master's government that shall meet together or be entertained in any house without the consent of parents or guardians after 9 o'clock . . . or make a rout or disorder at any other time shall pay 10 shillings or be set in the stocks for two hours.
>
> —*Acts and Laws of His Majesties Colony of Connecticut,* 1702

As the previous chapters have illustrated, protecting the lives and properties of Connecticut residents was a major feature of both statutes and case law in Connecticut from the seventeenth to the nineteenth centuries. The founders of Connecticut not only incorporated English values concerning property into its laws, but also, according to Everett Goodwin, had created its legal system "not merely to preserve traditions but to promote and encourage the Puritan vision of future social and political development." As Bruce Mann has pointed out, law as defined by statutes and as administered through the courts was part of the way people "attempted to assure what they valued as a society - what behavior was permissible, how people should act toward one another."[1]

Puritan attitudes toward society and social order influenced the move from England to Massachusetts, then from Massachusetts to Connecticut, as Puritan leaders sought to create a Christian commonwealth. Colonial leaders incorporated their interpretation of God's will into civil government. In Puritan eyes, as Perry Miller observed, the people created the laws and the government, but the actual institution of government came from God. John Winthrop put the question of the role of the government most succinctly, saying in 1645 that the great questions were "about the authority of the magistrates and the liberty of the people." Winthrop saw one of the principle functions of the magistrates in a Puritan community to be to restrain natural liberty, defined as "a liberty to evil as well as to good. This liberty is incompatible and inconsistent with authority and cannot endure the least restraint of the most just authority." For Winthrop as well as for other Puritan leaders natural liberty made men grow even more evil. This natural liberty of man "to do what he lists" was "the great enemy of truth and peace which all the ordinances of God are bent against to restrain and subdue it."[2]

Although Winthrop directed his remarks at adults who were discontented under the rule of the magistrates, his words had a wider significance as well. The role of civil authority was to restrain the unfettered exercise of natural liberty; the role of law and government was to establish and maintain order. Similarly, Edmund Morgan claimed the Puritans had an "evident concern with social virtues" and paid "homage to good conduct in their social life." Yet Morgan posed two questions: "First, why did the Puritans wish to be socially virtuous themselves; and second, why did they wish to force social virtue on others?" Morgan answered his own queries by saying that Puritans "felt obliged to be civil in order to convince themselves they were sanctified." He explained the desire to force others to live a moral life as an outgrowth of that same impulse with the examples of Massachusetts' John Cotton and Connecticut's Thomas Hooker. Cotton advocated bringing "all thy children and family" to a shared obedience to God's law, "that all thy family may be God's friends." Hooker declared that "the true convert" sought to eliminate all sin. Hooker in his book 1669 book *The Application of Redemption* gave the rationale for a Christian's responsibility for setting moral standards and interfering in the lives of others: "What ever sins come within his reach, he labors the removal of them, out of the families where he dwells, out of the plantation where he lives, out of the companies and occasions, with whom he hath occasion to meet and meddle at any time." Morgan claimed the responsibility to "enforce good behavior in the family was the germ of all civil and ecclesiastical authority."[3] Thus part of being a Puritan necessarily involved interfering in the lives of one's family and neighbors and setting standards of moral behavior for the entire community, believers and non-believers alike.

Connecticut's Puritans applied the laws they created most rigorously to the maintenance of order, an order not only of relationships between residents but an order imposed on the daily activities of ordinary people, including children. Living a goodly and obedient life was the responsibility of all Christians. Nevertheless, as Edmund Morgan made clear in *The Puritan Family,* Puritans viewed children as both evil and ignorant. Children would sin because they did not know any better. As a result, parents bore a heavy responsibility to teach their children not only how to read but how to behave and to follow God's laws. Connecticut's first published set of laws in 1650 delineated the responsibility of parents to "teach their children and apprentices, so much learning, as may inable them to read the English tongue, and knowledge of the capital laws." The same section of the statutes directed parents to instruct their servants and children "in the grounds and principles of religion." Here is an early example of the civil authorities standing by to enforce the moral code of the community because the law further provided that if parents failed to teach their children the proper principles of religion, the selectmen could take children from their parents and place them with masters who would fulfill that direction. Illustrating the uncertainty about the age of majority, that law bound such children to different terms of service; boys had to remain in an involuntary placement until they reached twenty-one; girls were free to leave at the age of eighteen. In addition seventeenth-century voluntary contracts of indenture supported the official mandate, often explicitly directing the master to instruct the apprentice in the principles of religion. Even with that official direction to educate children in their Christian duties, parents, masters, and guardians evidently were failing to do an adequate job. At the New London town meeting in June 1662, freemen voted to pay the sexton forty shillings a year "to order the youth in the meeting house."[4]

As the influence of the Puritan vision of morality and order declined over the course of Connecticut's history, laws rather than the churches of Connecticut gradually played an increasingly important role in establishing and maintaining that order. In 1702 a new law directed that when "young persons" resided with a family other than their own, they had to attend church "subject to the domestic management of the family." Providing even more oversight, only town selectmen could authorize youths to live outside their families. Since not all members of the community shared the Puritan vision, the General Assembly passed a law in 1713 to protect children from persons of "evil name and fame." The statute said that since people and wanderers "have by their vile and prophane discourse and actions provided a snare to youth generally and tends to the great detriment of religion and is of pernicious consequence," authorities could punish anyone convicted of "reviling, prophane speaking, or misbehavior." The law granted the magistrates great discretion in how they could punish such lawbreakers, allowing them the option of jail, a sentence to the workhouse, or a whipping of up to fifteen stripes. In 1715 the colony passed a law directing that selectmen in the towns were to order households without Bibles to obtain them. So concerned were the lawmakers with maintaining proper knowledge of religion that they further directed that the selectmen provide Bibles for householders who could not afford to obtain one. In 1722, legislators passed a new law specifically directed at preventing and punishing riots and rioters.[5] While not all of the new laws directed at maintaining public order and respect for religion specifically targeted minors, their existence made it clear that the secular side of Connecticut's society reinforced the earlier Puritan morality.

In the nineteenth century members of General Assembly continued to legislate on public behavior and morality. In 1821, the state legislature prohibited exhibitions of games, tricks, or shows, setting fines that ranged from sixty to two hundred dollars. In recognition that children might break this law, legislators directed that when an offender was under twenty-one, the parent, master, or guardian had to pay the fine. In 1838 concern over alcohol use by minors led to the passage of a law that reiterated the old prohibition against selling liquor to minors. This statute banned the sale of "any ale, wine, or spirituous liquor" to any minor, apprentice, or student of any college, academy, or boarding school. In theory this prevented college students who were over twenty-one from drinking. The punishment was ten dollars for each offense and the possibility of the loss of the license to sell alcohol. The continuing desire to maintain public order even extended to restrictions on firecrackers. In 1853 a new law assessed a fine of five dollars against "every person who shall use firecrackers on any other day than the 4th of July or other public holidays."[6] Perhaps legislators could no longer control the religious beliefs of Connecticut youths, but they could continue to restrict their activities.

SABBATH BREAKING AND PROFANE SPEAKING

Statutes prohibiting breach of the peace covered many types of public disorder and disruption, but specific laws against the breach of the Sabbath were an important part of the close relationship between Connecticut's churches and its political governance. Laws reinforced the biblical admonition against working on Sunday and prohibited profane speaking or actions that brought religion into disrepute. The statutes distinguished between those who actually challenged the authority of the ministers or committed profane swearing and those who merely disrupted public services by laughing or playing or who worked on the Sabbath. By 1650 the civil law of the colony was responsible for maintenance of religion in a law that proclaimed, "That the civil authority here established, hath power and liberty to see the peace, ordinances and rules of Christ bee observed in every church, according to his word." The law gave the civil authorities the right to prosecute anyone who "made God's wayes contemptible and rediculous." The first offense brought public correction by a magistrate and required the posting of a bond for good behavior. A second offense resulted in a five-pound fine. In dealing with Sabbath breakers, the statute directed that if "any person" absented himself from "the public ministry of the word" he would forfeit five shillings for each church service he missed. Initially those fines for breaking the Sabbath were uniform with no differentiation for minors.[7]

Apparently the original law did not bring about the desired respect for religion. In 1702 the General Assembly of the colony passed a new law making parents and masters responsible for seeing that their children or servants did not break the Sabbath. An additional law increased the punishment for profane swearing, raising the penalty to a ten-shilling fine or three hours in the stocks. The wording of the statute on keeping the Sabbath changed just a decade later by adding the proviso that masters and governors of their families had to make sure that their children and servants and others under their control obeyed the laws concerning the Sabbath. Even this alteration did not result in the desired social control because the Assembly passed yet another law in 1721. It set the fine at forty shillings for any rude or unlawful behavior on the Lord's Day, prohibiting such behaviors as "clamorous discourse, shouting, hollowing, running, riding, dancing, jumping, winding horns, or the like." At this point the law did not reduce the fine against children; it instead added an additional deterrent to make sure parents controlled their children. Calling for a more effectual preventing of the disturbance of the Lord's Day, the newest law ordered an additional two-shilling fine assessed against any parents or masters whose children broke the Sabbath. If the responsible adult refused to pay, he or she, not the child, was to be whipped up to twenty stripes. This additional law also finally addressed the issue of what to do about the youngest children in the community if they transgressed the Sabbath. If any child or servant under the age of discretion (age fourteen) did any act that violated the Sabbath, the punishment was the same as for lying. That meant the child's parent or guardian was to correct the guilty minor in the presence of some town officer if a magistrate ordered the punishment. Furthermore, in what may have been recognition that gossip could be a problem in the community, the law added that if no one charged a child within one month of the act of the alleged Sabbath breaking, the colony could not assess the fine against the parent. In addition, the law refused to accept hearsay accusations.[8]

In 1795 the state updated the law against Sabbath breaking. When children or servants under fourteen profaned or disturbed the Sabbath, the parent, master or guardian still had to correct the child in front of some officer of the court. The change was that parents who refused to punish their children would have to pay a fine of fifty cents.[9] Documents from the records of numerous justices of the peace made it clear that prosecutions for breaking the Sabbath continued into the nineteenth century but that children or their parents generally did pay for breaking that law.

In an early eighteenth-century case of profane speaking, penitence earned a minor a reduction in the prescribed sentence. In 1727 twenty-year-old Joseph Elderkin of Norwich had used "reviling and profane speaking" at the house of Joseph Reynolds, telling several people that they would go to hell because "they had sinned against light and knowledge." Sentenced to a one-year term in the New London jail, Joseph issued a memorial to the New London County Court saying he was remaining in jail under great difficulty. He acknowledged that he had acted "to the grievous dishonor of God," and begged for clemency. In addition he pleaded that he had committed his transgression "through inadvertancy." Noting Joseph's "very penitent frame," the Court agreed to drop the charges against him if he paid the costs of prosecution. At no time did the Court summon Joseph's father, also named Joseph Elderkin, to assist him in his defense.[10] While the sentence to jail seemed excessive, it could have reflected the community's continued agitation over religion fomented by the Rogerene sect in New London County in the early eighteenth century.

Though the court might have been merciful because Joseph was underage, it had provided the same clemency for an adult a few years earlier. John Ward of New London was in the New London jail for profane speaking and petitioned the court for release from jail. In his confession he admitted that in the company of several women he had "foolishly and wickedly" taken the Lord's name in vain. He claimed that he was now "showing a humble frame and disposition, signifying his hearty sorrow for his folly and wickedness." The court released Ward from jail upon his payment of thirty shillings in court costs.[11] Thus, in the early eighteenth century, the courts appeared to treat both minors and adults in a similar fashion when they showed sufficient repentance.

While no formal change in the laws directed leniency for children, in practice by the end of the eighteenth century the fines for minors who broke the solemnity of Sabbath meetings were generally half the amount assessed against adults. In 1773 nineteen-year-old David Beckwith of New London confessed his guilt for breaking the Sabbath to Justice of the Peace John Hempsted. The youth admitted to laughing and rude behavior. Hempsted, without bothering to summon the boy's father for his defense, fined David three shillings and court costs. At the same justice court session twenty-four-year old Joshua Leach admitted he too had laughed and acted rudely on the

Sabbath. Hempsted assessed a six-shilling fine and court costs, twice what he had charged the minor. Nevertheless, just a year later, in 1774, New London Justice of the Peace Richard Hide charged Ebeenezer Waterman, Jr. of Norwich with talking in a loud, merry manner in church in order to make sport to disturb the other worshippers and assessed a higher fine. In line with the requirement for the testimony of witness, Hide summoned Elisha Edgerton and Samuel Tracy to support the charge. Though Hide identified Ebeneezer as the son of Ebeneezer Waterman, he did not specifically summon the boy's father to court. Despite clear recognition that the boy was a minor, the fine charged to the youth was 10 shillings with an additional 5 shillings in costs. Apparently, justices had some leeway in the designation of fines. In 1778 Justice John Hempsted reported in his personal records that Daniel Tinker and Caleb Douglas, both minors from New London, had confessed a breach of Sabbath at a public meeting by laughing. Without giving any explanation of the lower amount, Hempsted fined each just 3 shillings and did not assess any court costs. However, Hempsted neither identified the boys' fathers, nor did he summon them to represent their sons.[12]

Even in the 1790s, when children violated the sanctity of the Sabbath, the law differentiated between the punishment assessed against minors over and under the age of fourteen, the so-called age of discretion. The parent or guardian was to punish those under the age of discretion in the presence of some officer of the town. If the responsible adult refused to correct the child, the state fined the adult 50 cents. Minors who were fourteen or older were personally responsible for any punishments or fines, but if they refused to pay, the court had the authority to assess the fines against the responsible adults. The statute further directed that the magistrates could put children who did not have parents, masters, or guardians into service to pay any fines for breach of Sabbath.[13]

Ironically, many minors who were over the age of fourteen continued to answer charges of breach of the Sabbath without the assistance of either parents or court-appointed guardians, probably because justices of the peace rather than the judges of the county court ruled on nearly every case of breach of the Sabbath. Justices were less likely to have had formal legal training and therefore were less likely to know all the intricacies of the Connecticut legal system, including those protections applicable to children charged with crimes. In April of 1796 the Lyme tithingman complained to Justice of the Peace William Noyes that Selden and Joseph Ely, whom he identified in his complaint as the sons of Cullick Ely of Lyme, had broken the Sabbath. Noyes did not summon Cullick to the hearing, but he then determined that the charges against the two youths were not properly supported and dropped them. Nevertheless, claiming that there was some cause for complaint against the boys, Noyes said they had to pay the costs of their prosecution. If the youths were unable to pay, Cullick Ely would have been responsible even for those costs, yet nothing in Noyes' record indicated the father represented them at the justice court. Also in Lyme, three years later Justice Moses Warren prosecuted Moses Miller, identified as the son of George Miller of Lyme, for breaking the Sabbath by traveling from his father's house down to the sea on a Sunday and throwing a stone at one of the Indian houses he passed on his way. No mention of summoning the elder Miller appeared in the record. Warren marked on the case file payment in full of the fine of 84 cents and court costs of 25 cents, but he did not record by whom, making it difficult to determine if Miller ever had notice of the case against his son.[14]

By the second decade of the nineteenth century, justices of the peace seemed to be more aware of procedural rules applicable when trying cases of minors accused of Sabbath breaking. In 1815 three boys violated the Sabbath by harvesting hay on a Sunday in Goshen. Theodore Norton, Justice of the Peace for Goshen, charged all three with Sabbath breaking. He carefully identified the miscreants, John Jennings, Josiah Jennings, and Thaddeus Jennings, all of Cornwall, and summoned Samuel Burnett Jennings, their father and natural guardian, "to appear if he see cause at said time and place to protect and defend" them. At the hearing, Norton found only Josiah guilty, fining him $1.67. The files revealed payment of the fine but did not indicate by whom. An adult arrested for the same crime on the same day paid a fine of $2.[15]

Nevertheless, in the nineteenth century the practice of assessing a lower fine against children who broke the Sabbath was not always consistent. In 1819 Justice of the Peace Theodore North of Goshen charged Horatio N. Beach of Goshen for haying on Sunday. North summoned Beach's father Jesse Beach to court to appear if he saw cause, found the youth guilty, and fined him $1.67. North also charged the elder Beach with haying on Sunday and charged him an identical $1.67. In three other breach of Sabbath cases prosecuted by the justice of the peace on August 1, 1819, two other adults paid fines of $1.67 while one paid only 25 cents. Nothing in the justice's files indicated any reason for the variation in the fines for the adults or why he assessed the full fine against the child.[16]

A far more egregious breach of Sabbath took place in New London in 1826 resulting in equal punishments for some of the adults and children involved. Again, the justice of the peace assessed equal fines against all whom he found guilty. William P. Cleaveland, Jr. charged George Rider, George Jeffrey, Thomas Hewlett, Elijah Lax, Henry Jepson, Jr., Peter Larkey, and

Sylvester Keeney, all of New London, with taking part in various sports on a Sunday, including pitching and turning cents, "a game whereby money is hazarded," causing "a great disturbance and inconvenience to the good citizens of this state." Cleaveland identified both George Jeffrey and Elijah Lax as minors and notified Charles Jeffrey and William Lax to appear to defend their sons if they saw cause. He also identified Hewlett and Keeny as minors but appointed H. Douglas their guardian to represent them in court rather than notifying their fathers. Nothing in the file indicated that the elder Jeffrey or Lax had appeared in court. Cleaveland then proceeded to find all the defendants not guilty except for George Jeffrey, a black youth, and Henry Jepson, Jr., one of the three adults charged in the case. The fine for each was $1. While nothing in the records of the justice of the peace indicated why he assessed an equal fine against the youth, it might have been because he viewed the child as a hardened offender against the public order. Cleaveland was probably quite familiar with the Jeffrey family. In 1825 another New London justice of the peace had charged young George with assault, notified his father, brought in a guilty verdict, and then fined the lad seven dollars. In that prior case there had been no evidence that the elder Jeffrey had bothered to protect his child's interests.[17]

A paucity of records from those who served as justices of the peace in the 1830s until the 1850s made it difficult to determine whether the authorities continued to prosecute either minors or adults for breach of Sabbath. Nevertheless, reports from the first year of operation of the State Reform School for Boys in Meriden in 1855 did reveal that the state continued its efforts to try to reinforce the authority of organized religion while maintaining order in the community. Though only one of the one hundred and fifty boys serving sentences at the school was actually serving a sentence for breaking the Sabbath, the Reform School Superintendent's report gave a different story. In assessing the "moral condition" of the boys at the time of their commitment to the institution, the superintendent claimed ninety-six of the total were Sabbath breakers and that one hundred and twenty-five were "prophane in language." Overlapping these were the one hundred and fifteen who were merely "obscene in language." The chaplain of the Reform School addressed the religious deficiencies of his charges, bemoaning the fact that thirty of the boys had never attended Sabbath school and that ninety-two more had attended Sabbath school only a few times. Since regular religious instruction was part of the curriculum at the Reform School, it was clear that as late as 1855 the state was still reinforcing religion at the public level. A poignant letter home from R. E. and James Griffing, two brothers at the Reform School, illustrated that influence:

> Mother, we will try to seek heaven, for it would be horrible to go to the other place. We will try to seek the Lord. and we want you to do the same. We want you to encourage father to go to church and to love God. We pray to the Lord that our souls might be saved and that your hearts may be softened and given to the Lord. We pray to the Lord that his blessing may rest down upon us and that He will guide father safe across the ocean and bring him back, freed from the bondage of sin. . . . We hear about the Lord every Sabbath. We want you both to become Christians and members of the church.[18]

Though Connecticut no longer had a direct relationship to the religious institutions of the community, it certainly continued to use its control over children in its custody to impart religious standards.

DISORDERLY CONDUCT

Since children were often one of the most disorderly groups in any society, it is not surprising that many Connecticut laws established standards of behavior that applied to children as well as adults. George Haskins has correctly claimed that the family was a vital factor in social control in the colonial period, but it is clear that various statutes served to provide support for fathers or heads of household when they failed to achieve that control at the level of the family. This was evident from the number of laws establishing the limits on acceptable behavior. Yet status rather than age seems to have been an early determinant in applying some such laws, at least during the earliest years of the colony. As early as 1650, Connecticut lawmakers passed a law restricting the freedom of "young men" to live where they wished without limiting the restriction to those under twenty-one. The law directed that no masters or families could allow a young man to live with them without the specific permission of the inhabitants of the town. The fine assessed for breaking this prohibition was twenty shillings for each week that the young man lived in the town, charged to the head of the household with whom he resided. The opposite side of this attempt at social control was a law that prohibited a single male who could not afford to employ a servant from maintaining an independent household without the permission of the town residents. Both of these laws make it clear that the issue was status rather than simply age. Based on the specific language of the statute, apparently a wealthy single male under the age of twenty-one or a married minor could maintain a separate household, free of the regulation by his neighbors.[19] Enforcement of such laws regulating specific behaviors depended on the oversight of the rest of the community. Judging from the lack of court cases to punish breaches of these regulations, community members did an effective job of policing the living arrangements of young, single males in their communities.

Clearly, adults perceived that youths could threaten the peace of the community, and equally clearly, the colonial courts held them fully responsible for their actions. Though many of the early records lacked specific evidence as to age, dependent status may have indicated when the lawbreakers who disrupted the public order were under age. In 1651 Sarah Gibbs, the daughter of the widow Gibbs, "carried herself sinfully and disorderly." Though the Particular Court did not explain what it meant by "sinfully," it still put Sarah into service as punishment for her transgression of the community standards and assessed court costs as well. In 1680 the New London County Court charged New London resident Jonathan Stevens with swearing, cursing, and breaking the peace, and with hitting and threatening his uncle. The Court fined Jonathan two pounds ten shillings and bound him for future peaceable behavior. In neither of these cases did the authorities summon responsible adults into court to represent the interests of the defendants; therefore it is not clear whether they were, in fact, underage.[20]

Perceptively recognizing that youthful lawbreaking and disruption of public order were most likely to occur away from the restraining eyes of adults, colonial legislators passed several laws to restrict the freedom of movement of young people. To prevent "unseasonable nightwalking," one such law prohibited individuals under the care of a parent or master from being out of their homes after 9 at night, nor could young people meet or be entertained at any house without the consent of parents or guardians. Youths also could not meet together or "associate themselves in company, or make any rout or disorder" at any other time. Minors who violated the law paid a fine of ten shillings or sat in the stocks for two hours. Heads of families who tolerated such gatherings of disorderly youth were also to pay a fine of ten shillings. Apparently the law was not a sufficient deterrent. In 1678 Jonathon Start, Samuel Packer, Mary Fish, and Margaret Culbro faced charges of "accompanying together unseasonably in the night at a haystack." In the same year Jonathan Wickwase answered to the charge of night walking and to the additional charge of lascivious conduct for being found asleep with a girl in a haycock and paid a two-pound fine.[21]

Limiting children who gathered outdoors or at the homes of friends still did not create the desired orderly behavior. As a result, the General Assembly sought an additional way to control the activities of young people. In 1712 a new law prohibited innkeepers and tavern owners from allowing "any single persons being boarders or sojourners, or any young persons or inhabitants whatsoever under the government of parents or masters to convene or meet together in company" on a Sabbath evening or after any fast day or lecture. Authorities clearly were trying to impose a form of curfew on youths in Connecticut. Further reinforcing the social order aspect of the new law, the statute directed that if an innkeeper could prove he or she had told the young people to leave and had asked the constable to break up "such disorderly meetings," he or she would not have to pay the fifty-shilling fine.[22]

At times children transgressed community standards in ways not covered by the existing laws, forcing adults in the community to pass new laws for the maintenance of public order. Parents apparently could not trust their children to stay in line even when indoors. In 1713 William Harris of New London was certainly outside the bounds of acceptable social behavior when he chose to "filthily, lasciviously, and corruptly dance naked before several maids." Although Harris was just a few months short of twenty-one, he was still legally under the control of his father. The court identified him as a minor in dealing with his lawbreaking, though it did not order Harris's father to appear with him in court to provide for his defense. Officials identified fellow participant and defendant in the alleged lewd dancing, Richard Mitchell, as a minor as well. Following a corn husking that must have taken place with the permission of Harris's father; the youths had gone to an upstairs room in Harris's father's house and, according to eyewitnesses, were not studiously discussing the week's religious lesson. Gabriel Woodmancy testified that Harris and Mitchell had merely taken off their shirts and hung them on their arms as they danced, but young Amos Tinker asserted both had stripped down until their bodies were "naked." Sarah and Mary Lester, ages fifteen and nine, said they had been hiding behind the bed curtains and could not see what was happening but had heard Samuel Harris tell the two youths to stop stripping themselves. An additional witness, Sarah Gidins, did see Harris and Mitchell pull off some clothing. She testified that she had tried to leave the room when they did so. Because Amos Tinker held the door shut to keep her from fleeing the bedroom, Sarah claimed she had then taken refuge behind the bed hangings with the Lester girls. Yet despite eyewitness evidence of this private disorder, the court could only convict Harris of lascivious dancing, fining him forty shillings and assessing court costs of over 4 pounds, in part because of the cost of calling the number of witnesses required to testify in the case. Mitchell, who claimed Harris had drawn him into the affair, paid a fine of only twenty shillings and correspondingly lower court costs.[23]

Though there is no direct evidence that this incident in 1713 influenced an additional measure for adding to the colony's laws on social control, the Connecticut legislature reissued its law against nightwalking and created yet another law to regulate the activities of minors in 1715. The newest law prohibited the "unseasonable meetings of young people in the evening after Sabbath Day and at other times," and directed that any minors who were under the government of parents or guardians and who broke the law would have to pay a fine of five shillings or sit in the stocks for two hours. The statute added the proviso that it was not intended to keep young people from attending religious meetings, making it clear that the purpose was to prevent rowdy misbehavior of the young.[24] Creation of such a law was itself evidence of a society that believed in the necessity of reinforcing parental control over its young people.

In a 1720 case that may have been an outgrowth of an apparent challenge to the religious orthodoxy of the community in New London County, magistrates made it clear that at times they would hold children to adult standards of behavior and even ignore their own procedures when trying minors in the courts. The orthodox Congregational Church was still in control of the religious beliefs and morality of the majority Connecticut's residents, but a challenge from John Rogers, founder of the Rogerene sect, and his followers had disrupted that religious unity in New London County. Rogers and his supporters misbehaved during church services, worked on the Sabbath, and generally challenged the power and control of the mainstream ministers and magistrates. Rogers served repeated jail sentences for his disorderly conduct and challenges to the authority of civil and ecclesiastical leaders in New London. In 1720 the New London County Court charged two of his supporters, John Bolles and John Waterous, both of New London, with breach of the peace. Authorities in New London knew Bolles and Waterous well. So egregious was their past behavior that the Connecticut General Assembly had taken direct notice of their "stupidity and stubbornness" in refusing to abide by public orders. The disorderly conduct alleged by town jailer Benjamin Starr was that someone had broken into the New London County jail, removed the two doors, the locks, and the irons and had carried them away. Starr also said that several times previously "great violence had been used upon the door of the said jail, as also upon the yard erected around the same, by persons in the night time." Starr stated in his complaint that Waterous had been in jail on charges that he had disturbed the church congregation in New London by singing and blowing a horn. Apparently the theft of the doors was part of an attempt to break Waterous out of jail. Nevertheless, Waterous would only admit that he had been in jail on the night the doors disappeared but said that he saw no reason to answer the magistrate's questions as to whether he had taken the doors or if he knew who had taken them. Despite Waterous' failure to cooperate with the authorities, the Court directed the arrest of both Waterous and Bolles and also ordered the arrest of any of Bolles' sons who were over the age of fourteen on suspicion that they had assisted in the vandalism. The warrant did not even bother to list the sons by their names. The Court also ordered the arrest of John Rogers and any of his sons over the age of fourteen on the suspicion that they had also assisted in the vandalism. The Court did not require any additional notice of the arrest warrant to the fathers of the youths, apparently holding the youths fully responsible for their actions, despite their being under the age of twenty-one.[25] The official refusal to recognize the rights of the minors charged with aiding in the attempted jailbreak may have been a result of the seriousness of the adult challenge to the public order.

Perhaps because all male minors sixteen and older had to serve in the colonial militia, when a teen refused to answer the call to march or deserted from the militia service, the colony sometimes notified the youth's parent or guardian. At other times the magistrates treated youth as adults when charging them with failure to serve, without providing notice to the youth's parent or guardian. This seems somewhat strange because colonial law mandated when a community impressed minors for military service, officials had to supply the names of the youths' parents. Furthermore, the law directed that if a male between the ages of sixteen and twenty-one refused to serve, the boy's parent or guardian could be responsible for the resultant fine. Nevertheless, the treatment of minors varied from case to case. In 1748, the colony recognized the protection due a minor in the case of desertion charges against nineteen-year-old Christopher Dickinson of Stonington. When the Court arrested Christopher, it noted that he was a minor and appointed Joseph Fowler, attorney, as his guardian. This reflected what Zephaniah Swift later termed the inability of minors to either defend or initiate lawsuits because of their age and lack of experience. Though failure to sue through a guardian provided grounds for dismissal of civil lawsuits, colonial authorities often did bring criminal charges against children without providing the requisite protection. Provision of a guardian for the duration of a trial to protect a child's interests represented a type of public defense, but the child usually paid the cost of that representation in the court costs charged by the courts. When Christopher pleaded guilty, the Court assessed a fine of twenty pounds and court costs. Since the magistrate marked the file as paid in court but made no mention of the either the boy's father or his temporary guardian, Christopher might have paid his own fine and costs.[26]

Despite this fairly recent precedent of the County Court appointing a guardian in a case of desertion, a number of cases during the French and Indian War revealed the anomaly of treating minors as adults. In 1757 the colony charged five New London residents with refusal to answer the call to march to the relief of Fort William Henry. One, Enoch Bolles, Jr., was just eighteen years old. According to the testimony of Samuel Bill, all the accused had refused his direct order to report for militia service, an order that he had issued under the authorization of the Connecticut General Assembly. Bill used the term "impressed" in describing his failed attempts to corral the unwilling militiamen. At no time did either Bill or the magistrate identify Enoch as a minor. The youth entered a not-guilty plea along with the adult defendants; the court found all not guilty but ordered that they pay the costs of prosecution. Enoch apparently paid along with the rest. In a separate case in 1758, the court charged another seven New Londoners with refusal to march to the relief of the fort. Again, one was a minor, twenty-year-old Arariah Beebe. As in the prior case, the Court did not identify him as a minor, treating him just as it did the adults. Again, the Court found all not guilty but charged them court costs. In 1759, the colony charged four more New London residents with "failure to march against the king's enemies." In this case, the writ identified two of the accused as sons of New London residents, but only one of those, Samuel Bolles, was actually a minor aged eighteen. Though the warrant identified Samuel's father as Joshua Bolles, it did not order an official notification of the elder Bolles concerning the charges against his son. As in the previous cases, the Court did not provide any special treatment or legal protection for the teen, though again it found all the defendants not guilty. Since boys sixteen and older had the adult responsibility of assisting in the defense of the colony, it appears that the Court correspondingly treated them as adults.[27] Perhaps more interesting was the evidence provided by these and other cases in which juries brought in not-guilty verdicts against any of the defendants charged with failure to serve. New London jurors apparently sympathized with those who did not want to fight in the war. Various resolutions passed by Connecticut's General Assembly during the course of the war revealed that the problem of failure to answer the call to serve in the militia was quite common. Clearly, not all Connecticut's residents, young or old, supported the colony's military endeavors.[28]

By the middle of the eighteenth century, although the various night-walking laws restricting the movement of minors remained in force, usually only those children who were extremely unruly appeared before the courts to face criminal charges of disorderly conduct, or even of inciting a riot. In

June of 1758 the New London County Court accused New London minors John Dishon and David Allen along with twenty-two-year old Nathaniel Shaw, Jr. of "alarming and terrifying" the inhabitants of New London at night. The accuseds' answer to the charges was that they had fired the town cannon to celebrate the news of the king of Prussia's victory over Austria, "an event so interesting that it would naturally elate the heart of every true Briton and well wisher to his country and the Protestant cause." They also said that they didn't actually cause any alarm. Nothing in the file indicated that the parents or guardians of the youths appeared on their behalf. Despite the ingenious excuse in their defense, the court found the two youths and Shaw guilty as charged and fined each four pounds. Compared to fines for assault or trespass, this was a greater punishment, perhaps reflecting the broader impact of the disorderly conduct. Another possible explanation of the amount of the fine could be that young Nathaniel was the son of one of New London's wealthy merchants. Though the trial documents provided no evidence that any adults represented the young men, it is apparent that they might have had legal advice from some source because they and Shaw filed for a review of their conviction in November of 1758. At that hearing the defendants admitted that they had entered the New London fort and had discharged four or five of the cannon but claimed they had not caused any alarm to anyone and should not have to pay the four-pound fine. The court refused to abate the fine, perhaps as a deterrent to others.[29]

Just two years later in 1760 the conviction of fourteen-year-old Benjamin Billings and two of his friends, John Miller and Ephraim Baker, all of New London, for public disruption made it clear that fines were no deterrent to youths who wanted to disturb the peace of their community. At the same time the noticeably lower fines in this case revealed the wide discretion available to magistrates prosecuting those who disturbed the peace. According to the warrant, the youths fired the town cannons, screamed, broke glass, and burned wigs and hats to disrupt public order. The boys claimed that they were celebrating the "joyous news " of the fall of the fort at "Louis Burge" and meant to make some public appearance of rejoicing. They asserted that since their actions had not endangered any house they should not be fined. Nevertheless, the court found all guilty. Despite evidence that the youths not only fired the cannon but also broke windows and set fire to the wigs and hats, actions seemingly more disruptive than those of Nathaniel and his companions, the court fined each just forty-five shillings. The smaller fine could have been because Benjamin was only fifteen or because the magistrate himself shared their elation in the victory over the French. As in the prior case of public disorder, there was no mention of notification of the boys' parents or guardians.[30] Although neither an adult nor another minor could bring independent charges against a minor in a civil lawsuit without legal notice to the child's parent or guardian, apparently a differing standard of responsibility applied for cases concerning the personal actions of minors, at least when those children disrupted public order.

By the 1780s the dependent status of children convicted of public disorder was more apparent because of the wider recognition of the responsibility of adults for the legal costs of their behavior. The requirement for formal notice to the parents of minors charged with rude and unlawful behavior in Stonington in 1783 was clear from the fact that the court dealt with the white boys in the same way it dealt with African Americans who also participated in the disruption. Stonington Justice of the Peace Nathaniel Minor arrested Stonington youths Wilbur Palmer, Amos Sheffield, Ebeneezer Cobb, Jr., Jesse Parker, Paul Rhodes, and Matthew Green in February of 1783 for being disguised and for terrifying the people at Long Point in Stonington. Minor brought the same charges against Frank Jagger, the "negro of Mr. Jagger," Ned Waldron, "the negro of Mr. Waldron," and Seazar, "the negro of Mr. John Denison, 3rd." According to the writ, the group had assembled at night and shouted, screamed, jumped, and made other "rude and other unlawful noises and were guilty of masquerading and disguising themselves and terrifying and affrightening divers people." Once he had arrested the boys, all age seventeen or younger, Minor ordered notice to the youth's parents, guardians, or masters to "appear if they see cause" to defend the teens. He also notified the masters of the three African Americans. All of the defendants pleaded guilty except for Ebeneezer Cobb, Jr. and Paul Rhodes. Minor rejected their not-guilty pleas and fined all the participants three pounds for the disruption and one pound for court costs, noting in the file that according to the state laws, execution for the fines was "to go forth not against the minors but against parent, guardian or master after conviction." At this point the fathers and masters of the white youths paid the fines and obtained the release of the boys. The justice of the peace marked "fine not paid" next to the names of the three African Americans. Apparently their masters had refused to accept the financial responsibility for their actions.[31]

Nightwalking was just one of three charges levied against three New London boys in 1784, but the authorities did notify the accuseds' parents and guardians of the legal action. Justice of the Peace Moses Fargo charged Amos Smith, Joshua Comstock, and Daniel Fox with creating "disorder in the night season" as well as tearing down a haycock, cutting down six young apple trees, and destroying a hovel on the property. At the original justice court hearing Fargo directed that because Joshua and Daniel were minors

Elisha Fox, father of Daniel, and Caleb Comstock, father of Joshua, be notified that they could appear to defend their sons. The magistrate ordered the arrest of the three accused, but Amos Smith could not be found. At the New London County Court trial, both boys pleaded not guilty in pleas entered by their fathers. After hearing evidence from Esther Johnson that she saw all three of the accused at 9 o'clock in the evening in the field where the "mischief" took place, the court found the two youths guilty as charged and ordered that they pay Fargo four pounds ten shillings in damages and court costs of over eight pounds. There was no evidence of an additional fine or a specific punishment for the boys breaking the law against nightwalking.[32]

In post-revolutionary Connecticut children who evaded the control of their parents and disrupted society were apparently still a problem. The state legislature reflected this concern with a 1795 reissue of the law against nightwalking. The language of the new law was very similar to the statute of 1702 in ordering that any persons who were out after nine o'clock at night without parental permission would be subject to a fine of one dollar. Continuing the 1715 practice of holding parents responsible for their children's activities, the new law maintained the practice of fining parents who allowed disorderly gatherings in their homes, charging them one dollar as well. However, the new law did make an addition to the old statute. It directed that if any persons charged with disorderly conduct could not provide a satisfactory explanation of where they were going, they would be liable to pay damages to any person who complained about their behavior, limiting the amount of such damages to seventeen dollars.[33] This alteration might have been a way to reinforce social control by encouraging witnesses to follow through on their complaints against rowdy activity by children.

Notable in the early nineteenth century was the increasing attention that magistrates and justices of the peace paid to identifying culprits as minors, even in the case of petty crimes. Paralleling that was the increasingly consistent notification to the parents, master, or guardians of under-age defendants. One reason for the more regular protection of the procedural rights of children might have been the 1795 publication of Zephaniah Swift's two-volume explanation of the laws of Connecticut, *A System of the Laws of the State of Connecticut*. Hereafter, magistrates and jurors alike did not have to be lawyers to understand the operation of Connecticut's laws and court system. Publication of this book along with increasingly formal training for aspiring attorneys raised the level of legal expertise within much of the community.

This attention to proper procedure was evident in a case against three children who not only faced prosecution under the night-walking statute;

Justice of the Peace Josiah Isham also accused them of being "common rogues, idle, dissolute, disorderly persons, and common pilferers." While this might be a description of transients with no connection to the community, Isham's complaint identified twenty-year-old Hannah Smith and her younger siblings Elizabeth and Robert as New London residents, the children of James Smith. James Tilley of New London also accused the three of hanging around his shop yard and stealing scraps of old bordage. Isham issued notice to James Smith as the children's parent and natural guardian to appear if he saw fit to defend them. There was no apparent resolution of the case, but the notice to Smith indicated that Isham was familiar with the legal requirement to notify the parents of a minor defendant accused of unlawful activity.[34]

A case in 1813 also revealed the role of a justice not only in punishing children for disrupting the community but in notifying responsible adults of their misbehavior, even when the adults were female. In 1813 Justice of the Peace William P. Cleaveland, Jr. charged five New London youths with nightwalking and breach of the peace. Ezra Harris, Charles Sisson, Isiah Mills, William Hilt, and Henry Rogers supposedly assembled at night without the consent of their parents, guardians, or masters and went to the house of Samuel Peters, "a house of great disorder, ill repute, and bad fame, there to be entertained in a most dissipated manner." Cleaveland also charged that afterwards the youths assembled in the streets of New London and disturbed the peace of the citizens by "hallowing, swearing, cursing, and other disorderly and unbecoming conduct, contrary to all good breeding and moral public decency." That these may have been boys without fathers seemed apparent from the summons by Cleaveland. When he issued warrants for the boys' arrest, he ordered notification to the mothers rather than the fathers of the boys. He summoned Betsy Harris as parent and guardian of Ezra, Elizabeth Rogers as parent and guardian to Henry, Elizabeth Sisson as parent and guardian for Charles, and Nancy Ramsey as parent and guardian for William Holt. Notably, Cleaveland did not identify or summon any adult to represent Isiah Mills but tried him anyway with the other youths. Though the files contained no evidence whether the mothers did appear to assist in their sons' defense, Cleaveland found all of the youths guilty as charged and fined each one dollar. Of all the boys only Isiah did not pay the fine. In this case, notification to the mothers apparently ensured payment to the court.[35]

Although justices of the peace or judges in the county courts tried most charges of breach of the peace, disorderly conduct, and even riotous behavior, in September of 1814, ten New Londoners created a public disruption that the authorities deemed a riot. By definition a riot was more severe than mere disorderly conduct; a riot was a violent act by persons who were part of a crowd of at least three people "which act or acts shall constitute a clear and present danger of, or shall result in, damage or injury to the property of another person or to the person of another individual." Clearly rioters put life and property at risk in addition to disturbing the peace. Tensions resulting from the August 1814 British attack on nearby Stonington during the War of 1812 or even the widespread opposition to the war shared by many Connecticut residents may have influenced local authorities to crack down more forcefully than usual on challenges to public order. The accusation of participating in an actual riot resulted in several youths standing their trial before the Superior Court, a venue that usually heard cases involving more serious charges. A trial at the Superior Court was necessarily before more experienced judges. As a result the judge directed that the children involved obtain adult representation by attorneys appointed to serve as their guardians for the trial. He was not willing to have only the youths' own parents present to protect their legal interests. The state's attorney charged the New Londoners with participating in a riot, asserting that they attempted to tear down the house of Isaac Thompson as well as the town jail and in addition had broken numerous windows in other houses. The judge identified four of the ten rioters as under age: Charles Mallory, John Rogers, Japhet Thorp, and Walter Roath. Rather than going through the motions of providing notice to the youths' parents to appear and defend them if they saw fit, the judge appointed Isiah Isham, Esq. as guardian to Charles, John, and Japhet and named James Lanman, Esq. as guardian to Walter. All the defendants entered pleas of not guilty, but the jury found three of the adults and the minor Japhet Thorp guilty of the charges and fined all four $34. Although being under age before a judge of the Superior Court apparently ensured Japhet a more skilled form of legal representation, it did not reduce the penalty for him.[36]

In contrast, the 1814 case of Henry Deshon of Montville made it clear that having a knowledgeable adult to assist in the defense against charges of breach of the peace could help a child evade the consequences of his actions. Justice of the Peace Loomis charged Joseph Deshon and Henry Deshon, identified as a minor, with swearing and breach of the peace, for threatening to beat people. That the state would still bring criminal charges of swearing against the boy was evidence of the continuing connection between religion and civil society. The original case documents do not make it clear whether John Deshon, Henry's father, did appear to defend his son; he probably did not because the justice found both of the accused guilty as charged and fined them one dollar for the swearing and $1.50 for the breach of the peace. In response to the guilty verdict, John Deshon later petitioned the Superior

Court in New London County for a writ of error to reverse his son's conviction, claiming the ruling by the justice of the peace was erroneous. The elder Deshon's claim was that the arresting constable was not authorized to present the original complaint since he had not notified Deshon as well as his son of the arrest. Only an adult familiar with Connecticut's legal system would have known the legal maneuvering necessary to obtain a reversal. The Superior Court agreed with Deshon's argument and reversed the lower court's verdict, freeing Henry from both fines.[37]

A pathetic case in 1814 revealed that the legal protection afforded "disorderly" minors was still far from uniform. It also showed that the seventeenth-century social control inherent in the law restricting where single males could live continued into the nineteenth century. New London Justice of the Peace Eben Leonard responded to a complaint filed by the New London selectmen that John Baum was an idle and dissolute person without any way of supporting himself. Learned wrote in his file that John was "a black boy without hands or feet" who was not a legal inhabitant of the state but who was living in New London. The selectmen did not allege that the boy had broken the peace or behaved in a particularly disorderly fashion. It was his very residence in the town that challenged the social order. Town officials sought the boy's removal to avoid having to pay the cost of his support. Even though Learned clearly identified John as a boy, he complied with the selectmen's request. In what seems to have been a clear-cut example of ignoring normal legal procedures in the case of an African American child, Learned's files gave no indication that he provided an adult to look out for the unfortunate boy's interests. Without appointing a guardian for the child and despite the fact that it was January, Learned ordered the boy to leave New London.[38]

In contrast to this callous treatment of a transient black youth, even though being without visible means of support was still a crime in the 1820s, the New London County Court did appoint a guardian in the case of New London resident Jeriamiah Potts, Jr. The difference in the judicial treatment may have been that Jeremiah, despite his sorry condition, was a resident of New London, or it could have reflected the racism that was rampant in Connecticut society. Justice of the Peace William P. Cleaveland, Jr. charged that Jeremiah was an idle person who had no way to support himself. He said the youth wandered about from place to place without any lawful business, misspent what money he did earn, and failed to provide for himself. Despite the boy's certain inability to pay for the cost of legal assistance, Cleaveland appointed Ebeneezer Watrous as guardian to Jeremiah, then convicted the youth of the charges and sentenced him to the workhouse for a thirty-day term.[39]

What was not clear from Cleaveland's files was if the unfortunate Jeremiah also had to pay for Watrous's services as his guardian *ad litem*.

Nightwalking continued to be a catchall charge to control the disorderly activities of rowdy children. In July of 1827, Justice of the Peace Cleaveland charged Charles Jeffrey, Jr., a black youth, Mortimer St. John, and Joseph Halliday both with night walking and having no visible means of support. The arrest warrant indicated that the three wandered from place to place, sleeping in barns, out houses, and the open air and that they "could not give a good account of themselves." Since both Charles and Mortimer were minors, Cleaveland went through the motions of notifying Charles Jeffrey, the father of Charles, and William Isaac, the guardian to Mortimer, to appear and defend the boys. Cleaveland was already familiar with the Jeffrey family because in 1826 he had tried George Jeffrey for breach of Sabbath and in April of the 1827 he had prosecuted young Charles for assault. In that case the justice had had to provide a court-appointed guardian for the boy when his father had failed to appear in court. After the elder Jeffrey again failed to protect his son's interests, Cleaveland appointed Thomas West, Esq. to represent both boys. Whatever assistance West provided did not forestall a guilty verdict. The sentence for each youth was a fourteen-day term in the New London workhouse.[40]

At times the Connecticut justice courts appeared to adapt the charges against minors to the circumstances of the case. In 1842 New London Justice of the Peace Henry Douglas originally charged fellow New London resident William Bolton, Jr. with "tumultuous carriage, threatening and traducing the character" of Joseph Mason and his wife Fanny. Connecticut had no specific prohibition against tumultuous carriage, but Douglas seemed to be using the charge to indicate a particularly egregious breach of the peace. Although the writ did not identify William as a minor, Douglas had added at the bottom of the charge a summons to William Bolton, "father of the said William, Jr. to appear." At the trial on charges that the justice had reduced to a mere breach of the peace, William, Jr. pleaded "for himself" not guilty, an indication that his father had not responded to the summons to represent his son. Douglas found the youth guilty but fined him only fifty cents plus court costs. The elder Bolton may have neglected to come into court because of the minor nature of the charges against his son.[41]

While disorderly conduct was not a major criminal act, support for the creation of a State Reform School for Boys relied in part on Connecticut residents who wanted to limit "that class of juvenile offenders, living in habits of vagrancy, wandering from place to place, . . . doing wanton mischief, sleeping in outhouses and in the hall of public buildings, without home, without instruction." When the school opened in 1855 with one hundred and fifty residents, only three were serving time for disorderly conduct or breach of the peace, but various courts had committed forty-one boys for vagrancy. A more notable statistic was that the school's chaplain identified fifty-six boys whose parents had lived a life that was "morally pernicious." Furthermore, the chaplain counted seventy-two boys who were at the school not because of any conviction for a crime but because their parents had had them committed for their unruly behavior. What made this factor interesting was that parents who voluntarily committed their sons to the Reform School had to pay room and board charges for their children. Clearly, the school met the need of adults who believed a certain number of children were outside the bonds of normal social control.[42]

DAMAGE TO PROPERTY AND WINDOW BREAKING

Disorderly conduct by a minor could apparently extend to charges of willfully damaging property. In 1833 the state charged Richard Reed of Montville with putting dirt, leaves, and iron into the upright shaft of the machinery at the cotton mill of Charles and George Lewis of Montville. The court charged that the youth intended to destroy the machinery. Noting that Richard was a minor, in the original writ the justice appointed William Tillotson as guardian to defend the youth against the charges and ordered the boy bound over to the County Court for a trial on the charges. Whether Tillotson's assistance would have helped the youth became moot when Richard defaulted by failing to appear in court.[43]

Disorderly conduct by youths also included something as simple as window breaking. Surprisingly, until the nineteenth century, there were no cases dealing solely with window breaking, yet by the 1830s the charge appeared on court dockets with some regularity. Often the perpetrators were underage. Three Montville residents, two of them minors, faced charges in 1834 that they had willfully and maliciously broken fifteen panes of glass in a single window of Asa Grant's house in Norwich. The crime was supposedly more dangerous and damaging because at the time of the vandalism, Grant's daughter was "dangerously sick and in the last stages of disease." The arrest warrant issued by the justice of the peace originally called Eben Woodworth and Daniel Ray transient minors, but that designation was questionable because the justice named Joshua E. Woodworth of Montville as their guardian. Woodworth may have been a relative of Eben. When the case came to trial at the County Court, the judge then identified the youths as residents of Montville but appointed an attorney to serve as guardian to defend them against the charges of breach of the peace and breaking the windowpanes. Under the advice of their legal guardian the boys pleaded not guilty to the charges. The jury found them not guilty and discharged them from custody.[44]

Window breaking was only one of many charges against five Norwich youths who comprised part of a crowd of twenty-five "evil disposed persons" who created a riot in Norwich on November 11, 1837. The state charged that John Spencer, Thomas Spencer, Jr., Warren Hill, James Wilson, 4th, and John Cornell made a "great noise, riot, and tumult" near the house of Sheffield Corey of Norwich, throwing "stones, sticks, clubs, and bricks . . . breaking windows and shutters." The boys and adults also made loud noises with drums, horns, and fifes, and shouted "loud, horrible, blasphemous oaths." The riot continued for over two hours, observed by at least thirteen witnesses. Perhaps because one of the adults charged was Thomas Spencer, Sr., father to two of the boys, the court did not specifically summon or name the father as guardian to represent the youths. Instead the judge appointed Asa Child, Esq. to defend all five minors in the case. Under Childs' advice, the boys pleaded not guilty to the charges, as did all the adults charged. Even with the testimony of the thirteen witnesses, the court found all defendants not guilty. What was not clear from the case file was whether Childs' assistance played any role in the acquittal of the minors since the jury also found the adults not guilty.[45]

Clemency based on age was possible in some cases of breach of the peace. In 1839, the state brought charges of breach of the peace and window breaking against Adeline Truman of Norwich and Charlotte Miller of Preston, asserting the two had broken a window in the house of Julia Robinson. The County Court appointed John Wait, Esq. as guardian to Charlotte because she was a minor. At the actual trial, the state's attorney dismissed the charges against Charlotte without comment but found Truman guilty as charged and fined her $8. Because the state's attorney did not indicate why he dropped the charges against the minor, it is not clear whether West helped her escape punishment or whether her age or lack of evidence was the deciding factor.[46]

Window breaking continued to be the most common breach of the peace perpetrated by children. In 1843 disorder on Guy Falkes Day resulted in three different charges against two New London residents, minors Nathaniel Robbins and Alden Lewis. The warrant identified the boys as being of "unruly, turbulent, and mischevious dispositions" and said the two "unlawfully, willfully, and maliciously" broke windows in the houses of Albert G. Crocker and Henry Spencer. The state further charged that the two youths had assembled with ten others, "unknown to the state attorney," and made a "great noise, riot, tumult, and disturbance" for over an hour on November 5, 1843. At the original justice court hearing the justice of the peace appointed Benjamin Brown as guardian to the two boys "to assist and advise them." After finding the youths guilty on all three counts, the justice transferred the cases to the New London County Court. At that level, the judge appointed Hiram Wiley, Esq. as guardian to defend the boys. While Wiley's appointment was as a guardian rather than as legal counsel, his presence or advice may have influenced the jury to find the youths guilty on just the first count of window breaking and not guilty on the other two charges. The boys' punishment was a twenty-dollar fine and a four-month sentence in the New London County jail, a severe punishment when compared to other resolutions of window-breaking cases. Yet without Wiley's advice and assistance, the two might have been convicted on all three charges and ended up serving their time at the state prison.[47]

In 1844 a New London youth compounded the crime of breaking windows by targeting the windows of the New Methodist Meeting House in New London. John Grace, Justice of the Peace for New London, charged William Marshall, Jr. and George Lyman with breaking seven panes of glass at the church at 1 A.M. in the morning of July first. The original complaint identified George as a minor and named William L. Marshall as guardian for his defense. Having legal representation did not help the boy avoid conviction. Grace found both George and his fellow defendant guilty and fined them $7 each.[48]

Perhaps in response to the increase in the frequency of incidents of window breaking, the Connecticut General Assembly passed a new law in 1852 to deal with the crime. The statute did not limit the law to adults. It directed that every person who "maliciously and willfully" broke a window or caused any other harm to a dwelling, a barn, or any other building faced a fine not to exceed $100 or imprisonment not to exceed six months in the common jail, or both. Similar to the earlier change in the laws against arson, this change applied the full punitive weight of the law to all, regardless of their age.[49]

As with cases of assault, by the 1840s Connecticut courts handed out more severe sentences for breach of the peace when the accused were minors of African or Irish descent. Even though the legal charge did not include a claim of malicious intent, when Henry Ellis, a seventeen-year-old transient black teenager, fired a gun at a horse, the magistrate charged him with breach of the peace. The justice of the peace who issued the original warrant did identify the boy as a minor who was living in Lebanon at the time of the crime and saying the boy had "no father, master, or guardian," appointed

Robert Champlin of Lebanon as his guardian. Under the advice and direction of his guardian, the teen pleaded guilty. The justice of the peace transferred the case to the New London County Court for sentencing where the magistrate assigned John D. Park, Esq. as his guardian *ad litem* to represent him in court. The higher court found the youth guilty of breach of the peace and fined him twenty dollars and court costs of twenty-six dollars. When Henry did not pay either the fine or the costs, the court jailed him for nonpayment.[50]

In 1848 when a transient Irish youth placed large stones on the railroad tracks located in Lisbon, supposedly with the express intent to impede passage of the engine and cars of the Norwich and Worcester Railroad and to injure the passengers, the sentence was four months in the county jail. Although the state did identify William R. Lewis as a minor, the notice was quite cursory. On the face of the original writ the magistrate wrote only, "Hill, guardian." The court documents were somewhat more detailed, but merely indicated that George Hill, Esq., was the guardian *ad litem,* "Lewis being a minor." There was no indication of any specific advice or representation by the guardian, just the notation that the boy pleaded not guilty. The County Court found him guilty as charged, fined him twenty dollars, and sentenced him to a four-month term in the county jail. Because this conviction took place after the implementation of Connecticut's discretionary sentencing law, the incarceration in the county jail could have been an indication that the boy was under fifteen.[51]

STUBBORN CHILDREN

While statutes that criminalized the act of Sabbath breaking were evidence of institutional support for the maintenance of Christian society and laws to prevent breaches of the peace reflected the social control exerted by the community, throughout the colonial era and even into the nineteenth century the Connecticut laws that emphasized the desire for order were those concerning stubborn and disobedient children. The specific laws clearly revealed the perceived need for the legal system to reinforce the ability of parents to control their children. Despite a lack of evidence that the magistrates ever applied the full consequences of the laws, on their face the statutes were a stark reminder of adult fears. Taking the text nearly straight from Deuteronomy 21.18, the Connecticut law directed that if any child over the age of sixteen struck his or her parent, the ultimate punishment was the death penalty. The only allowable defenses were if the child was defending himself or herself from being maimed or murdered or if the parents had failed to educate the child properly. The law did not specifically restrict the applicability of this law to children under twenty-one; at least on paper it applied to any offspring of any age who physically assaulted his or her parents. Equally stark was the law mandating the death penalty for a son over the age of sixteen who was stubborn and rebellious and who would not obey his parents, even after they had corrected him. On the face of this act there were no exceptions to exempt a youth from the death penalty, and again there was no upper age limit. Furthermore, extending the reach of the laws to children of even younger ages, the law allowed the magistrates to send any child of any age or gender to the house of correction as punishment for stubbornness, and to keep the child there under hard labor and severe punishment as long as the magistrates deemed necessary to affect a transformation in the child's behavior.[52]

Though there is no record during the colonial period that the magistrates ever executed a child or an adult under the stubborn child law, prosecutions resulting in lesser punishments illustrated its ongoing use to maintain order. In New Haven in 1643 the local court had to deal with Andrew Low, Jr. who was "obstinate and rebellious against his parents, and incorrigible." Because Low compounded his crime against the order of the community by breaking into the house of a New Haven resident, stealing his rum, and ransacking the house, the record is not clear on whether he went to jail for the disobedience to his parents or for the crimes against property. Low then escaped from custody, further illustrating his incorrigible nature. Despite the youth's repeated transgressions against the public order, the court issued a surprisingly mild sentence, perhaps a reflection that the child was under the age of sixteen. The magistrate was to whip the boy as severely "as the rule will bare" and then to require that Low work with his father literally as a prisoner, chained by the leg to prevent his escape.[53] The maximum punishment for Low's crimes under other aspects of the criminal code could have included fines and branding for the theft and imprisonment for the stubborn conduct.

In practice the stubborn child law applied equally to disobedient apprentices. In 1644 the Particular Court of the colony convicted Susan Coles of rebellious carriage toward her mistress, sentencing her to a term at the house of correction where she was to remain at hard labor and harsh diet. Apparently the harsh regimen did not affect the necessary change in the girl's attitude because a further sentence directed that she undergo weekly public correction.[54]

Correction under the terms of the stubborn child law did not change attitudes for the better in the case of John Lewis. In 1670 he faced charges of absenting himself from home at "unseasonable times of the night to the great grief of his parents." He also distressed both his parents and the community for sitting with Sarah Chapman under an apple tree on a Sunday. The magistrate ordered him to obey his parents but did not impose a fine for his transgressions. Mild correction was ineffective. John obviously did not reform, because in 1672 his father again complained against his son, citing his disorderly conduct. At this breach of the social order the Court fined the younger Lewis twenty pounds and ordered him to perform well for his parents and placed him under a bond for good behavior. Only after the passage of a full year of good behavior did the Court release Lewis from that bond. Though the younger Lewis married in 1677, three years after the release of the bond, the court records do not specifically mention whether the son was under 21 at the time of his rebellious and stubborn conduct.[55]

That stubborn children continued to be a problem for colonial society was evident in the passage of a law in 1727 concerning the building of workhouses in the colony. The new law directed that each county must build a house of correction to house "common pipers, fiddlers, runaways, stubborn servants or children, common drunkards, common nightwalkers, and pilferers." The law also directed that when the courts sent stubborn children to the workhouses, the children's parents had to provide the material for them to work on. In addition to making parents pay for their inability to control their own children, this extra cost may have been a reflection of some concern for the well being of the children though housing them with the other disorderly persons of the society did not reflect that same concern.[56]

That the issue of stubborn children was one of status as well as of age was clear as late as the 1730s. In January of 1732/33, Solomon Stoddard of Norwich, who had reached his twenty-first birthday a few weeks earlier, assaulted his father and threw him from his house. Norwich Justice of the Peace Backus charged the young man with abuse and misdemeanors against his father, apparently using the stubborn and disobedient child law. Thomas Stoddard, the father, complicated the disposition of the case because he quickly found reason to forgive his son. The dispute seems to have been over possession of the house Solomon was living in. Thomas Stoddard had gone at night to the house where Solomon was living. Two witnesses to the attack, Samuel Spicer and Moses Chapman, said that Thomas Stoddard had asked them to go with him, perhaps an indication that Stoddard expected trouble from his son. When they got to the house, Solomon stood in the doorway and told his father he could not enter. The elder's response was that he had not come to hurt his son but that the house was his because he had built it. The father then tried to enter the door with Samuel Spicer, but Solomon seized them and "hurled them both out of the house." After arresting the young man for his crime, Backus jailed him until the case came to trial in June of 1733. At the hearing Solomon at first tried to exonerate himself, saying it had been dark when he had taken his father by the collar and thrown him out the door and he had thought he was a different person. The testimony of the two eyewitnesses contradicted this. The jury found that Solomon had "wittingly and willingly" committed the crime and sentenced him to ten lashes and to payment of court costs of seven pounds. Because Solomon was unable to pay the costs, the judge sent him back to jail.[57]

After spending additional time in jail, Solomon had an apparent change of heart. He wrote to the judge admitting that he had behaved himself "unbecoming to his father" and had reflected on and repented his poor treatment of his father. He asked for the Court's forgiveness and sought divine assistance to turn him from his evil ways. He pleaded for mercy to allow him to return home to his "poor, indigent, and distressed wife and children." This request made it clear that he had been living as an independent adult. In March Thomas himself had written to the magistrate seeking Solomon's release from jail saying his son was sick and likely to die. Thomas wrote in another letter in June that he was convinced his son had not recognized him the night of the attack and that once he did he was "very humble and sorry for what he had done." He again asked for his son's release, saying he had forgiven him. What may have been more to the point, he promised to pay Solomon's court costs. In the face of Solomon's repentance, Thomas's forgiveness, and the agreement to cover court costs, the New London County Court released Solomon, taking surety from Thomas to guarantee the son's good behavior.[58] Apparently Solomon's status under the stubborn child law was still directly related to his position as a child, whatever his age.

The law to control children who ignored normal parental controls changed over the course of the eighteenth century. In a 1750 revision of the colony's statutes, rebellion against parents by sons lost its status as a capital crime. Zephaniah Swift noted in the 1790s that if either children or servants were convicted of stubborn or rebellious carriage against their parents or master, two assistants or justices of the peace could commit the offender to the house of correction, to "remain under hard labor and severe punishment at the discretion of the court."[59] The state was continuing its role in enforcing parental discipline and control, but it reduced the consequences for rebellious children.

In one of the most disturbing cases of a "rebellious child," the state apparently imposed the punishment appropriate for attempted murder rather than the revised punishment mandated by this change of the 1790s. In 1804 the state brought charges against Azariah Beebe, Jr. of Waterford, claiming that "regardless of the filial duty of a son towards a father," the youth had struck his father, Azariah Beebe, on the head with a club, knocking him to the ground. The nineteen-year-old had then beaten his father on the head with a large stone, "with the intent to murder," fracturing the elder's skull and endangering his life. The justice of the peace arrested the youth the day after the assault and set bond at $500. He did not identify the boy as a minor, nor did he assign a guardian for his defense. Azariah admitted he had assaulted his father and refused to provide bond. At his trial before the Superior Court, again without the assistance of a court-appointed guardian, he also pleaded guilty, The failure to provide a guardian at the Superior Court is somewhat inexplicable, since a judge at this upper level of the court system ought to have been familiar with the requirement that the state provide guardians for those under age charged with crime. Most certainly the elder Beebe would not have raised the question of whether the court had followed its own procedures. The Superior Court sentenced the twenty-year-old to a three-year prison term at Newgate Prison.[60]

In the nineteenth century the law against stubborn children remained a way for parents to bring extra force to bear in keeping their children in line, whatever their ages or their complaints against their parents. Revisiting the colonial law for the creation of a work house, in 1800 New London incorporated a "Poor and Bettering House" for use as a home for "rogues, vagabonds, sturdy beggars, idle, dissolute, and disorderly persons, runaways, and stubborn children and servants." It was also to house all persons who were "under distraction." The state legislature revised its law on stubborn children in 1821. The new version proclaimed that if children were rebellious and stubborn and resisted the authority of their parents, the parents could complain to the justice of the peace. In response the justice had the authority to issue an arrest warrant against the child. If, after a trial, the justice found the child guilty of stubborn and rebellious behavior, he could send the minor to the house of correction or the county jail for a term not to exceed thirty days. The law also provided that if a stubborn child reformed while in custody of the state, the magistrate could release the child to his or her parents. As with the earlier law against stubborn children, there was no age limit designated within the statute. Surprisingly, even as the statute retained some of its reach against children, it eliminated the specific punishment for a child who cursed his or her parents.[61]

When children disobeyed their parents, judges at times seemed unconcerned with the potential conflict of interest of having the parent represent the child in court. In 1844, Ledyard Colvart ran a house of prostitution and had numerous convictions for breach of the peace. Despite these factors

New London Justice of the Peace John Grace charged Colvart's daughter Miranda under the stubborn child law, saying she was "stubborn and rebellious, and did refuse to obey the commands, and resisted the authority of her parents." The file noted that Miranda Colvart was a minor, but the court did not assign her a separate guardian even though her father certainly could not have provided effective legal counsel since he had filed the original complaint against Miranda. Furthermore, in considering the evidence, no one took into consideration the type of family from which the girl was trying to escape. In 1848, a frustrated father rather than the state brought suit under the stubborn child law, one of the few such cases in the nineteenth century. John Noyes of Stonington sued his minor son, Charles Noyes, saying that for more than a year the boy had been stubborn and rebellious and had refused to obey his father or to perform various duties for him. In this case Stonington Justice of the Peace Francis Sheffield recognized the potential conflict of interest and appointed Henry Sheffield to defend the child. Although Charles pleaded innocent, the justice found him guilty and sentenced him to serve up to thirty days in the New London County jail since Stonington did not have a house of correction. Sheffield directed that if the boy reformed before the end of the thirty days, the county could release him back to his father. Sheffield also noted full payment of fees on the case, but the justice did not record if the elder Noyes had taken responsibility for the cost of prosecuting his own son.[62]

As with other crimes against the public order, stubbornness and disobedience to parents were still problems for parents in the 1850s when the State Reform School for Boys opened. Of the one hundred and fifty inmates in 1855, thirty-five boys were serving sentences for stubbornness, clear evidence that some parents still depended on the state to reinforce their authority over their children. Stubbornness, in fact, was the third most common complaint, after theft and vagrancy. Moreover, the chaplain of the Reform School reported that over one hundred of the youths in his charge had been truants and that fifty-nine had "visited improper places of amusement;" both could have been prime examples of disobedience to parental orders. The chaplain also claimed that forty-six of the boys had regularly "drunk ardent spirits, most of them to intoxication" and that sixty-five slept out at night in stables, sheds, and boxes. None of these moral failings were crimes punishable by a jail term, yet the boys were in the Reform School. While some might also have committed thefts, assaults, or breaches of the public order resulting in fixed terms of imprisonment at the school, nearly half the children at the school were not serving sentences for committing crimes. Parents or relatives of seventy-two of the boys had voluntarily committed the children to the Reform School. This was especially noteworthy because in the case of a voluntary placement, the parent was responsible for the costs of maintaining the boy in the Reform School. This usage of the school to bring unruly children in line by the power of the state rather than their parents illustrated the way the stubborn-child law supported and reinforced parental control. Since the minimum stay at the Reform School was ninety days, punishment for stubborn behavior was far harsher than under the old system that limited the stay to thirty days in the workhouse or jail.[63]

CRIMES OF SEXUALITY: FORNICATION AND RAPE

From the seventeenth century, Connecticut treated fornication as a criminal act rather than the subject of civil action; it was thus a crime against the public morals and order of society. Though fornication prosecutions were numerous in both the seventeenth and eighteenth centuries, they declined markedly after the American Revolution. Similarly, rape prosecutions were relatively rare in the first two centuries but became more common as actions for fornication declined. In both crimes, the colony and then the state treated minors first as the equivalent of responsible adults, holding them to the same standards of behavior, but by the nineteenth century the laws and the courts began to change the way society looked at sexual activity by minors.

The original Connecticut law against fornication was similar to many other early colonial laws in that it did not distinguish the age of the accused, directing that "if any man shall commit fornication with any single woman, they shall be punished by being made to marry or by fine or by corporal punishment." By the early eighteenth century the law set a specific fine of not more than five pounds and limited the corporal punishment to ten stripes when a single man and a single woman committed the crime but still set no specific age limit. Since civil suits by the women seeking support for the resulting birth of a child out of wedlock often accompanied many public charges of fornication, the intent of the laws appears to have been to identify the participants and hold them accountable, freeing the towns from responsibility for the maintenance of illegitimate children. Despite civil laws that required notification of the parents of minors in civil lawsuits, the courts initially treated minors who committed fornication as adults and apparently did not require notification to the responsible parent or guardian. Certainly for purposes of contracting a marriage, the law considered that a boy was a "man" at fourteen, and a girl was a "woman" at twelve (though both needed parental consent to enter into a marriage contract); the same age distinction seemed to apply to sex outside marriage.[64]

Status rather than age may have played an important role in early fornication cases. Though her age was not available, the defendant in a fornication case in 1668 was certainly in a dependent status. Before the New London County Court, the colony charged Nan, maid to Captain George Denison, with fornication with the Indian Domurk. Since Nan was already in service to Denison, the court suspended its punishment. In 1702 in the case of *Rex v. Joanna Tubbs,* the New London County Court found Joanna Tubbs guilty of fornication. Though there was no mention of Joanna's mother being called to represent her at the trial in the case files, the court ordered her mother to pay ten pounds as surety to guarantee her daughter's appearance at the trial. At trial the magistrate ordered Joanna to pay a forty-shilling fine upon her conviction for fornication, but noted that her mother, the widow Mary Tubbs, had paid the fine. While this was not conclusive evidence that Joanna was underage, certainly her mother would have had no legal obligation to pay the fine if she were over the age of twenty-one. In a parallel case, the court examined evidence on the condition of Joanna's stillborn child to make sure there had been no interference in the birth. There was no evidence that anyone assisted Joanna in her defense. Accompanying this examination was an accusation against John Fox that he had fathered the bastard. The court concluded that the child had in fact died before birth; one witness claimed that Joanna had been frightened by mice while pregnant, an apparent explanation of the miscarriage. Because the child had died, the issue of Fox's responsibility for support was apparently moot.[65]

While the lack of clear records of vital statistics for the above cases made it uncertain if women under twenty-one received the same treatment as older women, a case in 1720 made it clear that the courts held both minor men and women to an adult standard of behavior. Town officials charged nineteen-year-old Marcy Walker of Norwich with fornication and having a bastard child. She in turn accused twenty-year-old Zebediah Gates of Preston of fathering the child. Testifying in her own defense, Marcy claimed she had allowed Gates "to have to do with her" because he had said he would marry her. The court fined both fifty shillings and ordered Gates to pay child support of two pounds six shillings per quarter until the child reached the age of four. At no time during the proceedings did the court summon either minor's parent to answer the charges against the two underage defendants.[66]

In 1732 a minor female faced the charge of having had a bastard child, yet she received no legal assistance for her defense. At the time Ann Darkis of Groton was an apprentice bound for a number of years to Robert Stoddard, also of Groton. The New London County Court found the girl guilty and fined her fifty shillings. Though Stoddard, as her master, was legally responsible for the girl, he did not represent her during the trial. Nevertheless, when Ann said she could not pay her fine, Stoddard paid the amount and asked the court to bind her to work for him an additional two months beyond her original term as compensation for his expense. The court accepted his suggestion. In a parallel civil lawsuit, Ann brought charges against Thomas Murrer of Groton, charging him as the father of her bastard child. Though the New London County Court had not charged Murrer with fornication, it jailed him for his refusal to provide a surety after his denial of the charge of fathering the child. In spite of the fact that Stoddard had not provided any formal protection for Ann in her criminal case, in the civil case, he stood as her surety. He may have helped her pursue the alleged father of the child to avoid being saddled with the support of a child born to his apprentice.[67]

Additional cases in the 1730s revealed that neither men nor women under the age of twenty-one who committed fornication received special treatment or protection of their rights as minors by Connecticut's courts. Aptly named Freelove Frink of Stonington was twenty when she paid the fine for her conviction for fornication and named Joseph Avery as the father of her child in 1739. Though John Holmes was her surety, the court record had no evidence that Holmes or any other adult had formal notice of the proceedings against Freelove or assisted her in her defense. In the same year in the case of *Rex v. Gatherit Greenman,* at a justice court the nineteen-year-old Gatherit confessed herself guilty of the crime of fornication and accused Johnwell Frink of being the father of her child. Her father, Silas Greenman, stood as her surety for payment of the fine and then forfeited his bond because she failed to appear at the New London County Court to answer the charges against her, but the justice of the peace had not formally notified the father of the case against his underage daughter.[68]

Apparently, not until the 1740s did the Connecticut courts begin to provide any sort of legal assistance or protection for minors who committed fornication, but even then the assistance was not uniform. In 1749 the selectmen of New London charged Mary Manwaring, "one of the poor of the town," who was already under the care of the selectmen with fornication and having a bastard child. The selectmen also charged Benjamin Chappel of New London as the father of the child. Though Mary was thirty-six years old, Benjamin was underage, the apprentice of George Sheffield and the son of George Chappell of New London. To complicate the case, the court deemed Mary incapable of giving an oath in the case because she was *non compos mentis.* In her place, the selectmen testified that she had identified young George as the father of her bastard while she was in labor. The arrest warrant for Benjamin ordered notification of his guardian, George Sheffield, to be present at the hearing "if he sees cause," but it did not require notification to the boy's father Though the evidence against Mary's veracity was damning, including testimony from Rachel Tinker who said Mary was so weak-minded that, "I could persuade her to swear her last child upon any man in town," perhaps it was because of the assistance of an adult that Benjamin proved himself innocent of being the father. The court awarded him costs of fifteen pounds, to be recovered from the town selectmen. It certainly would have been in Sheffield's interest to represent the youth since the boy would have had to pay child support had he been found guilty. As in previous cases, Sheffield might have paid the fine and costs in the face of a guilty verdict and added time to the youth's indenture.[69]

The inconsistency of the colonial legal system was apparent in a case the next year when nineteen-year-old Ziporah Reed of Norwich brought suit against Jesse Spaulding of Norwich, charging he had fathered her child born March 11th, 1750. Jesse was the apprentice of Steven Johnson of Norwich, but the court did not notify Johnson of the case nor had it notified Ziporah's father, Aaron Reed, to defend her against the original charges of fornication. At the New London County Court trial on the bastardy and support charges, Jesse failed to appear and defaulted. Despite the youth's absence the judge heard testimony from Susanna Lawrence, the midwife at the birth of Ziporah's son, that the girl had named Jesse as the father while she was in labor. Thankful Reed and Elizabeth Mordock corroborated Lawrence's testimony. The judge found the boy guilty of fathering the bastard and ordered that he pay eighteen shillings a week to Ziporah, dating from the birth of the child. Judging by the execution issued against Jesse in February of 1752, he failed to make those payments as ordered, yet there was no record that either the Court or Ziporah pursued the boy's parents or his master for the support payments.[70]

A variation in the legal procedure was apparent in a 1751 civil suit for maintenance of a bastard child. Lyme resident Margarett Burnett, Jr. brought a case against twenty-one-year-old Nathan Latimore of Lyme charging he had gotten her pregnant. The difference in procedure was that she sued by her father, James Burnett of Lyme, rather than bringing the lawsuit in her own name. Though she obtained the protection of an adult to assist in the case, the court did not take notice of the fact that Nathan himself had been a minor at the time of the birth of the illegitimate child on April 19th, 1750. The New London County Court found Nathan to be the reputed father and ordered that he pay support of two shillings six sixpence weekly. Acting on his own behalf, the youth appealed the decision, but in

1752 the court again found in favor of Margarett. By the time of his appeal, Nathan was now over twenty-one, but he did not raise the issue of his minority as a bar to the original action.[71]

Assistance by a parent was eventually critical to the success of Jerusha Powers' prosecution of an action against William Angell, Jr. of New London in which she charged him with fathering her bastard child. Jerusha, a New London resident who was only nineteen, initially brought suit against the twenty-year-old William in 1762. The court identified neither party to the lawsuit as a minor and found for the defendant, charging court costs to Jerusha. A year later, Jerusha again sued William, this time "by her father and natural guardian," Samuel Powers. However, the case had indeed gotten more complicated, perhaps requiring Jerusha to seek her father's help. Jerusha claimed that William had originally promised to marry her and later paid her three notes of hand to induce her to withdraw the lawsuit against him for fathering her bastard. Apparently at that point he again said he would marry her. The line between civil and criminal action gradually emerged In the 1763 renewal of the lawsuit William pleaded that he had paid Jerusha thirty pounds to release him from any obligation for the child. In response Jerusha said that at the time she made the bargain with William she was under twenty-one and "by law could not make any agreements as aforesaid and the said agreement was made entirely without the knowledge, privity, or consent of said guardian." Furthermore after William had given Jerusha the notes, he changed his mind and absolutely refused to marry her. In court Jerusha's father, Samuel Powers, "disclaimed and utterly refused to consent" to the agreement and returned the notes to William. By the time of the second suit, William was legally an adult, but he did not offer in his own defense that he also had been legally incapable of entering into any contract with Jerusha when he was underage. In the second round the court found William to be the father of Jerusha's child and ordered child support of two shillings nine pence per week.[72]

RAPE

Of the crimes against public order, rape was amongst the last for which the Connecticut courts accepted arguments concerning the age of the accused to excuse the act or mitigate the punishment. In the earliest of Connecticut's laws, though age was a mitigating factor in the crime of sodomy, perhaps, as claimed by George Haskins, because of a belief that boys under fifteen were not capable of the crime, the legal system accepted no such differentiation for rape. In its earliest form the law concerning rape assigned the death penalty to "any man" who with force and without consent ravished any maid or any woman who was engaged to be married. By 1702 the law defined ravishment as the act of carnal copulation with any maid or woman, thus providing punishment for those who raped married women or widows, but the revised statute added the proviso that the complaint and ensuing prosecution must occur immediately. Again the law did not excuse those who were under age twenty-one or even fifteen from responsibility for the act. In 1795 rape itself was still a capital crime, but the state legislature introduced a separate punishment for the crime of attempted rape: life in prison or any shorter term set by the Superior Court. Once again, the law made no distinction based on the age of those convicted of rape or attempted rape.[73]

Although the law thus made minors equally culpable for the crime of rape and despite numerous fornication prosecutions of both male and female minors, few cases in either the seventeenth or eighteenth centuries had brought minors into court to answer charges of rape. Even in the early nineteenth century the crime was rare. Lists of prisoners at Newgate Prison in 1810 and 1811 reveal few convicts serving time for attempted rape; only one was underage, Deming Latimer of Lyme, a white boy of just fourteen when he began his seven-year term in prison. Nevertheless, perhaps consideration of his age was evident in this sentence; the sentences of the four adults convicted of attempted rape were for life. By the time of an 1812 prisoner list from Newgate, Deming had apparently gained an early release or had died in prison because he was no longer listed as a prisoner. Furthermore, not a single one of the minors then in the prison was serving time for either rape or attempted rape.[74]

Not until later in the nineteenth century did a number of minors face charges of rape or attempted rape, and many of those defendants tried to claim youth, lack of understanding, or even physical incapacity as a defense against rape charges. In 1825 in an unusual plea for clemency, Julius Skiff of Kent, the father of a four-year-old victim of attempted rape, sought an early release from prison for his daughter's assailant. Skiff wrote that in 1824 the state had convicted Joseph Mawwee, an Indian boy who was then about fifteen years old, of attempting to rape Skiff's daughter Delia. The sentence for the attempted rape was life in prison at Newgate. Skiff may have developed doubts about the boy's guilt because in his petition to the state for immediate release of the youth, he cited the fact that prior to the crime the boy had always behaved himself well, with a "propriety proper for his age," considering that he was poorly educated. He went further, asserting that since being imprisoned in Newgate Prison, the boy had been a model prisoner, behaving with greater propriety and morality than the typical prisoner. Skiff declared himself satisfied that the boy had been confined long enough and asked the General Assembly to release young Joseph. Staff from the prison presented a concurring petition, citing the boy's youth and good behavior. In response, the Assembly voted to release Joseph immediately.[75]

Age at the time of the crime was apparently a factor in clemency in another rape case. In 1828, a young man who was serving a life sentence after his conviction at age sixteen for an attempted rape sought release from his life sentence. Now age twenty-seven after eleven years at Newgate, Philip Vincent petitioned the General Assembly for freedom. He claimed that he was a native of Spain and still had great difficulty understanding even the simplest directions in English. Though his petition did not specifically mention that his age at the time of conviction should be taken into account, his repeated mention of that age made the same point. The Assembly granted Philip's petition on the condition that he would leave Connecticut within one month of his release from prison.[76]

Obtaining early release from a life sentence for attempted rape proved more difficult for Long Island native James Mitchell, also known by the name of Shadrach Burr, perhaps because he was part Indian and part mulatto. In 1817, the New Haven Superior Court convicted Shadrach, then just sixteen, of two counts of attempted rape and sentenced him to life at Newgate Prison. In 1828 in his first petition for clemency or a reduction in his sentence, the young man, now legally an adult, pleaded that his sentence was unusually long and that his youth at the time of the crime ought to have been a mitigating factor. The Assembly rejected the plea without comment. A year later, Shadrach tried again. He repeated that he had been only sixteen at the time of the crime and added that he had also been intoxicated. He asserted that he had been orderly and well behaved while in prison and asked if twelve years were not sufficient for reformation. He added that since his incarceration the state had reduced the criminal penalty for attempted rape to as few as three years. This time the General Assembly committee when reconsidering the petition for clemency approved the request for early release and recommended that, "considering the age of the prisoner at the time of committing the crime and the circumstances under which the same was perpetrated," the Assembly should release the petitioner. The Assembly as a whole concurred and voted to release Shadrach in June of 1829.[77]

Just one year later the General Assembly received a petition for clemency from seventeen-year-old Thomas Wesley of Lyme, who in 1830 was in the State Prison facing a death sentence for the rape of a young girl. This plea was notably different from the petition of Shadrach Mitchell since Thomas was still under the age of twenty-one when he appealed for clemency. The request for mercy originated from the boy's two court-appointed guardians, Josiah Isham and C. J. McGurdy. The two men argued that although the young girl had given testimony based on her "honest impression," their client had not succeeded in completing the offense of rape. In case their argument for a reduction of sentence based on the lesser crime failed, they also played up the boy's youth and neglected upbringing. They averred that Thomas has not been brought up in Connecticut and therefore had not had "the benefit of its moral and religious institutions." The boy had had no one to direct or protect him, his guardians claimed, and he had no knowledge of his duty to man or God. In fact, they said, at seventeen he had less knowledge of right and wrong than any ten or twelve-year-old child. Because of this deficient upbringing, Isham and McGurdy claimed that the crime was not one of malice but was rather the result of the youth's immaturity, his ignorance, and the "sudden violence of his passions." Because the General Assembly did not record its reasons for accepting the plea for clemency and commuting the death sentence to one of life imprisonment, it was not clear which aspect of the plea by the court-appointed guardians swayed their judgment.[78]

The issue of a child's sexual capability and the strength and age of the supposed victim were key factors in a citizens' petition for the early release of sixteen-year-old George Hamlin of New Hartford, serving a three-year prison term for attempted rape. The petitioners, also from New Hartford, believed the jury had erred in its original conviction of George who had been only fourteen at the time of the alleged crime. The victim, whom the petitioners identified only as a "black wench" working for a New Hartford family, accused George of an actual rape but had not reported the crime until six weeks after it took place. She was the only witness against the boy, and the indignant petitioners claimed that she was stronger and more muscular than the teenager and could easily have repelled any attack by the boy. Though the specific issue of whether or not George had passed puberty was not raised in the petition, the reference to his being only fourteen certainly alluded to that factor. Based on the facts they presented in the petition, the boy's supporters said that the guilty verdict at the Superior Court had been a surprise to all, including the judge. Without comment, the General Assembly voted to release the boy immediately.[79]

The case of Joel Doolittle of Wolcott may have influenced the passage of a new law assigning a lesser penalty for the rape of a child under ten, perhaps because the court reconsidered his original life sentence for rape. In 1829 the state charged thirteen-year-old Joel with having carnal knowledge of Finette Churchill, the one-year ten-month-old daughter of Lewis Churchill of Wolcott. The boy appeared originally before Justice of the

Peace Fitch A. Higgins in 1828; the initial writ neither identified him as a minor nor did it note the appointment of a guardian. Higgins took the boy's plea of not guilty but found probable cause to hold Joel and jailed him pending the Superior Court trial because the youth could not provide a surety. After the youth had spent two months in jail, the Superior Court at New Haven indicted Joel for the rape and appointed Charles Chapman, Esq. as his guardian. Because of Finette's age, it is clear that she could not have testified against Joel, but the file did not contain transcripts of any of the evidence against the boy. Chapman's failure to raise the question of the boy's sexual maturity was rather surprising. Furthermore the guardian did not challenge the boy's lack of representation at the justice court, nor did he seek an abatement of the conviction when the court convicted Joel and sentenced him to life in prison. The prison warden's report listed Joel as a convict for life for the crime of "abusing a female child" rather than for rape. In 1833 Joel petitioned in his own name, seeking a reduction in his sentence. The youth claimed he had been but an "unlearned and ignorant boy . . . and had never been instructed in the principles of chastity." He also claimed that he had been intoxicated at the time of the crime, though he did admit his guilt. The General Assembly rejected the petition without comment. Surprisingly, just two years later, while Joel was still under age, one hundred Wolcott and Waterbury residents presented a petition for clemency to the Connecticut General Assembly. Their first line of attack was that they now had evidence that Joel had not committed the crime, a surprising claim considering Joel's earlier admission of guilt. In case that claim did not pass muster with the Assembly, the petition also claimed that Joel had been an "ignorant boy" at the time of the crime, having been an orphan since the age of ten with no one to look out for him or guide him. The petitioners said that Joel had been unable to write or even read when arrested but had since learned to do both while in prison and had been well behaved. Astonishingly, the first two signatures on the petition were of Lewis and Sarah Churchill, the parents of Joel's alleged victim. This time the General Assembly accepted the plea for mercy and released Joel, but since it ordered his release without comment, the members' specific reason for clemency was not apparent.[80]

The reliability of girls who testified against their assailants was at issue in the aftermath of the conviction of Daniel Garfy of Hartford for the 1845 attempted rape of Bridget Conway of Hartford. Though the Hartford Superior Court found Daniel and two other boys guilty as charged, within a year Garfy petitioned the Assembly for release from his three-year sentence at the State Prison. He presented a deposition from

Lydia Ripley who testified that Bridget had "the reputation of a very bad girl" and that Bridget had accused the three boys of the attack because her uncle had threatened her. The Assembly voted to release Daniel in May of 1846 but made no reference to the other two youths serving time for the same assault.[81]

The issue of a minor's sexual capabilities was the heart of an 1848 appeal by Cyrus Osborn. Convicted of rape at the age of 14 in 1841, Cyrus in 1848 sought release from his life sentence. Despite the fact that the legal system was not always consistent in providing mandated legal protections for minors who were African Americans, Cyrus was a black boy for whom the Litchfield County Superior Court had provided W. S. Nolalion, Esq. as guardian *ad litem* to assist him with his defense at his trial for rape. The guardian apparently limited his advice to presenting a plea of not guilty. Not surprisingly, the jury convicted the boy and sentenced him to life in prison. Cyrus' petition for clemency asserted that the alleged victim was a full-grown woman and that "the circumstances of the case make it doubtful a crime was actually committed." Ironically, in its report on Cyrus' request for release from prison the General Assembly committee concluded that mercy was necessary, not because of the prisoner's youth or inexperience at the time of the crime but because "the prisoner is a colored man, very ignorant and stubborn, and there is no good reason for his discharge except that which arises from his having been improperly convicted." Without explaining the facts that had led them to that conclusion, the Assembly voted to release Cyrus.[82]

The differences between sentences for minors and adults convicted of rape or attempted rape were a clear indication that adults did make allowances for children who broke the law. In the 1840s and 1850s, most minors' petitions for clemency or reduction of sentences for rape received a favorable response; the typical adult male who sought mercy for the crime of rape was not so fortunate. Only rarely did the General Assembly find exonerating circumstances for adult rapists. In one of the rare instances of a minor who failed to gain a reduction in his sentence for sexual assault, in 1851 residents of Enfield presented a plea for the release of Theodore Rhoda, serving a sentence for an attempted rape. The petitioners said that the boy had been but fifteen when accused of the crime and was known to them all as an honest, quiet, and peaceable youth. Perhaps because Theodore himself did not plead for mercy or perhaps because he was not sufficiently penitent for his crime, the Assembly did not approve releasing the boy but instead gave the citizens permission to withdraw the petition without rejecting it outright.[83]

ADULTERY AND BIGAMY

Two unique cases involving charges of adultery and bigamy reveal community concern over the legal capacity of minors charged in sexual activity. In 1832 Deming C. Darling, who identified himself as a "colored boy," petitioned the Connecticut General Assembly for clemency on his conviction for adultery in 1829, when he had been just seventeen. He claimed that he had been brought up in the household of Samuel Wheeler of Monroe and had "gained the esteem of his master as an honest and obedient boy." Deming said that part of his daily chores had required him to go to an old house owned by Wheeler, where he stored potatoes to feed the cattle. Every day he came into contact with a woman who lived in the house who was "of intemperate and dissolute habit" and who enticed the youth with her nakedness. Deming claimed the woman was a miserable, abandoned, dissolute woman while he had been but a boy, knowing little of the world. Apparently recognizing the danger the woman posed for the youth, Wheeler had tried to evict the woman, but before he succeeded, she had "committed the act" with the hapless Deming. Since she was a married woman, the state had charged and convicted the unwitting boy of adultery, sentencing him to the state prison. Upon receipt of Deming's petition, the General Assembly voted to free the youth from his sentence.[84]

An 1839 petition for clemency on the charges of bigamy revealed some confusion about the age of consent for marriage. Rufus Fuller, serving his sentence for bigamy in the Hartford County jail, claimed that he had been between the ages of thirteen and sixteen when, in 1836, he had married Julia McKeith in Uxbridge, Massachusetts. Soon after that marriage, Julia had left Rufus and married another man. Rufus claimed that in his youth and inexperience he believed his marriage had not been binding on either party because he was, he thought, under age. In fact Connecticut law did recognize that the age of consent for children to a marriage was fourteen for the boy and just twelve for a girl, but since a marriage was a contract, under state law no child under twenty-one could contract a marriage without parental consent.[85] This conflict may have contributed to Rufus' confusion about the legality of his marriage, though the case did not address the question of whether Rufus did obtain parental consent. As a result, believing he had never been legally married to Julia, in February 1838, he had married Charlotte Hoxie in Manchester, Connecticut. Upon an informer reporting the second marriage to state authorities, the state convicted him of bigamy. Without specific comment, a special committee of the Assembly granted Rufus's request for a pardon in 1839. Apparently though Connecticut law still allowed men as young as fourteen to enter into valid contracts of marriage, the Assembly accepted the boy's claim of ignorance.[86]

PROSTITUTION

The issue of prostitution raised the question of how to deal with underage female defendants who transgressed community moral standards. In the seventeenth and eighteenth centuries, prosecution of persons for lascivious carriage apparently had encompassed charges of visiting bawdy houses or having sex for money because the state had no specific statute against prostitution. By the nineteenth century, the charge began to appear on the court records, as did the accusation of running a bawdy house.[87]

In New London County in the 1820s a number of young women faced charges of prostitution. Since local justices of the peace heard the cases and often were not concerned with the age of any defendants facing charges before them, the ages of the accused were unavailable. Nevertheless, differences in the sentences meted out may have been an indication of differences in the ages of the women. In 1822, William P. Cleaveland, Jr., a New London justice of the peace, charged Lucinda Edwards (also known as Lucinda Davis), Catherine Noble (also known as Catherine Thompson), and Rue Dart as prostitutes. Cleaveland sent all three to the New London workhouse for thirty days. In July of 1828 Cleaveland ruled that Mary Mason was a prostitute and nightwalker, of lewd and dissolute character, but he sent her to the workhouse for only eight days. At the same session of his justice court, Cleaveland found Hannah Baker guilty of identical charges yet imposed a ten-day sentence. Just two months later he charged Catherine Beckwith of Waterford with being a common prostitute, saying that she was a lewd and dissolute person who frequented houses of bad fame. Yet he sentenced Catherine to only five days in the workhouse. Since the charges against the various women appeared to be the same, the lack of consistency in the punishments might have related to the age of the defendants.[88]

Yet in an 1848 case the age of defendants seemed irrelevant. The state's attorney charged three transient women with frequenting a house of ill fame for purposes of prostitution and brought them to trial in the New London County Court. Being less than twenty-one did not shield one of them from the full consequences of her actions. Elisebeth and Sarah Richards were young African-American women; Lucinda Fowler was also an African American, but she was only twenty years old. The files in the case asserted that the three lived in the house of prostitution owned by Frank Samson, an African American, but did not identify Lucinda as a minor. Nevertheless Lucinda obtained legal representation from attorney Watkins. Even with legal advice, the girl pleaded guilty, as did the two other women. The New London County Court sentenced both Lucinda and Elisebeth to three months in jail and a $25 fine, but assessed only a $15 fine against Sarah. At least in this case, even women under the age of majority bore full responsibility for their illegal sexual activity.[89]

BESTIALITY

Even though Connecticut's colonial law protected boys under the age of fifteen from prosecution for the crime of sodomy, neither the colony nor the state imposed such a limit on prosecutions for the crime of bestiality. In its earliest form, the law relied on biblical authority by citing Leviticus 20.15, 16. The prohibition mandated the death sentence: "If any man or woman shall lye with any beast or bruit creature, by carnal copulation, they shall surely be put to death, and the beast shall be slain and buried." Though the lack of records of vital statistics makes it difficult to determine the ages of many seventeenth-century defendants in bestiality cases, the differences in punishments imposed might be an indication that colonial courts stopped short of imposing the maximum penalty on minors. When the magistrates of Connecticut's Particular Court accused Aaron Starke of buggery with a heifer in 1640, he had admitted that he had twice committed the act but complained that the heifer was too narrow. Despite this confession, the Court sentenced Aaron to be kept locked up, put to hard labor, and fed a coarse diet. Failure to sentence Aaron to death was likely a reflection that Aaron was a minor. Similarly, in 1647 John Nuberry confessed to several attempts at bestiality yet received no punishment at all. Again, though Nuberry's age was not available, the clemency of the Court might have reflected that colonial society recognized differing culpability in minors.[90]

Although this case presented possible evidence of the mitigation of punishment for minors charged with bestiality, cases in the eighteenth century revealed that the law officially held minors to the adult standard of behavior. In the 1767 case of *Rex v. Amos Green* the colony charged Norwich resident Amos with assaulting and carnally knowing a dun cow belonging to John Kurtland. The judge identified Amos as a minor. Perhaps because this was a capital case, he assigned the youth legal counsel. From the record it appears that this was the same as naming a guardian to advise the youth. Unable to make a decision on the evidence, the New London County Court transferred the case to the Superior Court, which also failed to make a disposition of the case. Being unwilling to come to a verdict might have been a reflection of the opinions of jurors who did not want to sentence the boy to death.[91]

In 1770, a slander case provided evidence that minors still faced the death penalty for bestiality. Fifteen-year-old Pardon Clarke of Stonington, suing by his father and natural guardian, Benjamin Clarke, charged Stonington resident Asa Minor with trespass and slander. In the case files Pardon claimed that he had always been honest, true, and faithful and been "innocent of imputation of sodomy, buggery, and bestiality and all such shocking and detestable crimes." Yet Pardon said that Minor had defamed him intending to injure his reputation and "subjecting him to capital presentation for the heinous and detestable crime of buggery or bestiality" because he had said he had caught the boy in the act of buggering a mare. Pardon denied that he had ever done such an act. The County Court found Minor guilty of the slander and did not prosecute any charges against the boy. Nevertheless, the case made it obvious that children as young as fifteen did still face the death penalty for the crime.[92]

Into the nineteenth century, the state continued to impose the death penalty for the crime of bestiality. The relative harshness of the punishment may have reflected the continuing influence of religion on Connecticut lawmakers. In 1817, in another slander case, fourteen-year-old Jonas Satterly of Groton, a minor who brought suit by his next friend and natural guardian, Elisha Satterly, sued Lydia Sholes, also of Groton, for $1,000 because she had told people that "Jonas Satterly has done a dreadful thing; he has had to do with a cow in a criminal way." Lydia claimed she had seen the boy in the act with the cows belonging to Ebeneezer Morgan. Young Jonas claimed he had not committed the act and that Lydia's false claim had slandered him and made him subject to the death penalty. Furthermore, he added that her accusation had caused him to lose both his peace of mind and body. The New London County Court found Lydia and her husband Jonathan guilty of slandering the youth, awarding him $100 in damages and court costs. Though officials never charged the boy himself with bestiality, his complaint against the Sholes showed that the death penalty for the crime of bestiality still applied for youths.[93]

In an 1821 revision of the statutes of the state, the Connecticut General Assembly reduced the punishment for bestiality to life in prison but did not make an exception for those under age twenty-one. At the same time the Assembly had preserved the age-based protection for those under age fifteen charged with sodomy. That this led to questionable justice was clear in the 1824 bestiality conviction of thirteen-year-old David Jackson from Sharon. At the original trial the State's Attorney had objected to the admission of evidence concerning the boy's age and had obtained a conviction, resulting in a life-sentence for the child. The boy had made a motion for a new trial that the Litchfield County Court granted. Unfortunately, lacking legal advice and "being wholly destitute of funds," the boy had not been able to obtain a new trial. After serving seven years of his sentence, the twenty-year-old youth petitioned the Connecticut General Assembly for clemency. In his petition, filed without adult assistance, David claimed that at the time of the crime he had been a "mere child and had not yet attained to the years of puberty," being under fourteen years old. He asserted that the state's attorney had improperly denied the evidence concerning his age and incapacity to commit the crime. Without comment the Assembly ordered the boy freed in May of 1831 but required him to sign a note for the court costs. His plea concerning his youth and his sexual immaturity made an obvious impact on the legislators, yet there was no attempt to soften the impact of the law on other young offenders.[94]

What these prosecutions against children who disturbed public order or who transgressed against community standards of behavior revealed was that legislators continued to have a vision of what constituted an orderly society, decades after the disestablishment of religion in Connecticut. When parents could not control the behavior of their own children, the state continued to provide laws that reinforced, and at times, superseded parental authority. As has been noted, the 1854 opening of the State Reform School for Boys gave parents another big stick in the arsenal of parental discipline because parents could send their children to the school for a minimum of ninety days for "correction" even if the child had not broken any laws of the state itself. In 1854, in a speech to the General Assembly advocating an increase in state support for the school, Dr. Clark had compared the reform school favorably to private educational academies, saying he "would rather have a ten-year-old guarded, watched, and educated at the Reform School than at the most reputable Boarding Schools." He said in the future Connecticut citizens would look to the Reform School "as a place where they were turned from the road that leadeth closer to death, into a temple in which they were born again, into a new condition of existence, reformed and redeemed men." If families could not impart the moral and behavioral standards required by Connecticut's society, the state would do it for them.[95]

Chapter Four

Legal Standards, Community Justice: The Problem of Child Abuse

> A master may reasonably and moderately chastise his servant for negligence and misbehavior.
>
> If a servant or apprentice flees from the tyranny and cruelty of his master to the house of any inhabitant of the town, he shall be protected and sustained until an order is provided for his relief.
>
> —Zephaniah Swift *A System of the Laws of the State of Connecticut*, 1795

As the laws and court cases make clear, Connecticut law from its earliest days accepted the concept of differences inherent as a result of age that gradually resulted in differentiated treatment of children when they broke the law. Yet the criminal laws of the colony and the state did not initially provide a different quality of protection for children to protect them from physical or sexual abuse by those adults responsible for them. Surprisingly, especially in view of the sports of bearbaiting and bull baiting in seventeenth-century England, Connecticut's earliest laws were clear on the prohibition of the abuse of animals. The same legal code had no similar legal protection specifically for children. Unlike the law that protected animals against "tyranny or cruelty," Connecticut's laws permitted the "reasonable" physical correction of children by responsible adults. In fact, many early Puritan writers advocated the use of physical punishment to correct children, including John Robinson who wrote in 1628 that parents should beat a child's stubbornness out with the rod. Furthermore, the criminal laws themselves directed the use of physical punishments. Whippings under the criminal code itself were to be "severe and sharp" as an example that others might "hear and fear" and thus resist breaking the law themselves. Connecticut's Puritan heritage may have influenced the acceptance of physical punishment of children because of the belief that all humans were sinful. Therefore the issue of when society owed children protection from potential or actual abuse was a gradual outgrowth of changing attitudes toward children and religion.[1]

This change reflected a softening of the Puritan viewpoint of the innate sinfulness of human beings and the rise of the idea that adults owed certain responsibilities toward children in their care. Such an attitude appeared in print in 1690 in John Locke's *Second Treatise of Government* when he wrote that, "all parents were, by the law of nature, under an obligation to preserve, nourish, and protect the children they had begotten." Locke asserted: "the power, then, that parents have over their children, arises from that duty which is incumbent on them, to take care of their offspring, during the imperfect state of childhood." Locke was also opposed to most use of physical punishment, at least in the process of teaching children. Even religious authors began to alter their views on punishment. In 1706 Cotton Mather advocated the use of what modern parents would recognize as a "time out" and advised using physical punishment rarely. By the end of the century John Witherspoon told parents to establish their authority over their children at an early age, but not to be severe. In 1833 John S. C. Abbott advocated recognizing that children had differing dispositions and advised that parents should not punish their children "in anger."[2] Though Locke directed his focus on parental responsibility mainly at educating the child to become an independent adult and the other writers were discussing discipline within the home, the question of protection from excessive punishment and abuse would gradually enter the community consciousness of what duties parents, and in fact all adults, owed to children.

While Howard Cohen has claimed that the protection provided children in the colonial period was largely academic and did not actually provide protection from abuse, George Haskins went further in claiming that early colonial laws and courts in Massachusetts did not recognize any need to protect children within their families from social or economic harm. On the other side of the debate over early attitudes toward children, Michael Grossberg has asserted that as early as the seventeenth century courts did start to oversee the welfare of minors under the doctrine of *parens patriae.*[3] This allowed the courts or colonial authorities to interfere with parental control "when the morals or the safety of the children" were at risk. This was behind Connecticut's 1650 law that ordered selectmen "to have a vigilant eye" to see that parents educated, trained, and corrected their children, especially to instruct and catechize their offspring "in the grounds and principles of religion," reinforcing Connecticut's Puritan outlook. The statute also gave selectmen the right to take children from parents who failed to meet community standards "whereby children and servants became rude, stubborn, and unruly." That law also authorized town officials who removed children from their parents to "force them to submit unto government," implying that the authorities themselves could and would use violence against unruly youngsters. Yet nothing in those earliest laws concerning children directed authorities to protect children from physical harm.[4] Nevertheless, what emerges from an examination of the early Connecticut court records is evidence that not only did the laws themselves eventually provide some protection for abused children but also that Connecticut residents often had differing opinions on what constituted reasonable treatment of children.

The "stubborn child" laws of the colonial period ironically made it apparent that colonial society did not sanction serious abuse of minors that threatened their lives. Connecticut in one of its earliest laws followed the lead of Massachusetts in providing an "escape clause" for children who assaulted their parents, masters, or guardians. Both colonies under their stubborn-child laws mandated the death sentence for children who struck their parents, but each added a proviso implying a form of protection for children. If there were sufficient proof that the parents had neglected the education of the children or that they had imposed "extreme and cruel correction" as to put them in fear of their lives, the authorities would not hold children responsible for striking their parents in self-defense. The very existence of such an exception revealed that society had some concept of what constituted appropriate correction for children. While Joseph Hawes has asserted that the 1641 Massachusetts law was revolutionary in that it was the first to provide legal protection of any kind to children, he undercut that claim by saying he had found no cases in the colonial period in which a child successfully prosecuted an abuse claim against his or her parents. Connecticut's 1642 law that utilized identical language to the Massachusetts statute similarly appeared to provide protection for children. Nevertheless, it was not until 1702 that the General Assembly passed a specific law against "inhumane, barbarous, or cruel punishment," but applied the law to all punishments and persons, not just to those administered to minors. This new law may merely have been a codification of the common law prohibition against chastising unreasonably and not representative of a softening of attitudes toward punishment itself.[5]

Writing about the legal system in Connecticut from the viewpoint of the 1790s, Zephaniah Swift cited the inequities in a system that provided some protection against abuse for older children and servants but did not provide the same protection for those too young or too afraid to flee from an abusive master. Noting that Connecticut law directed that a "parent may give reasonable correction to his child" and a master could "reasonably and moderately correct and chastise a servant for negligence and misbehavior," Swift appeared to dislike the use of physical punishment. He was instead an advocate of a separate, long-standing Connecticut law that directed that if a servant or apprentice fled from the cruelty of his or her employer or master to the dwelling of an inhabitant in the same town, the authorities in the town would "protect and sustain" the child until the court investigated the charges of abuse. The negative side to this law directed that if the court did not confirm the child's complaint of cruelty, a different Connecticut statute mandated that any apprentice or servant who fled his or her master's service would have to serve triple the time away once returned to his or her master. Furthermore, this statute allowed constables to use force to return runaways to their employers. That could have deterred many youths from fleeing their abusers because many apprentices in Connecticut served indentures outside their native communities; they might not have believed strangers would uphold their complaints.[6]

Nevertheless, if the magistrate or judge found the master had corrected the child unreasonably, he could require the master to post a bond for good behavior. In the most severe cases of abusive punishment, the law provided for the release of the child from his or her indenture. Yet the law also provided that if a child died as the result of the physical punishment by a parent, guardian, or master the death was a case of misadventure rather than murder if the correction was moderate. Only if the court ruled that the punishment "exceeded the bounds of moderation" in the form, the amount, or the instrument of punishment could the adult face charges of either manslaughter or murder. Swift was obviously amongst those who opposed the most severe forms of physical correction of children when he wrote:

> Perhaps in the improvement of society, it will be discovered that the power of parents and masters ought further to be restrained and controlled, and that cruelty to children in those tender years when they are incapable of defense, shall be punished in such a manner as to secure for them mild and humane treatment in all cases.[7]

STANDARDS OF PARENTAL CARE

Inquests provide some evidence that Connecticut colonists in the early years of the eighteenth century had standards similar to Swift's: that parents had a responsibility to take care of their children. In 1717 a jury of inquest investigating the death of an Indian child ruled that the child had been burnt and bruised from the middle of its body downward resulting in death, but the jurymen did not assign blame to the parents for the death. In an apparent effort to include Native American standards of adequate parental care, the inquest report included four Indians on the eighteen-man jury, natives who signed the inquest report by their marks: Wabeyayohu, Honoss Will, George Pall, and Samson. A 1743 case of the drowning of a "Negro boy called Prince" resulted in the ruling of accidental death, because the jury had looked for evidence of abuse or injury and "could find no wounds or other causes of suspicion of his being murdered or injured by any person." In 1779, the deaths of three Killingworth children brought in a charge that their mother, Sarah Higgins, had cut their throats, "she being delirious and bereaved of her reason." A few years later in 1781 an inquest brought in a ruling of accidental death, despite what modern ideas would rank as clear evidence of neglect or abuse. A Native-American woman, Molly George, the wife of Isaac George, had gotten drunk and fallen asleep in an open field while carrying her child. When she awoke, the child had frozen to death. The jury declared this an accident because, "we do not find to be in malice, but entirely by her being in liquor." Similarly, the jury of inquest did not hold Mary Pothiage, whom the inquest report identified as an Indian, responsible for the death of her daughter, Maryannah, when the girl froze to death on the way to Stonington with her mother in 1786. Instead, it ruled that the two had gotten lost in an October storm and the girl was so poorly clothed that she was chilled by the storm and died.[8]

In the nineteenth century, standards of care in looking after the well-being of children appear to have become more rigorous, perhaps because of the increasing influence of John Locke's ideas and of books such as Rousseau's *Emile,* which detailed maternal responsibilities of care and nurturing. In addition, a softening of the harshness of Puritan theology had given rise to the view that children themselves were "too good for this world."[9] In 1815 Stonington officials discovered the body of a black child near the home of Oliver Dennison, Jr. The members of the jury of inquest ruled the boy had been willfully murdered, though there was no evidence of wounds or physical abuse. In 1834, in contrast to the George and Pothiage cases, the jury found that a "female child of color" whose body was found in Lebanon was the victim of parental neglect. Similarly, in 1841, the inquest ruling following the investigation of the death of a female Indian child was that she had died as a result of neglect by her mother and the cold. When Thomas Church, the son of James Church of Groton, died in 1854, the jury had to deal with a report of willful murder by poisoning. Instead, the men found the six-year-old had died because of "convulsions produced by exposure, want of food, medical assistance, and proper care."[10] The number of indictments that resulted from inquests into the untimely deaths of children revealed that by the nineteenth century the laws of the state held parents to a higher standard of care in looking after their children.

APPRENTICESHIP: AN INVITATION TO ABUSE?

Because Connecticut utilized the system of apprenticeship to provide occupational training for children, to remove children from neglectful parents while providing for their education and maintenance, and to keep orphans or poor children from being a burden on the town's taxpayers, the status relationship between master and apprentice was one that had the potential for the abuse of children. Three types of apprenticeship existed in Connecticut from the seventeenth century through the early nineteenth century: charity apprenticeships in which town selectmen took orphans or children from poor families and placed them with adults who would educate and sustain them, voluntary trade apprenticeships arranged by a child's parent in which the master was to teach the child a trade, and business apprenticeships that provided somewhat less on-the-job training. In charity apprenticeships, magistrates, justices of the peace, and even town selectmen would place a child with an adult until boys reached the age of twenty-one and girls reached eighteen. Those placements were as fully binding as if the children's parents had entered into the agreement on their behalf. Neither the colonial authorities nor the courts placed limits on the actual conditions of the indenture; the document could be as generous or as miserly as the master desired, especially in charity cases. Not until the nineteenth century brought a growing concern about both education and the well being of children, did state law direct specific conditions of the indenture. Those requirements included teaching the child to read and write and to master the first four rules of arithmetic. Most notable of the mandates was that as the Puritan heritage of the state was lessening, the law on involuntary apprenticeships ordered religious and moral education for the children, requiring that "due attention be paid to the preservation of their morals and that they be required regularly to attend public worship."[11]

A few examples of differing types of indentures of apprenticeship reveal both the potential for abuse of pauper children in the earlier period and the increasing oversight by the nineteenth century. In a voluntary indenture, with the consent of his parents in 1661, James Redfin of New London bound himself to New London tanner Hugh Roberts for a period of five years. Under the indenture Roberts was to pay the boy five pounds ten shillings per year, to provide "good diet, comfortable lodging and washing, and teach him the trade of tanning." In contrast, in the same year the involuntary indentures of John and Joseph Jennings revealed little concern for their personal wishes or their health and well being. The Particular Court ordered placement of the boys, orphaned after the colony executed their parents for murder. Though John was fourteen, above the statutory age to consent to the choice of a master, the Court did not allow either child the freedom to choose. Jeremiah Adams took John as an apprentice for seven years; the only requirement in the indenture was that he was to pay the youth seven pounds and provide two suits of clothes when the lad reached twenty-one. The master made no promise of specific training, education, or care. Richard Treat took on eleven-year-old Joseph, guaranteeing nothing but to pay the boy ten pounds at the end of his term and to clothe him well.[12] The community seemed to have little concern for the boys.

Eighteenth-century involuntary indentures revealed some improvement in the community's concern for the education of children but still paid little attention to their personal needs. In 1750 the indenture of Appleton, a four-year-old mulatto child, reflected the relative lack of concern for the child's care by the New London selectmen. Saying the child's mother was unable to provide for him, the authorities bound the boy to John Hewitson for sixteen years and ten months, directing that Hewitson teach the child to learn husbandry, to read English well, to write, and to know the "ordinary rules of arithmetic." Notably, the articles of indenture said little about the maintenance or living conditions required for the child, merely noting that the master was to feed and clothe the child as "suitable for an apprentice." Other eighteenth-century indentures binding black and Native-American children revealed an apparently ongoing lack of concern for the living conditions for children of color. New London selectmen bound Betty, a five-year-old black girl, and Mary Fogg, a nine-year-old mulatto girl, until they reached the age of eighteen, requiring of their respective masters only that they teach the girls housewifery.[13]

Articles of indenture in the nineteenth century reflected somewhat more concern for the children, but voluntary placements continued to provide a higher quality of care. In 1820 Lodowick Frederick Adams, an eighteen-year-old German boy recently arrived in Waterford, put himself into the service of William Champion of Waterford for two years to learn farming. In addition to mandating on-the-job training, the articles of indenture directed that Champion would take the boy "into his family and treat him kindly and provide suitable victuals, board, washing, medicine, and clothing." Contrasting to that was the agreement the Lyme selectmen entered into with John Gillitte of Lyme in 1824. The selectmen bound six-year-old William Moore, "a poor boy of Lyme," to serve Gillitte for fourteen years and five days. The master agreed to teach the child the art of farming and to provide food, clothing, lodging, and washing, with "physic when necessary." Though a child of six would more certainly need kindly treatment, the indenture did not require it from Gillitte. In an indenture that openly reflected the 1821 revision of the law that mandated moral education for apprentices, Philip A. Capen of East Haddam as guardian to eight-year-old William Wadsworth Scovil apprenticed the boy to learn the trade of farming from fellow East Haddam resident Robert W. Chapman. Chapman undertook to teach the boy farming in the best manner, to have the child learn to read, write, and cipher to the rule of four, and "to educate him in the principles of virtue and religion and to train him in habits of faithfulness, industry, and economy" as well as provide for his bodily needs. Clearly, having a caring adult to look out for a child's interests could result in more protection under the terms of a contract of indenture.[14]

The factor that had the greatest potential for the possibility of abuse of apprentices was that in the practice of apprenticing poor children, many placements were outside the child's native town. As noted before, being in a strange town among strangers often undercut the colonial and state laws that allowed an abused apprentice to flee to a neighbor's home for protection. A child who did not know his or her neighbors might have been less willing to flee from abuse. Despite this apparent lack of concern for poor apprentices, colonial law did provide a measure of protection of the potential well-being of children, permitting boys over fourteen and girls over twelve to agree to the choice of master, perhaps on the theory that if the child accepted his or her placement freely, there would be less cause for complaint or disobedience. However, if the child refused to make a selection, authorities or parents could still make a binding contract of indenture in the child's name. Once parents or colonial authorities had signed the contract, the master had complete control over the child unless the authorities sustained an apprentice's complaint of failure to fulfill the terms of the contract or an allegation of physical abuse. Nevertheless, as a hedge against the potential abuse of an apprentice, by the late eighteenth century the law specifically provided if a child aged fifteen or older fled the cruelty of a master to the safety of a neighbor, an assistant or a justice of the peace had the authority protect the child from further abuse as long he notified the master. This created a problem for younger children who faced abuse; they had no such recourse. As Zephaniah Swift complained, when a child was "too young or too afraid to flee a cruel master," the legal system provided no remedy. The only recourse was for the child's parent or guardian to sue the master "under the common law for chastising unreasonably and immoderately." Such a provision would be of little use to a poor orphaned child apprenticed outside his or her home town; such a child would have no one looking out for his or her interests.[15]

By the nineteenth century, Connecticut's legislators apparently realized that more positive oversight was necessary and amended the laws on apprentices, providing a modicum of protection for all apprentices, poor or not. The new law said it was the "right and duty of parents or selectmen to inquire into the treatment of apprentices by their masters; and if they find that the masters are guilty of any personal cruelty or abuse," the parents or selectmen were to complain to the justice of the peace. In such a case, the justice was first to try to reconcile the child and master, but if he found the master guilty of cruelty or abuse, he could "discharge the apprentice, cancel the indenture, and award costs against the master." The justice could also cancel the indenture if he found the master had failed to teach the child a trade or had failed to provide suitable maintenance for the child. This new view of the duties owed to children showed up in the prosecutions of charges of abuse in the nineteenth century courts, but rarely did the selectmen who had placed poor children into involuntary apprenticeships initiate lawsuits charging abuse of those poor apprentices.[16]

Under Connecticut's system of apprenticeship, the question of what constituted excessive punishment by masters changed between the seventeenth and nineteenth centuries. The fact that minors could bring suit against adults who employed them or who were responsible for their support and maintenance was evident in several cases from the 1600s. In 1643 Thomas Wainwright sued his master, Mr. Henry Smith, charging battery and trespass. This meant Smith had physically struck the child. Though the jury found the master not guilty of the accusation, the minor bringing the action clearly believed his employer had exceeded the bounds of reasonableness in his treatment. In 1653 Connecticut's Particular Court imposed a severe whipping on Edward Messenger for his "unmercifulness" towards his servants and for "lying to extenuate his fault." Six years later, the Particular Court freed Gervis Benbree from his apprenticeship to Mr. Witchfield and ordered the master to provide the "covenant clothes" promised in the indenture. This may have reflected the provision in Connecticut law that allowed the court to free an apprentice from his indenture if the courts found the employer guilty of abuse.[17]

By 1690, it was clear that Connecticut courts did have a standard of acceptable behavior toward minor apprentices, but the case of Hugh Peck revealed that masters often rejected that standard. Before a special session of the probate court, Hugh complained that his master, Mr. Samuel Wolcott, had treated him cruelly, "beating and abusing him most unreasonably sundry times." The court found that Wolcott had indeed acted in a cruel manner when he stripped the boy, tied him to a stadle (the lower part of a stack of hay), and beat him with "three great sticks until he had bruised and wounded him in a grievous manner." Had Wolcott accepted the court's censure, he might have merely had to pay a bond to ensure his future good behavior. Instead, he challenged the court's ruling, asserting the law allowed him to beat his servant. When the magistrate examined Wolcott further, Wolcott stated that he would beat the boy more severely in the future. In response to this attitude that clearly exceeded the community standard, the court fined Wolcott three pounds for his cruelty to the child. Furthermore, the magistrate ordered that the master could not regain custody of the boy but that the child would remain under the protection of the Wethersfield constable until Wolcott procured another master for Hugh, subject to the approval of two Assistants of the colony. In addition, nothing in the court record indicated that Wolcott received compensation for the loss of the boy's services.[18]

The 1703 case prosecuting a vicious assault against fifteen-year-old Martha Tomson of Lyme revealed that while both the colony and Connecticut residents had standards for the treatment of children by their masters, the abused children had to take active steps to gain protection. Poor Martha had faced severe physical abuse for over a year before she finally fled to the protection of a neighbor's house in Lyme. The case first came to light when Sarah Waterus of Lyme, of lawful age, testified to the New London County Court that a week before, in July of 1703, Martha Tomson had arrived at the house of Isaac Waterus "in a lamentable condition crying out and all bloody about the face and head." The girl claimed her aunt Tilison had beaten her, jumped on her stomach, and almost killed her. The girl was afraid to return to her uncle's house until he came home because her aunt had said she would "be the death of her by day or by night." Sarah Waterus then went to the Tilison house to discover what had happened. She asked Goody Tilison why she had beaten the girl. At first the woman denied having beaten Martha and refused to answer Waterus' questions. In her testimony Waterus said Tilison was "in drink" but that the woman denied she had been drinking. After the woman told Waterus that the affair was none of her business, Waterus then said she would inform the authority of what had happened. At that point, Tilison became belligerent and said no authority could come near her or the girl. She repeated that she would not account for her treatment of the child "for the girl had been a plague to her and if she had her near she would break her bones. She would bring her down to her feet and would make the girl sorry she was ever born and she would rue the day she came to your house to complain." Though Waterus deposed that Tilison "had lost her reason with drinking," she held the woman responsible for her actions and notified the Lyme justice of the peace, William Ely.[19]

On July 23, 1703 Martha Tomson herself brought charges of assault against Mary Tilison, wife of Jonathan Tilison, for beating her and threatening her life. John Borden acted on her behalf in the filing of the charges. In her complaint, Martha identified herself as a servant to Jonathan Tilison rather than as his niece. Ely, the justice of the peace, ruled that such charges were not suable in his court but that the county court did have jurisdiction. After hearing the testimony of a number of Lyme citizens, he issued a ruling that Martha was to remain at the home of John Borden of Lyme until the New London County Court heard the case, thus temporarily releasing her from her contract of indenture. Borden paid 20 shillings to maintain the legal action to the next level, and Jonathan Tilison paid 10 shillings recognizance to defend his wife against the lawsuit.[20]

The testimony Ely relied on for his decision to remove Martha from the home of her uncle and master provided ample evidence of Mary Tilison's mistreatment of the fifteen-year-old girl. Steven Scofel said that he had been at Tilison's house earlier in the spring and had heard Tilison's wife say she would be the death of that Tomson and that she would break her bones and stomp her to pieces. Thomas Champion seconded Scofel's evidence, adding that he heard Tilison say she would be the death of the girl. Isaac Tubs and Jabez Watrus testified to the justice of the peace that in March or April of 1703 they had heard Mary Tilison, the wife of Jonathan, say she would beat Martha Tomson into powder if she was not better. Liddy Watrus said she went to Tilison's house after seeing Martha's condition after the July assault to ask her why she had beaten the girl. At first Tilison denied hitting Martha; then she claimed the child had done it. Watrus accused Tilison of drinking, but the woman (who had staggered as she came to the door) said she had had nothing to drink in a week. Nevertheless, Liddy Watrus deposed that Tilison was "worse for drink, her face and actions much altered." John Borden and Joseph Robinos both declared under oath that they feared Tilison would cripple Martha if the girl had to continue to live with her, especially if the older woman was "in drink or passion." Elizabeth Greves told the justice of the peace that in January of 1703 she saw Mary Tilison beat Martha Tomson unmercifully and cut her arm with a scythe. As the witnesses made abundantly evident, Mary Tilison had regularly maltreated the girl under her care; yet until the child fled for help to the house of a neighbor, no one had reported the abuse to any person in authority.[21]

When the New London County Court heard the case of Martha Tomson against Mary Tilison, others from Lyme testified that the girl had faced severe abuse for more than a year, but that none of the witnesses to the abuse had tried to intervene to help her. The actual assault that had driven the teen to flee her home was the culmination of escalating abuse. Isaac Tubs said that in October of 1702, he was at Tilison's house when he saw Mary Tilison seize Martha by the hair and fling her down on the floor and beat her several times. In the winter he saw the woman grab Martha by the hair again and strike her head against the corner of the chimney. Jabez Watrus saw Mary Tilison beat Martha against the doorjamb in 1702 and threaten to break her bones. Samuel Watrus testified that he too saw Mary Tilison beat the girl against the chimney stones, but that one of her sons (the oldest was only ten at the time) had pulled her off the girl and told her to go to bed. Thomas Wate, also of Lyme, swore that he had been at Tilison's house in August of 1702 and had seen Mary Tilison beat Martha down to the floor behind a door and say that she would be the death of her. Other than the intervention of one of her young cousins, not a single person took any action to protect Martha from the abuse by her aunt.[22]

What provided protection for the beleaguered Martha was that the final assault drove her to seek help from a neighbor, thus bringing into play Connecticut's law that provided protection for a servant who fled the cruelty of his or her master. Martha's own testimony revealed that on the day of the assault her aunt had ordered her to do some chores and had hit her with a stick when she wasn't quick enough. Martha had then hidden "until her passion might be over." When Martha reappeared, the older woman took a leather whip and chased the girl outside, caught her, and flung her to the ground. She then straddled the child, hit her in the face, grabbed her by the hair, and smashed her face into the ground. In addition she kicked the girl as she lay on the ground. Martha testified that she was in fear of her life and was afraid that if she returned to her uncle's house, her aunt would kill her. As a result of the testimony, the Court refused to return the girl to service with her uncle, holding him responsible for the acts of his wife. Surprisingly, the court did not award monetary damages to Martha. The disposition of the case made it obvious that the legal system could protect children from abuse, but only if they fulfilled the legal requirement of fleeing for protection.[23]

In a 1716 case brought by New London apprentice Gaston Clap, Jr. against his master and employer Jonathan Rogers, the charges included both physical abuse and Rogers' failure to fulfill the terms of the indenture. Gaston first alleged that in the two years he had served of his apprenticeship, Rogers had often beaten him "without cause and without mercy" so that he had fled the cruelty of his master, going to the house of Jeremiah Wilson of New London. Furthermore, Gaston alleged that Rogers had never properly clothed or fed him, with the result that he had to pay for his own clothing and food. In addition, the boy said Rogers had not provided suitable lodging but had made him sleep on the floor by the fire with an Indian and a Negro. The final accusation was that Rogers had failed to teach him either to read, as required in the articles of indenture, or to practice his trade. Rogers denied all the accusations and tried to justify his beating of the boy, but others testified that Gaston could not read and that Rogers had not provided suitable clothing for the boy while he was in service. The New London County Court ordered the release of Gaston from his indenture, ruling that the boy return to the custody of Simon Roy of Block Island, the executor of his father's estate. What was not clear from the disposition of the case was which charge bore the most weight with the jury: the physical abuse or Rogers' failure to live up to his agreement with the youth.[24]

That the system designed to protect children from the abuse of their masters did not always work immediately was apparent in the case of Benjamin Bump of Preston. While ultimately the New London County Court released Benjamin from his obligation to his master, John Rudd of Preston, testimony from close neighbors revealed a known pattern of abuse. In November of 1720, Benjamin fled from Rudd's farm to the neighboring house of Mr. Stanton. Stanton testified that the boy had come to his house with blood running out of his mouth, saying that Rudd was murdering him. The boy's back revealed welts from a whipping, welts that were covered in brine. Benjamin said that he had come to Stanton for help because his master had threatened to kill him or geld him. Then Rudd arrived at Stanton's house, looking for the boy. Stanton testified that he told Rudd that "he was a wretch for abusing him in such a shameful sordid manner," and in response Rudd threatened to beat Stanton as well as Benjamin. In Stanton's opinion, the beating inflicted on the boy was so severe as to threaten poor Benjamin's reason. Based on Stanton's evidence, Timothy Pierce, Justice of the Peace in Preston, decided to remove the boy from his master's house and to place him with his brother Philip Bump of Plainfield until the case could come to trial, thus fulfilling the intent of the law to protect a child fleeing from abuse.[25]

At the formal hearing of Benjamin's charge of cruelty by his master some neighbors made it clear that they had known of the ongoing abuse and had failed to protect the boy as required by the law, even though he had previously fled to escape his abusive master. Mrs. Philips of Preston said that the prior time that Benjamin had run away she had returned the boy to Rudd. She witnessed Rudd beat the child until he cried out, and she heard Rudd threaten to salt Benjamin if he ran away again. Despite the colonial law that provided protection to apprentices who fled abusive masters, Mrs. Philips had returned the child to his abuser. Sarah Prentice, also of Preston, testified that Rudd had hung Benjamin up at least twice and whipped him because the boy had stolen two shirts and two scythes. She further testified that Rudd had beaten the boy for over a quarter of an hour, striking him many blows with a birch rod. John Prentice countered his wife's testimony, saying Rudd had beaten Benjamin just once previously, but that he had used a leather whip rather than sticks. Mr. Prentice added that he had never heard Rudd threaten to kill his apprentice and that he did not believe the whipping had damaged the child's reason. Yet other neighbors apparently had a different standard by which they judged Rudd's treatment of his apprentice. Anna and Sarah Stanton testified to the miserable condition of the boy's back while John Hall and Ephraim Fellows judged that the bruises that covered the boy from his shoulders to his thighs revealed that Rudd had beaten him "with a stick of considerable bigness."[26]

Despite this apparently conflicting testimony, the New London County Court extended legal protection to young Benjamin. In taking the boy from his master and canceling the articles of indenture, the jury ignored Rudd's plea of not guilty, a plea that he had justified by claiming he had corrected the child in a moderate manner as was his right. Rudd may have undercut his own defense because his neighbors testified that he had threatened harm to various witnesses in the case. The Court ordered that Rudd pay for the medical costs incurred for healing the child's injuries, that he pay court costs, and that he pay a thirty-shilling fine to the county. The Court not only removed Benjamin from Rudd's control; it ordered a full release of the boy's term of indenture, perhaps because of the concern over his sanity as a result of the abusive treatment.[27] Nevertheless, had neighbors acted to protect the child when he first had fled his abusive master, the boy's physical and mental suffering would have been far less serious.

Compared to the resolution of the case of apprentice Thomas Dickens of New London in 1723, Benjamin had been fortunate. While the court record did not detail whether Thomas had actually fled the cruelty of his master, Nathaniel Otis of New London, Thomas did appear before Justice of the Peace Richard Bushnell and filed a legal complaint (without the assistance of an adult or legal guardian) against Otis, charging Otis with abusing and cruelly beating him with a stick. The Justice of the Peace recorded that the boy showed him the wounds that had resulted from his beating. As in other cases of alleged abuse, Thomas also charged that his master had not taught him his trade nor taught him to read and write. The boy had an additional complaint; his indenture was illegal. He claimed that the selectman of Fall River, Massachusetts had originally apprenticed him to Nathaniel House of Lebanon, Connecticut to learn the trade of weaving. Creation of the contract of indenture by the selectmen was evidence that young Thomas had been one of the poor of the town. Without obtaining the approval of the selectmen, House had then assigned the original indenture to Thomas Bishop, and Bishop had sold it to Otis for 20 pounds. This, according to the boy, was contrary to Connecticut's laws. Perhaps because the child had been a poor boy assigned into service, the New London County Court agreed with Otis' plea of not guilty to the charge of abuse and did not even consider the issue of the legality of the transfer of the boy's indenture. The jury assessed court costs against Thomas and issued an execution for collection of the costs as well. In this case, the child was worse off after using the legal system in an attempt to protect himself since his only source of funds to pay the court costs would have been to remain in service to an abusive master an additional period of time.[28]

Abusive and cruel treatment of apprentices could take many forms in eighteenth-century Connecticut, but the court system did not always provide a remedy for the victims because community standards certainly influenced how juries viewed the alleged abuse. In June of 1723, Bothia Taylor of Norwich brought a complaint that Thomas Wills, her master, had committed "sundry hardships and cruelties on her." At the trial she testified that in the four years she had worked for Wills she had been "pinched with hunger" and had poor clothing with no shoes or stockings. In fact, she claimed that she was so ashamed of her poor clothing that she had been to Sabbath meeting just three or four times while in Wills' service. Bothia said that even her grandfather had urged her to run away because Wills was not properly providing for her. Margaret Foote testified on Bothia's behalf, saying the girl had suffered very much because of insufficient food and clothing, but Foote added that Wills' wife Ann and his children also lacked enough food and had inadequate clothing. Three other Norwich residents added their testimony that they had seen no difference between what Bothia had and what Wills' wife and children received. Ann Wills herself declared that she could get more food out begging in the street than she could get at home and that Bothia actually got more than she did. Laday Stubbins said that Bothia had suffered from lack of food because Wills locked the food up when he was away. Although the Court valued Bothia's clothing as worth less than one shilling and as so inadequate that "it could not cover her nakedness," it found Wills innocent of the charge that he had treated the girl cruelly. The ruling said that Bothia's suffering was equal to that inflicted on the rest of the family so the abuse was not intentional. Perhaps recognizing that neither Bothia nor Wills had any money, the court did not assess court costs against either party to the dispute, but it did not release the girl from her indenture to Wills.[29]

In 1744, the guardian of apprentice Stephen Leech of New London raised a new legal issue in claiming that beating of an apprentice was against the law. James Chapman, Stephen's legal guardian, complained to the New London County Court that William Cardwell, master of Stephen, had attacked the boy while the child was "faithfully attending the commands of said master" and cruelly and unlawfully corrected him with a whip used for horses and "did beat, bruise, maim, and much hurt" the apprentice. After summoning Cardwell into Court to answer the charge of cruelty, the judge found him guilty not of abusing the child but guilty of a breach of the peace. Despite the guardian's claim that beating an apprentice was illegal, the court made no judgment on Cardwell's abuse of the boy. The sentence was mild. The Court did not release the child from his indenture, and Cardwell had only to post a fifty-pound bond for good behavior, especially toward Stephen. What stood out in this case was that the apprentice had a guardian attempting to look out for his well being so that he had not had to flee to the house of a stranger to seek protection.[30]

Even masters of slave children could not maltreat them with impunity under Connecticut's laws. Though in one case the final verdict was "ignoramus," the very existence of an inquiry into the death of a slave child revealed a society concerned with overly harsh punishment of both apprentices and slaves. In 1751 a New London County jury of inquest viewed the body of Zeno, "a negro child, slave for life" to Mr. Nicholas Lechmere of New London. The jurymen attributed the girl's death to serious wounds on her head and body. The colony brought formal charges against Lechmere, alleging he had beaten the nine-year-old with a two-foot long horsewhip. The wounds resulting were so severe that the girl "languished" for four days and died. While there seemed to be no question that Lechmere had caused the girl's death, the verdict of "ignoramus" may have indicated that the jury was not sure of Lechmere's intent when beating the child. The court imposed no punishment on him for causing the girl's death, but he did have to pay court costs for his own prosecution.[31]

That colonial officials would provide protection even to male slave children seemed apparent in the initial stages of 1754 case against New London resident James Rogers, 3rd. Rogers faced charges of "great cruelty" for abusing Sharper, a Negro boy whom he owned. The writ detailed that the master had nailed one of the child's ears to the wall of his house and nailed the other to a block of wood. Rogers had also forced a large corncob into the boy's mouth, overextending his jaw, and tied him up "hand and foot" for over twelve hours, inflicting extreme pain and torture. Mathew Griswold, king's attorney, characterized the attack as without any just cause and as "an immoderate and extravagant degree of correction." Though Rogers pleaded not guilty and tried to justify and extenuate his actions, the New London County Court found him guilty of "sundry misdemeanors against the peace." However, the Court did not remove the child from Rogers, nor did it impose any fine or damages. Furthermore, the magistrate granted Rogers the right to seek a review of the verdict.[32]

Six months after the original hearing, before a different jury of New London County residents, Rogers challenged his conviction, saying that his punishment of the boy had been neither immoderate nor extravagant, "nor were the corrections in any degree equal to the great crime by the said Sharper committed." Rogers presented what he said was a pattern of misbehavior and criminal activity by the child, prior to the alleged abuse. He claimed the boy had stolen various items from him and given them to "those who were the avowed enemies to God and King." After catching Sharper, Rogers said he had used "mild and moderate correction" to discipline his slave. Then the child ran away from Rogers. Rogers said he again corrected the boy in a mild manner but threatened to use harsher methods if the boy still misbehaved. Once more the boy escaped, this time fleeing to "enemies" of the King, according to Rogers. The final straw was the child's flight to "aid and assist the French King." Rogers described how, after recapturing the boy, he had in a "mild and calm manner even as a tender father would correct his only son" put a nail through each of the boy's ears, nailing one ear to the wall of the house. Rogers admitted he had kept the boy nailed to the wall, but offered in extenuation of the severity of the punishment that he allowed Janis True, the boy's mother, to care for the child while he was nailed to the wall. He further asserted that he had tied the boy's hands and feet only to keep him from pulling his ear free from the wall and running away. Because in 1755 Connecticut residents were concerned about the possibility of hostilities between England and France, the jury was apparently sympathetic to Rogers' claim that he was preventing the child from aiding Indians in Connecticut who were hostile to the English cause; the jury dismissed the abuse complaint against Rogers. Certainly an additional factor in the dismissal of the charges was Sharper's status as a slave; he had no one in the community to look out for his interests.[33]

Following the American Revolution, juries began to find consistently in favor of abused apprentices, perhaps reflecting changes in the view of children presented in books such as Rousseau's *Emile.* Rarely did masters claim in their own defense that they had a legal right to use physical punishment to correct apprentices. In two cases from the 1780s, the children brought suit unassisted by adults and succeeded in having their indentures ended by the Court. In 1783 Perry Button of Preston filed a complaint against his master, Roswell Smith of Preston, complaining of the cruelty of his master. Perry said his master had beaten him in a "cruel and dangerous manner to threaten his life so that he fled his master," but the case did not contain the supporting testimony from neighbors or witnesses marking earlier abuse cases. Nevertheless, the New London County Court found in favor of the minor and dissolved the indentures binding Perry to Smith. In 1787 Betty Freeman of Groton brought a complaint against her mistress, Rebecca Morgan of Groton, after she had fled from the tyranny of her employer. Betty asked the New London County Court to provide her "the protection and liberation as the law directs." Again, the Court simply ruled that the facts alleged by the girl were true and freed her from her indentures.[34]

ABUSE ON THE HIGH SEAS

Not only did Connecticut's courts become more consistent in protecting apprentices from abusive masters in the post-Revolutionary era; the courts also started extending a similar protection to underage employees who were not under formal terms of indenture. This change was particularly evident in the handling of cases alleging cruelty and abuse against underage sailors working for Connecticut's ship owners and captains. A problem for children who went to sea to work was that shipmasters and captains maintained discipline on board ship. Unlike the case of abused apprentices on land, abused underage seamen had no one to whom they could flee for protection. Furthermore, there were no state laws that controlled the behavior of ship captains toward their employees. Because children had to wait until the ship returned to port for them to seek a remedy for alleged abuse, most such cases appeared on the trial dockets as civil suits for specific damages caused by the abuse. The preponderance of verdicts in favor of the minor plaintiffs even in a maritime community such as New London reflected a society that sought to limit the power a ship's captain had over his crew, at least over those who were minors.

In 1781 Thomas Gardiner, Jr. of Stonington brought a lawsuit with the assistance of his father, Thomas Gardiner, against Oliver Norris of Saybrook, alleging Norris had beaten him while he was employed on the sloop *American Revenue* on a voyage from the Mystic River to the West

Indies. Thomas sought two thousand pounds in damages in the case. At the trial witness Joshua Weaver of Stonington identified the ship as a "revenue privateer" and said that while at sea the master had summoned all hands on deck, but that some had not turned out, Thomas Gardiner among them. Oliver Norris, the first mate, had then used a rope end and flogged several of those who had not come on deck, including Thomas. Asked if Thomas had ever disobeyed orders before, Weaver responded, "Never when it was his watch upon deck nor at any other time that I know of." Weaver added that Thomas was as good a hand as any on board the ship, except for one or two others. Asked about the conditions aboard ship, Weaver said that the weather had been good that day but that the crew had just faced ten days of bad weather and were all very fatigued. The testimony thus established that Thomas was neither a disobedient nor an incompetent hand. The jury found the first mate guilty of abusing the boy, but greatly lowered the damages from the original claim for two thousand to just nine pounds with an additional nine pounds of court costs.[35]

In 1796 minor John Chapple, Jr. of Montville, with the assistance of his father, John Chapple, brought a lawsuit seeking twenty pounds from ship owner and captain Nathaniel Dickerson of New London, alleging that the captain had arbitrarily assaulted young John "to show his importance as commander." The boy testified that he had a rupture that Dickerson knew of, but that Dickerson had beaten him on the rupture on purpose and kept him on deck after the beating to torment him. The beating, said John, had so aggravated his rupture that he was still bedridden and would probably be a cripple for life. Without comment the jury, many probably former seamen themselves, found in favor of the plaintiff, awarding him seven pounds in damages and court costs.[36]

The 1800 lawsuit of twenty-year-old Joseph Camp of Stonington against Norwich resident John Langnos, the captain of the sloop *Dispatch*, made it clear that not all jurors sympathized with minors facing the rigorous discipline found on board ships. Assisted by his father James Melzer Camp, Joseph detailed a horrific pattern of abuse on a voyage from New London to the West Indies in September of 1799. During the trip the captain repeatedly knocked Joseph down with his fists, hit him with a rope, and made the poor boy crawl on his hands and knees under thirty oxen on board the ship. "To feed his vengeful disposition," the captain also made the youth sit in the shrouds for two hours until the boy almost lost the use of his limbs. Joseph also claimed that the captain threatened to throw him overboard to drown him. For the abuse and injuries he suffered, Joseph sought six hundred dollars in damages from his abuser.[37]

At the New London County Court trial, jurors, many of whom may have been mariners at some point in their lives, sympathized with the captain rather than with the abused youth. Testimony made it clear that Joseph had signed on as ship's cook under false pretenses; he had said he knew how to cook. Dan Cook, a mate of *The Dispatch,* testified that Joseph "poorly, carelessly, and negligently" performed his duties as cook, often falling asleep while he should have been working. Worthington claimed that at such times he and the captain had had to cook for themselves. He admitted that Langnos had frequently been angry with the boy, threatening to flog him or throw him overboard if he did not learn how to cook. According to Worthington's deposition, the captain even tried to teach the boy himself, giving up in frustration and angrily damning him. Worthing admitted that he saw the captain seize the boy by the collar, shake him, throw him on the deck, and kick him, but he asserted that the captain never offered violence against Joseph unless the youth neglected his duty. Clearly, the captain was a man pushed beyond endurance by a hand who was unable or unwilling to do his job. The County Court jury apparently sided with the captain because they found him not guilty of either abuse or assault. When the hapless Joseph appealed the verdict to the Superior Court, Captain Langnos did not receive such a sympathetic hearing from the jurors. After hearing the Camps' appeal, the Superior Court reversed the original ruling in favor of the ship's captain and awarded \$100 in damages to Joseph.[38]

Reflecting the division of jurisdiction based on the amount of damages at issue in lawsuits, justices of the peace adjudicated some cases involving abuse and cruelty by the early 1800s. In 1801 Justice of the Peace Elijah Palmer of Stonington heard Henry Noyes, a minor who lived in Stonington, direct a complaint against Jeremiah Haley, also of Stonington. Bringing the case with the assistance of his father, Henry charged that when he was a hand on a fishing voyage for mackerel on the schooner *Anne,* Noyes unlawfully beat and struck him. The boy sought \$7 in damages. Henry provided eyewitness testimony of the alleged assault. Fellow sailor Isaac Whittle of Stonington testified that on a calm day he went into the cabin and saw Haley strike Henry "with a fox, being two yarns twisted together, and the boy ran out of the cabin." Perhaps because the child did not allege any lasting injuries, Palmer dismissed the complaint. Nevertheless, the fact that Henry and his father brought suit for a relatively small amount and were ready to pay court costs to pursue the case reflected their belief that the captain had overstepped the bounds of his lawful authority.[39]

Four years later another justice court found in favor of a twenty-year-old plaintiff. Nathan Meech of Preston claimed that Christopher Stanton of Norwich, the master of the brigantine *Favorite,* had knocked him down and beaten him on board ship while the ship was at dock in Charleston, South Carolina. Nathan brought the suit with the assistance of his next friend Moses Meech of Preston who functioned as an informal legal assistant to the boy, perhaps because the child had no father available to assist him. Minors could not initiate civil lawsuits under Connecticut's laws without the assistance of a parent, guardian, or next friend. The youth claimed that Stanton had, without cause, knocked him to the floor and hit him ten hard blows with his fists on his head, face, and chest and also had kicked him. Even though Nathan did not provide witnesses to support his accusations nor did he allege lasting injuries from the beating, the justice of the peace found in his favor and awarded him $15 in damages and court costs.[40]

The question of when and how severely a captain could discipline minors under his command continued to evolve during the rest of the nineteenth century. In 1832 a minor brought suit against the captain of the whaling ship *Electra* seeking $200 in damages. The captain's defense was that he had a right "by law" to punish his hands as he saw fit. John Moore, assisted by his next friend George Moore, both of Norwich, claimed that while he was a hand on a whaling voyage on the *Electra,* Maxwell Griffings of Sag Harbor, New York, the captain of the vessel, had knocked him to the deck, hit him with his fists, and beaten him with a rope. Then Griffings tied the boy to the mast for three hours. John asserted that the abuse had made him sick and disordered for three months. At the New London County Court, the jury upheld the boy's claim, awarding him $140 of the $200 in damages requested.[41]

Unhappy with that verdict, Griffings appealed to the Superior Court for New London County. In his defense, the captain asserted that he was the captain of the *Electra* and that John had been a mariner under his command. He claimed that the boy had neglected his duty, had disobeyed orders, and had lied. Furthermore, the captain asserted that the youth was disorderly and insolent. Griffings admitted that he had used a small whip "moderately and reasonably to chastise and correct the plaintiff for his neglect of duty and disobedience to orders." He then stated that he had a legal right to use such physical punishment on his employees. The Superior Court disagreed and upheld the verdict of the County Court in favor of the boy.[42] Perhaps this resolution reflected new ideas toward punishment marked by opening of the new state prison at Wethersfield a few years earlier in 1828. More humane standards of punishment, including the elimination of physical punishment, were becoming the norm in Connecticut's penal system. This alteration could have had an impact on how judges and juries viewed permissible standards of punishment aboard ships.

The ameliorating trend continued into the middle of the nineteenth century as illustrated by the 1850 case of seventeen-year-old Hyms Waterman of Bozrah. Hyms brought an action against Riley Sweet, the master of the ship *Mentor*, claiming he had assaulted him while the ship was on the high seas. Gurdon Waterman of New London, the boy's father, assisted in the case even though Hyms clearly was not living with his father at the time of the trial. Seeking $1,500 in damages, the teen said that Sweet, a New London resident, had flogged him with a rope end, striking him on the back and shoulders seventeen times while he was aloft in the rigging of the ship. Hyms complained that the beating had cut and bruised him, so severely lacerating his back that he was sick and lame from his injuries for over three weeks. In justification of his abuse of the teen, Sweet responded that Hymes had stolen two quarts of molasses while on board ship and that the beating was only a moderate punishment. Sweet did admit to the Court that in administering the correction he "did necessarily and unavoidably a little beat, bruise, and ill treat" the boy. The Superior Court did not agree that the punishment fit the alleged crime and found Sweet guilty, awarding damages of $200 and court costs to the teenager. This sympathy with the abused teen reflected attitudes of reform in Connecticut's prison system where physical punishment for theft was no longer legal.[43]

FACTORY DISCIPLINE OR CHILD ABUSE?

Ship captains who abused minors under their control were not the only employers who faced challenges to their cruelty toward children. With the increasing number of factories in Connecticut in the nineteenth century, factory owners and overseers discovered they did not have a free hand to discipline employees who were minors. In 1838 Abby S. Branch, a fifteen-year-old from Lisbon, Connecticut, with the assistance of her father, Elisha Branch of Lisbon, charged that Ebeneezer Weaver of Griswold had cruelly abused her. Abby said Weaver had hit her on the face and side of the head, and pulled her by the ears. In a second assault he had again pulled her by the ears and struck her in the face. Abby and her father had obtained the services of an attorney, Layfayette Foster, in pursuing the girl's claim, a somewhat rare occurrence in this era. Foster warned the jury that Weaver would try to justify his actions by claiming that he was the overseer in the card room of the cotton mill in Griswold where Abby had worked. Weaver did claim the girl had refused to do her duty in the mill. Furthermore, he asserted that Elisha Branch had given permission for moderate correction. Though the court files did not include whether or not Elisha Branch refuted that claim, the jury found Weaver guilty and assessed damages of $25 and court costs.[44] Being a factory employer apparently did not allow the use of physical punishment against children working in the factory.

That the bias against punishment did not apply only to girls was apparent in a case the following year. Frederic Prentice of Norwich with the help of Fanny Prentice of Norwich, his next friend (a term used to describe an adult other than a parent who assisted a child in bringing or defending a legal action), claimed Chauncy Palmer of Norwich had abused him by hitting him with his fists and stomping on him. Palmer also allegedly seized the boy by the hair, pulled him about, and threw him down on the floor of the factory where Frederic worked. He then beat the youth again, jumping and stomping on him. At the original hearing of the charges at a justice court in Norwich, the magistrate had found in the boy's favor, awarding him $35 in damages. When Palmer appealed the verdict to the New London County Court, five of the six witnesses, all members of the Prentice family, apparently supported Frederic's version of the abuse. The jury agreed that the alleged abuse was an assault but reduced the damages to just $7. Palmer paid the damages without a further appeal to the Superior Court, perhaps realizing that public opinion would be against him.[45]

SCHOOLHOUSE DISCIPLINE: ANOTHER FORM OF ABUSE

Even as attitudes toward the punishment of minor employees by their employers changed, so did the leeway granted to schoolteachers to discipline the students under their charge. In the seventeenth century, laws concerning the education of children made it clear that children who disobeyed their teachers or refused to learn as directed could expect little sympathy from the community. One statute from 1650 directed that if children became rude, stubborn, and unruly, town selectmen could take them from their parents and place them under masters who would "more strictly look unto and force them to submit unto government." By implication, this included corporal punishment to bring children in line. In the 1790s Zephaniah Swift noted the existence of a Connecticut law that included schoolmasters among those adults who legally could "reasonably correct" the children under their control. Despite this tradition of corporal punishment by teachers, lawsuits brought against abusive teachers in the nineteenth century revealed that parents and juries no longer supported this right of correction. This may have reflected new attitudes toward both children and education that held that sympathy and understanding were more important to imparting education to children than was corporal punishment.[46]

In an 1836 case that pitted a minor plaintiff against a minor defendant, Charles S. Woodworth of Montville with the assistance of his father Joshua E. Woodworth brought what looked like a simple assault case against Joshua Perkins of Lisbon, seeking $500 in damages. Charles complained that Perkins had attacked him with a large stick, beating and bruising him and injuring his right eye. In the original writ, the Woodworths identified Perkins as a minor and provided legal notice to his father, Charles Perkins, to assist his son in the trial if he saw fit. However, this was not simply a case of two teens having a fight. At the trial, Joshua defended his actions by saying that Charles had been a student in his school. He asserted that Charles was" vicious, insolent, and ungovernable." He went so far as to claim that the punishment he had inflicted on his pupil had been "necessary and proper to reduce the plaintiff to obedience and to preserve order and good government in the defendant's school." The jury did not accept Joshua's justification of his actions, finding him guilty and ordering him to pay Charles $50.[47]

In 1842 a jury again found in favor of a student who protested physical punishment by his teacher. William M. Dodge, a minor of Norwich who brought his case with the assistance of his next friend Samuel Storey, Esq. of Norwich, sued Oliver P. Wattles of Norwich, a local school teacher, for assault, charging that Wattles had grabbed him by the back of the neck and gripped and pulled it, shaking him and throwing him down across a chair. When the boy was on the ground, Wattles allegedly struck and beat him with a three-foot-long stick that was about an inch in diameter. This beating was so severe, William claimed, that he suffered great pain and received such serious wounds that he could not "transact his ordinary affairs and business." William then claimed that Wattles had beaten him a second time on the same day. Furthermore, he complained he had to spend $10 to cure his bruises and sickness resulting from the beatings. At the original hearing before a justice of the peace, the justice found Wattles guilty but did not assign an amount for damages, allowing Wattles an appeal of the verdict. The New London County Court also found in favor of William but permitted the teacher another appeal to the Connecticut Superior Court. At the Superior Court hearing Wattles justified his actions, saying he was a schoolmaster and that William had been his pupil. He claimed on the day of the assault William had been rude and insolent and had refused to obey Wattles' "lawful and proper commands." The teacher asserted that to "induce obedience" he had to use force and moderately chastise the boy but said he used no more violence than necessary. While Wattles had probably used this defense of necessity in the two prior hearings, he managed to prevail before the Superior Court because William and his next friend failed to appear to present their side of the case.

With this default by the original plaintiffs, the jury directed a judgment in favor of the teacher and ordered Storey to pay Wattles' court costs because he was the adult who had assisted William in bringing the lawsuit.[48]

ABUSE BY PARENTS OR GUARDIANS

Whereas Connecticut law mandated some sort of protection for apprentices and other children who fled abusive employers, neither the colony nor the state had any similar automatic protection for children abused by their parents. Certainly authorities investigated the deaths of newborn infants, especially illegitimate children, to make sure their mothers had not murdered them. Yet, not until the late eighteenth century were many cases in which the state charged parents with intentionally abusing their children when death did not result from the abuse. In 1816 Tapping Reeve still asserted a parent had the right to govern children, with the authority to "chastise moderately." Nevertheless, Reeve claimed that the state recognized certain rights "which the law will protect against the brutality of a parent." Reeve asserted that when a parent appeared "unreasonably severe" in punishing a child, he would not be guilty of an offense against the law if he "acted conscientiously and from motives of duty." This appeared to provide parents a free hand in administering punishment, but Reeve added the proviso that if a parent had acted from "malice of heart," the law would not shield a parent from the consequences of abusing a child in his care.[49]

Infanticide was certainly a form of child abuse. Early Connecticut laws required an examination of stillborn infants, especially when their mothers were not married, to make sure that the babies had not been murdered. In 1699 the colony passed a law that imposed the death sentence on any woman who concealed the death of a child, who if it had lived would have been a bastard. This law said that if a woman tried to bury or "drown" a dead infant to conceal whether it had been born dead or alive, "she shall suffer death as for murder" unless she had one witness that the child was stillborn. Not surprisingly, many of the prosecutions for infanticide were against Native American women who had given birth to bastard children. This may have been because Native American women often did not employ midwives and thus had no acceptable witness to the condition of a child at birth. There was no question of stillbirth when in 1737 the colony brought murder charges against Kate, a Pequot Indian woman from Saybrook, alleging that she had killed her newborn male bastard by crushing its skull with a piece of wood. Kate compounded her crime by denying her actions. When her employer's wife, Mrs. Temperance Worthington, asked Kate if she had miscarried, Kate denied having given birth. Mrs. Worthington later found the infant, barely alive, buried under some rotten hay in the barn. When she lifted it, she "felt the back part of the skull crumble . . . as if broken." The local midwife examined Kate and testified that Kate had born a child the day the baby was found. The colony convicted Kate of willful murder and executed her on May 7, 1738.[50]

Nearly ten years later, abandonment rather than an alleged beating of her newborn illegitimate child brought murder charges against Betty Kiness, an Indian girl from Stonington. Betty gave birth in the house of her employer, Joseph Denison, Esq. of Stonington but neither let anyone know she was pregnant nor called for help while in labor. After the child died, Betty had tried to conceal it by burying it secretly. Witnesses found the body near an old fence by Betty's mother's wigwam. When midwife Pricilla Cheeseborough confirmed that Betty had recently given birth, Betty first compounded her crime by denying she had had a baby, and then she claimed that if she had, the child had fallen into the privy. At an inquest over the body of the child the jurymen said that the child had a loose string around its neck when found, but that they could not tell if the child had been born alive or dead. Despite that judgment, the colony went ahead and indicted Betty for murder, saying she had given birth to a living child but had concealed it and let it die. Perhaps because of the confusion over whether Betty actually caused the baby's death, at Betty's trial the court apparently dismissed the incitement but assessed court costs of over fifty-three pounds against her.[51]

Confusion over the cause of death was apparently a continuing problem in determining guilt for the death of newborns. In 1750, an Indian woman named Peg, held as a slave by Captain Elnathan Stevens of Killingworth, gave birth to a bastard child who died shortly after birth. Peg made the mistake of giving birth alone, in an uninhabited house, so she had no witness to the child's condition. The jury at the inquest ruled that the condition of the body proved the infant had lived after birth. Because the child's hands were crossed and held up to its face and the feet were flexed up to its buttocks, the members of the jury said the child had been able to move after being born. They said the cause of death was the result of the lack of covering or care, but the jury could find no sign of violence against the child. In this case despite what appeared to be clear evidence of neglect, the court dismissed the murder charge against Peg.[52]

The case of *Rex v. Sarah Bramble* in 1753 made it evident that while juries might not consider failure to care for a child the equivalent of murder, evidence of actual physical abuse of an infant leading to its death made a stronger case against the mother. Sarah, a single woman in New London who was a servant to Benjamin Palmer, gave birth to a female bastard on March 21, 1752. When witnesses found the body of the infant, they reported it was burned on all its parts. Sarah claimed the baby was stillborn; the court asserted that the child was alive at birth and that Sarah had then thrown the infant girl on the bed and failed to feed or care for her, so that she "instantly" died. Sarah admitted to concealing the dead body, claiming that the bruises and burns had resulted from her attempt to hide it but insisted again that the child had been stillborn. Despite Sarah's testimony, the Court ruled that she was guilty of willfully murdering her child and ordered her to be hanged for the crime on November 21, 1753.[53]

Surprisingly, several other cases charging infanticide did not result in executions. In 1759 the colony said Ann Hayden of Saybrook gave birth to a child of "white complexion" while alone, refused to nourish or support it, and concealed it so it died. In issuing their judgment that someone had murdered the child, jurors at the inquest described the body as bruised and mangled, with a broken right arm and a dislocated neck. Nevertheless when the Superior Court heard the case, it dismissed the charges without a verdict. The case file did not include testimony from a midwife, but it is possible that the injuries were consistent with a difficult birth. When the colony charged Abigail Wilson, a transient single woman, with the murder of her newborn child in 1760, the Superior Court brought in a verdict of ignoramus. Again in 1784 the verdict was ignoramus when the state charged Sylvia, a single Negro woman from Preston, with giving birth to a bastard, killing it, and concealing it. Without detailed evidence it is difficult to know what decided the juries that these cases, unlike that of Sarah Bramble, were not willful murder.[54]

Because juries of inquest had continued problems over deciding whether a newborn had been born dead, had died because of neglect by its mother, or had been murdered, Connecticut finally amended the law in 1808 to reduce the punishment for women who gave birth to bastards and concealed their deaths, an apparent attempt to protect helpless newborns against their own mothers. A woman who hid her pregnancy or concealed the birth of a bastard child had to pay a fine of $150. This law also penalized a woman who gave birth to a bastard child who died if the woman concealed the body to make it difficult to determine if the child had been born alive. When convicted, the culprit had to wear a halter around her neck and sit on the gallows for an hour. The Court could also choose to make her pay a bond for good behavior or imprison her for as long authorities saw fit. Shortening that open-ended sentence, in 1821 the state reduced the potential prison term to up to one year in jail.[55]

Despite this law that aimed at making women give birth in the presence of witnesses in order to provide some protection for their children, the nineteenth century saw continued prosecutions against mothers who killed their newborn infants, but in New London County the majority of such prosecutions were against women of color. This may have reflected a continuation of what Cornelia Dayton has identified in the eighteenth century as "a narrowly selective approach targeting poor, marginal women and sheltering the middling classes from public scrutiny, humiliation, and penalty." In 1807 Clarissa Ockery, a black woman from Preston, gave birth to a male bastard. After the death of the child, the state charged that Clarissa had suffocated her son and concealed the body by throwing it onto Moses Lester's land. Although Clarissa pleaded not guilty to the charge of murder, the state found her guilty and sentenced her to die. However, a petition to the Connecticut General Assembly alleging that evidence had not been available at the trial that might have exonerated Clarissa resulted on June 8th, 1808 in a commutation of her sentence to just six months to be served at the Norwich County jail. Tragically, she died in jail just a week after the reduction in her sentence.[56]

Another infanticide case against an African-American mother implicated her own mother as well. In 1832 the state charged Rue Benedict of North Stonington with strangling her newborn bastard with a piece of cloth and charged her mother, Betsy Benedict, with helping commit the murder. The jury of inquest viewed the child's body and ruled that it had died as the result of a linen or cotton cloth tied around its neck. In response to findings of the inquest, the North Stonington justice of the peace found Rue guilty of murder and ordered her jailed until a Superior Court trial. Though this seems to parallel prior cases of infanticide, the Superior Court ruled that the case was not a true bill and dismissed the charges against both women.[57]

While the legal records of New London County in the seventeenth or eighteenth century revealed not a single prosecution against a parent for abuse of a child not resulting in death, in the nineteenth century parents who assaulted or neglected children, even though they did not cause the death of the child, faced prosecution for their behavior. This new protection for children perhaps reflected a decline in the view that children were naturally evil, requiring harsh physical punishment to keep them in line. Nevertheless, as in cases of infanticide, the state tended to prosecute more cases against parents of color, and even when it brought charges against whites, those parents usually received more lenient sentences. The change in the idea of parental responsibility culminated in the 1830s with a specific statute that mandated a two-to-five-year prison sentence for abandonment or neglect of a child under the age of six. The state began to hold parents responsible for abusive actions as early as 1801 when Azubus Munsel, a minor female from Lyme, complained to the justice court of assault and "cruel, inhumane, and barbarous treatment" by her father, John Munsel, Jr. Because her abuser was her natural parent, the girl brought her complaint with the assistance of her maternal grandfather, Amos Huntley, also of Lyme. Lyme Justice of the Peace William Noyes rejected the father's plea of not guilty and found that the girl had reason to be afraid of her father. He required John Munsel to pay a bond for good behavior of $150 to ensure he kept the peace toward his daughter.[58]

Abuse in the form of overly severe punishment resulted in manslaughter charges against Billings Warden of Stonington in 1803. The state accused him of striking his five-year-old son Isaac on the head with a rough stick and fracturing his skull, causing his death the following day. At the initial justice court hearing in 1802, the justice ruled that Warden was not only responsible for his son's death but also that he had attempted to conceal the facts of Isaac's demise to avoid charges. Though the indictment at the Superior Court stated that the act was without malice aforethought, the case was not merely a charge of accidental death. Though found guilty of a high handed misdemeanor rather than the more serious charge of manslaughter, Warden paid a $100 fine, reimbursed the court for costs of $140.22, and served three months in the New London County jail. The verdict was probably indicative that the Superior Court found he had used excessive force in correcting the child since, as Zephaniah Swift asserted, death resulting from moderate correction of a child without malice was a crime of misadventure, whereas if the punishment exceeded the bounds of moderation, the charge could be as severe as either manslaughter or murder.[59]

Legal decisions after 1800 revealed that parents could not abuse their offspring with impunity. The specific charge of child abuse by a parent against a child appeared in a 1805 case in which Sarah Abbott of Norwich charged that her husband, Daniel, had become "addicted to spirituous liquors" and had abused both her and their children. One child still was in a languishing condition, so severe had been the abuse according to Mrs. Abbott. After his arrest, Abbott pleaded not guilty to the charges, but the New London County Court found him guilty as charged and bound him for good behavior, not only towards his wife, but also towards his children. Abbott may have recognized the changing attitudes in the legal system because he did not plead that it was his right to correct his children as he saw fit but merely paid the fine as ordered.[60]

In 1815 the Connecticut Superior Court imposed a seven-year jail sentence on a black woman who abused her child. Hannah Crosswell, also known as Hannah Niles or Mary Johnson or Mary Niles, pleaded not guilty to the charge that she had attempted to murder her child, but the court heard evidence that the mother had told others she intended to destroy the child. She battered and bruised the infant, throwing "junk bottles and other deadly weapons" at the child as well as throwing it on the floor with the intent to kill it. The imposition of such a severe sentence for attempted murder of a child might have been a reflection of the extreme level of abuse, but it also might have been because Crosswell was black. However, her sentence was less than sentences imposed on either white or black men convicted of attempted murder during the same period: records from Newgate Prison revealed that the state had leveled life sentences on males convicted of attempted murder.[61]

In Stonington in 1815, both parents faced charges of child abuse for putting a three-week-old infant in danger. Justice of the Peace Coddington Billings recorded that Lois Woodbridge had mixed tobacco in a dish of food she had prepared for her child. John Woodbridge had then beaten and choked Lois. Apparently he was not concerned with the threat to his child because he also violently bruised the infant, according to Billings, with the intent to kill the child. Billings did not resolve the case, perhaps because the only witnesses to the counter claims of abuse were the parents themselves. The fact that they were not black may also have been a factor in Billings' dismissal of the charges.[62]

Parental abuse continued to be a problem facing Connecticut's courts. In 1834 Atwell Tucker, Jr. of Lyme attacked his daughter Sarah with a club. The New London County Court termed the attack a violent assault, resulting in the beating, bruising, and wounding of the girl. Tucker had also threatened to kill Sarah. Though he pleaded not guilty to the charges, the court found him guilty but only fined him $20 for the abuse. Aside from the fact that Crosswell was white, the lack of a jail or prison sentence was inexplicable, considering the severity of earlier punishments for physical abuse of minors.[63]

A more bewildering case occurred in Groton in 1835. The state charged Matilda Davis of Groton with beating and abusing Jane Gardner, a four-year-old child who lived with Davis. A number of witnesses testified that Davis had maltreated the child for a period of over two months with the abuse culminating in Jane's death in January of 1835; yet no one had intervened to rescue the child. On November 1, 1834 Davis forced the child out into the street, exposing her to the cold and inclement weather, an abuse that evidenced the "lack of due care and attention she was bound to bestow."

Witnesses claimed Davis in early December beat Jane on the head, face, and stomach with a large stick, leaving several wounds over five inches long. Later in the month she attempted to choke the child and struck her on the head with such force as to knock her head on the wall and force her to fall to the floor. On December 25th, Davis again abused the girl in front of witnesses who later testified that "with her hands about Jane's throat (she) did violently squeeze and press, giving a wound half way around Jane's neck." On January 11, 1835, the woman whipped the child on her naked back, using a fourfold cord, even though the girl was so weak she could not sit or stand; the abuse continued when Davis seized the girl, shook her, and knocked her head against the side of the cradle, "bruising her with mortal strokes to the head, back, shoulders, and stomach." On January 12th the poor, abused child died of her injuries. In his indictment the State's Attorney detailed the accelerating abuse and called the culmination of the attacks willful murder, but inexplicably the jury accepted the woman's plea of not guilty and freed her. Nothing in the file indicated why the jury did not find Davis guilty of manslaughter or at least an assault against the child.[64]

The failure to hold Davis accountable for her actions stood out as the exception in the 1830s and 40s. In 1837 Charles Hobby, identified as "a transient man of color," broke into the Montville home of James Ashcroft with the intent to steal. Ashcroft's twelve-year-old daughter Harriet was in the house. Hobby threatened the child, putting her "in dread and fear of her life or bodily injury." Convicted of both the breaking and entering and the abuse, Hobby went to the State Prison to serve a two-year sentence. When in 1846 Edmund Freeman of Colchester struck, beat, and bruised eight-year-old Charles Morgan, identified as a "colored boy" who was the son of Colchester resident Henry Morgan, striking him on the head with a large stone, the state sentenced him to serve sixty days in the New London County Jail. When Catharine Dunn of Norwich pushed her two-month-old daughter Elizabeth into the Thames River in 1851, the State's Attorney brought a charge of murder. While the justice court limited itself to convicting Dunn of only pushing the infant into the water, causing it to drown, the Connecticut Superior Court expanded the charges, asserting Dunn had initially strangled her child with her hands, had then tied it into a bag to suffocate it, had beaten the child on the head, back, and belly, inflicting several mortal wounds, and had finally tossed the poor baby into the river to drown. Despite the comprehensive nature of the charges, the jury found Dunn guilty of only second-degree murder and sentenced her to life in prison. Nevertheless, the conviction clearly held the mother responsible for her abuse and killing of the child.[65]

An 1843 case of ongoing abuse that resulted in the death of a child seemed to mirror Davis's abuse of young Jane Gardner, but in this situation the state did hold the caregivers accountable. In this situation authorities initially accused not only the caregivers but also the parents of abusing and causing the death of their five-week-old infant. In October of 1842, a jury of inquest in Griswold found that the infant daughter of Isaac and Sarah Gardiner of Griswold "had come to its end by acts of violence." At the local justice court the justice of the peace indicted both the Gardiners in the death and also charged David and Mary Frost of Griswold, noting that all four were "persons of color" and indicating that the Gardiners had been living with the Frosts at the time of the crime. After hearing testimony that all four adults had beaten the baby, striking, kicking, squeezing, and burning her, the justice court exonerated Sarah Gardiner but found the other three guilty as charged. At the Superior Court review of the case, the state dropped the charges against Isaac Gardiner as well but added the accusation that the Frosts had exposed the baby too close to a fire so that she was "burned, choked, and suffocated." The abuse apparently occurred over a period of several days in October of 1842, but no one reported it until after the child's death on October 30th. Both the Frosts pleaded not guilty to the charges. The Superior Court found David Frost not guilty but convicted his wife and sentenced her to serve two years at the State Prison. The difference in the disposition of this case almost certainly was that the Frosts and Gardeners were black; the Court appeared to hold them to a more rigorous standard of care.[66]

A new form of child abuse began appearing in the court records of the 1830s: child abandonment. Rather than charging parents with neglect, the state treated the act as a more serious criminal matter. In 1835 Phoebe and Ozias Bogue of Lyme left their two-month-old son on the public highway in Montville. After charging both parents with abandoning the infant, the state then dropped the charges against the father without explanation. At her trial, the state assigned Asa Child as counsel to the mother, who pleaded not guilty to the charge. The jury accepted her plea and released her from custody. Without records of testimony in the case, the reason for the dismissal was not clear. Just two years later, a similar charge of abandonment resulted in a three-year sentence at the State Prison at Wethersfield for Mary Ann Francisco from New London. Ironically, Mary Ann was herself just sixteen when convicted, but the fact that she was an Indian may have prejudiced the jury against her. Initially charged at a justice court in Preston with the abandonment of her one-day-old son, Mary Ann pleaded guilty. Unlike the case against the Bogues, who were white, the state did not provide Mary Ann the benefit of either a court-appointed guardian or legal counsel. At the Superior

Court, the charges included the accusation that she had not only left the child, but that she had tried to conceal it in a stonewall. With no one to help her argue her case, again the girl pleaded guilty and ended up at the State Prison for a three-year sentence. Tragically she died of epilepsy in prison after serving two years of her term.[67]

In 1838, the Connecticut General Assembly formalized the protection of children under six. It enacted a new criminal law that mandated a prison term of two to five years for any parent who abandoned a child under six years old. The statute extended the sanction against any other person entrusted with the care of a child under six. In addition, those convicted under the law faced fines not to exceed $400. Clearly the state lawmakers had come to view children as people with special needs for care and recognized the need to protect children from their parents and caregivers.[68]

What was most evident in the gradual development of the concept that the state itself owed a duty of protection to those under the age of twenty-one was that the courts, magistrates, and juries were not consistent. Even as the laws and society itself came to view excessive punishment or physical abuse as wrong, the decisions of the cases revealed that determining what was excessive differed from jury to jury and case to case. An action that authorities seemed to view as acceptable punishment from a white father toward a white child at times became a criminal act by an Africa-American or Native-American parent. Juries apparently "trusted" most whites to know and do the right thing for their children while they did not allow the same latitude to African Americans, Native Americans, or the poor on the margins of white society. Conversely, the difference in outcome of cases against whites may have reflected their greater knowledge of the ins and outs of the legal system. When an adult "knew" the system and provided good advice to a child charged with a crime, such as theft, the records revealed that the courts at times dismissed the charges or reduced the punishment. Lesser sentences and lower fines for the physical abuse of children could have followed a similar pattern, though there were no explicit records of plea bargaining or other obvious manipulations of the legal system by white defendants.

Chapter Five

The Emergent Problem of the Sexual Abuse of Children

> Any person who shall carnally know and abuse any female child under 10 years old is to be imprisoned at Newgate for life or for such other term as the court shall determine.
>
> —Public Statutes of Connecticut, *1821*

> It is more than tongue can describe to think such a monster and hard-hearted wretch is now telling so many stories. The public does not know the feelings of an afflicted child . . . mourning over the inhuman deed of such a wretch.
>
> —Petition to the General Assembly in the 1825 incest case of, *State v. Ezekial Ball*

As the discussion of the problem of physical abuse of children has made evident, Connecticut residents had some concept of what constituted improper or excessively cruel treatment of children as early as the seventeenth century. In contrast the issue of protecting children from sexual abuse was problematic in the seventeenth and eighteenth centuries in part because many of Connecticut's laws seemed to hold children responsible for sexual activity. Though some cases in the earlier period did reveal that citizens recognized that certain types of contact between adults and children were inappropriate, aside from the crime of rape not until the nineteenth century did the regulation of sexual relationships between adults and minors appear in the state's statutes. The paucity of cases may also have reflected problems with the reliability of the testimony of children, especially of those under fourteen, the so-called doubtful period, or under seven, the age of discretion. While Connecticut's legal system accepted minors as witnesses and set no precise age at which courts should allow them to testify, there was an ongoing debate concerning the quality of their evidence. Cases existed in which court officers found children as young as eight competent to testify, but the general rule was that each case depended on "the discretion and capacity of the infant" and whether the child understood the nature of an oath and the necessity of speaking the truth.[1] A further problem that may have limited prosecutions for sexual abuse could have been the reluctance of parents to bring notoriety upon their families.

Unsurprisingly, the pattern of prosecution under laws that sought to protect children from sexual abuse followed the pattern of many of Connecticut's other laws directed at social control, with more vigorous prosecutions against parents and people on the margins of society. This could have been what Cornelia Hughes Dayton has identified in the eighteenth century as a feature of a system that insulated the middling sort from public scrutiny of their private actions. It could equally have resulted from the fact that poor people and people of color would have been less familiar with the legal culture and thus less able to negotiate within the courts, resulting in a higher proportion of guilty verdicts and imposition of more rigorous sentences against them.[2]

Connecticut's earliest legal code addressed the issue of inappropriate sexual acts in several of its laws but made no mention of age. The death penalty for adultery, sodomy, and bestiality initially applied equally against any man, woman, or person. The code also directed that fornication was a crime that applied equally to both participants, directing "that if any man shall commit fornication, with any single woman, they shall be punished, either by enjoining to marriage, or fine, or corporal punishment . . . most agreeable to the word of God." Since other laws, such as the law against lying, had provided separate, more lenient treatment for those under the age of discretion, the law code appeared to make it clear that no such exemption applied to children who committed sexual transgressions. Furthermore, the 1650 statute against lascivious carriage, a vague term applied to "several other ways of uncleanness," which included "wanton dalliances," "self pollution," "foul misdemeanors," and "inveigling the affections" of someone's maid, did not differentiate between adults and minors. This law directed that since "evils of this kind (were) pernicious and destructive" to society, the court could use its discretion in stamping out the offense, allowing "sharp and severe" punishments against any offenders, again without exempting those under twenty-one. In 1702, a restatement of the law directed that the County Courts had the leeway either to fine those who committed acts of lascivious carriage, to sentence them to a term in the house of correction, or to order corporal punishment so that "others may see and fear." Perhaps because of that need to regulate public conduct, in few of the early prosecutions of crimes of sexuality or of lascivious carriage did Connecticut authorities assume adults had victimized minors. Nevertheless, by the late eighteenth century, the state rarely prosecuted cases under the charge of lascivious carriage, perhaps sharing Zephaniah Swift's recognition that sexual activity "was hard to restrain by the fear of the penal laws."[3]

In addition to the reluctance to view children as essentially different from adults in the area of sexuality, the problem of the competence of children as witnesses was an ongoing problem for Connecticut's courts and juries when considering questions of sexual abuse of minors. The common law considered the victim of rape as a competent witness, but according to Zephaniah Swift "her credibility must be judged." Swift also asserted that when a victim of a rape was under the age of twelve years old, her testimony could be admissible if she had "sufficient understanding to be a witness."[4] The problem of the credibility of minor witnesses complicated prosecutions for sexual abuse of children even after Connecticut society recognized such abuse as a crime. By the nineteenth century those accused of sexual assault or sexual abuse of girls often claimed the girls had no understanding of the nature of an oath or that other adults had unduly influenced their testimony. As a result, questions about the reliability of a child's evidence eventually contributed to a law that reduced the length of the prison sentence for those convicted of the rape of a child under the age of ten.

Nevertheless, despite questions on both the responsibility and credibility of minors, early Connecticut courts could act to protect minors against sexual abuse. In a 1677 prosecution for abuse and sodomy, the colony charged Nicholas Sension of Windsor with several counts of sodomy against his own apprentices, especially in his acts against Nathaniel Pond. Eyewitness testimony declared that Sension would climb into bed with the boy and "hug and feel" of the lad. Another of Sension's apprentices, Daniel Sexton, testified that Sension had come to his bed but that he had "fought him off." Despite the fact that sodomy was a capital crime in the colony, the court merely took a bond of 200 pounds from Sension to guarantee his good behavior. Since the crime against sodomy explicitly said that "if any man lyeth with mankind as he lyeth with woman, they both shall surely put to death," the fact that Sension only touched the lad inappropriately may have saved him from the death penalty. Nevertheless, it was somewhat surprising that the sexual abuse did not result in the release of the apprentices from their contracts.[5]

A notable case in 1736 revealed that Connecticut's residents may have begun to have a differing standard for adults and children accused of lascivious carriage. While numerous earlier cases of lascivious carriage brought criminal charges against both participants in the act, the case of *Rex v. David Deming* of Lyme prosecuted Deming for "lascivious carriage against" Elizabeth Greenfield for "exposing her most private parts." The colony brought no separate charge of lascivious carriage against the girl. What made the case notable was that Deming was a Harvard-educated minister, owner of an extensive property and home in Lyme, and Elizabeth was the twelve-year-old daughter of one of Lyme's poorer residents, mariner Archabald Greenfield. The confrontation began in May of 1734 when Deming was acting as Lyme's schoolmaster. According to her later testimony, Susannah Loveland, who worked for William Borden in his house located just rods from the schoolhouse, had heard that Deming's behavior toward some of the children was "unsuitable," especially toward young Elizabeth Greenfield. When Loveland saw Deming dismiss the children for the day and then call Elizabeth back into the schoolhouse, she rushed over to the building and peered through a hole in the side of the school. She reported that she saw Elizabeth standing on a table, her clothes raised. Deming had his hand on the girl's "privities" and, according to Loveland, was attempting to enter the girl's body with a finger. Loveland rushed back to Borden's house and asked him to come with her to the schoolhouse as a second witness. When Borden looked in the schoolroom, he saw Elizabeth still standing on the table with Deming stroking her leg as high as the knee. Borden went in and questioned Deming why he was touching the child. The teacher replied that the girl had a black spot above her knee and was lame so he was checking for broken bones. As Borden left, Deming followed him, asking for a rag to tie up the girl's leg. Susannah Loveland challenged his explanation that the child was lame and said, "You know what you have been doing with that child." Loveland then asked Elizabeth what had happened, telling her that Deming had said she was lame. Elizabeth responded that she had been but was now fine. In her testimony Loveland claimed she saw the child playing later that same day, running with no sign of lameness.[6]

Although neither Borden nor Loveland filed a complaint charging Deming with a crime, two days later Deming came to Borden with a changed story, asking to speak to Borden and Loveland in private. He had a new explanation for his questionable conduct. The girl, Deming claimed, was afflicted with worms, and he had been stroking her belly to break the "knot" of the worms to get them to fall out. This new version did not satisfy either Borden or Loveland, nor did it resolve the concerns of other Lyme parents. They withdrew their children from Deming's school. As Sarah Alger of Lyme later deposed, Deming came to her house to ask her forgiveness. Alger said her response was that Deming had not wronged her. Then Deming asked that she return her children to his school. She said she told him that she would not until she was "better satisfied about what he was accused of." She asked him what was behind the report circulating about his treatment of Elizabeth. Again Deming said he was treating the girl for worms. When Alger asked Elizabeth herself what had happened, the girl said Deming had had his hand on her private parts three times. Deming admitted that action, but said he had "done it for a good end." Deming also went to the home of Jabez and Sarah Watrous to explain his conduct and induce them to return their child to school. He added a new justification of his acts. When Elizabeth had stood in front of him to "say her book," he said he had felt her belly and had found it hard near her navel, a sign of worms, or so he asserted. When the other children left, he had held up Elizabeth's clothes and chafed her belly to move the worms. Deming's explanations did not satisfy either woman because they refused to send their children back to school while he was still the teacher.[7]

Despite the fact that the mothers in Lyme had taken immediate action by withdrawing their children from school, not until six months later did the legal system react to the allegations of Deming's improper behavior. On November 11, 1734 Zachariah Marvin, a grandjuryman of Lyme, brought a formal complaint in the name of the king of England against Deming for his lascivious carriage against Elizabeth Greenfield. He cited the testimony of the Bordens, Sarah Alger, Sarah Waterhouse, and Susannah Loveland to support his charges. In response, Justice of the Peace Thomas Lee of Lyme issued a warrant against Deming and ordered him into court. Deming appeared in January of 1735 but pleaded not guilty to the charges. He added that in his opinion the charges should be quashed and set aside because they did not "sufficiently set forth a crime against him." Lee denied that request and bound Deming over for trial at the New London County Court, setting a bond for appearance at fifty pounds.[8]

Though courts usually heard most cases in this period in a timely manner, the New London County Court trial of the charges against Deming did not come to trial until June of 1736, more than two years after the alleged incident. This might have been because Deming, a minister with a Master of Arts from Harvard, was a leader in the New London County community. After graduating from Harvard and serving briefly as a minister near Middletown, Connecticut, he had been the settled minister of Medway, Massachusetts from 1715 until 1722. After relocating to Lyme in 1722, he had often filled in at the pulpit of the Lyme Congregational Church, had served as the visiting minister at other area towns, had held several positions of responsibility in Lyme, and had even been a candidate for the permanent position as minister in the new town of Salem, Connecticut in 1728. Against the eyewitness testimony of Loveland and Borden, at the trial Deming counterpoised the deposition of Elizabeth Greenfield herself. Elizabeth, who by the time of the trial was living with Charles and Elizabeth Hamlin in Middletown, Connecticut, asserted that Susannah Loveland's testimony was false, especially "with respect to Mr. Deming applying his hand to my private parts and with his finger to make an entrance into my body." The Hamlins signed Elizabeth's deposition, saying she had made it in their presence and signed it by her mark and that she had declared that it was a false report about Mr. Deming. Faced with contradictory evidence, the members of the grand jury at the New London County Court found Deming innocent of the charges; one went so far as to write on the back of Elizabeth's deposition, "A flat denial of the facts of the case." Another wrote "insufficient to prosecute." So little notice did the men take of the case that Joshua Hempsted, one of the justices presiding over the case and an inveterate diarist, did not even mention the case in his summary of the Court's activity for June 8th, 1736.[9]

The male-dominated legal culture of New London County had dismissed the case because the evidence did not stand up to scrutiny. The residents of Lyme did not accept this ruling, revealing they had a different standard of proof. Six months before the actual trial the members of the Lyme Congregational Church had voted to suspend David Deming from communion. Following the not-guilty verdict from the New London County Court, the members did not reinstate Deming. Instead, in January of 1737, the Church meeting appointed a three-man committee to call on Deming "in the name of the Church to persuade and urge him to offer some reflections upon himself for his conduct respecting Elizabeth Greenfield." The members even prescribed the form that such a reflection should take, requiring that he admit he had "been guilty of some misconduct toward Elizabeth Greenfield which has been very grievous to my good brethren of this and some other churches." The apology, that he was to give in public in front of the congregation, was to include a request for "the charity of you all as well as of all other churches and also (to) ask your prayers that I might, in whatever state or employment I engage, be more careful to adore the doctrine of God our Saviour by a good and unspotted life and conversation." Because in Connecticut those who had owned the covenant could vote on church matters, this demand for repentance issued by the Church meeting reflected the opinions of the women members as well as the men.[10]

Being ostracized by his neighbors for his inappropriate behavior finally had an effect on Deming, though it took him six more months to capitulate.

The Lyme Congregational Church members took the problem up again in March of 1737 and resolved that if Deming continued to refuse to issue the required confession, they would ask their pastor to give Deming a letter of admonition. Eventually, on July 10th, 1737, Deming gave in. In front of the congregation he read a confession of "his misconduct with Elizabeth Greenfield." The members accepted the confession and voted to restore Deming to full communion.[11] Though the Church restored Deming to membership, town and church records indicate that Deming never again preached for the Lyme church, never again taught in the school, and never again held a position of responsibility in the town commensurate with his educational background and economic standing. Public opinion continued to condemn him for his admitted sexual abuse of a twelve-year-old girl.

PROTECTION AGAINST RAPE

Though few other cases in the eighteenth century exposed community attitudes concerning the sexual abuse of minors as clearly as the Deming case did, cases that involved rape and incest against minor females did reveal that Connecticut society provided a measure of protection for minor females. The seventeenth-century law against rape was a blanket condemnation: "if any man shall forcibly, and without consent, ravish any maid, or woman that is lawfully married or contracted, he shall be put to death." *The Code of 1650* cited Deuteronomy 22:25 as the source of this prohibition. Nevertheless, perhaps because of the problem of determining the competency of witnesses, there were few reported cases of rape in the New London County Court in the seventeenth century, and none clearly involved sexual assaults against minors.[12]

In a revision of Connecticut's laws in 1702, the General Assembly altered the prohibition against rape to apply to all women, not only to maids (virgins) or those who were already married or contracted, thus apparently extending the protection of the law to widows as well. The statute still did not include a specific protection for girls under the age of discretion; they apparently came under the category of maids. Shortly thereafter, the county tried Thomas Hall of Norwich for the abuse of his wife's daughter Hannah Rood. Authorities may have had trouble categorizing the crime because one file referred to the case as one of incest, while another treated the case as one of support for the bastard child who resulted from the assault. Surprisingly, the resolution was neither the death sentence for Hall for rape nor the public humiliation mandated for incest, but instead the requirement that he provide sufficient security for the maintenance of Hannah's baby.[13]

Though the charges were clear in the 1756 rape prosecution of Bristoe, a slave for life owned by George Beckwith of Lyme, the question of the victim's competence as a witness affected the outcome. The indictment charged Bristoe with the forcible rape of Hannah Beebe, Jr. of Lyme. The files at first identified Hannah as a maid or single woman. Initially the New London County Court found Bristoe guilty as charged and sentenced him to death. On appeal, the judge overturned the conviction, noting that the "girl" had committed perjury. As noted earlier, at common law the victim of a rape was a competent witness, but authorities had the right to assess her "credibility." By overturning the original conviction, the judge certainly was questioning the victim's competence as a witness. Though Bristoe did not hang as a result of the girl's prevarication, he still had to pay court costs for his own prosecution.[14]

While few prosecutions for the rape of minors took place in eighteenth-century New London County, a law allowing recourse for parents of "debauched" girls indicated that Connecticut society recognized that girls could be the victim of a sexual act without actually being the victim of forcible rape. An individual who defiled a girl under the age of twenty-one and got her pregnant did not merely have to pay child support for the resulting bastard. The parents of the girl had the right under Connecticut's civil law to sue the man for a trespass against their daughter. The damages resulted not only from the cost of caring for the girl while she was pregnant, but also for the loss of her services to the family while pregnant and lying in. Though few such lawsuits came to trial, the law served as a possible deterrent to potential seducers and may have indicated recognition of the need to protect girls from the wiles of silver-tongued Romeos.[15]

The nineteenth century brought a rise both in the numbers of prosecutions for rape of underage females and in the concern over the competence of underage witnesses. Deming Latimer of Lyme, just fourteen when officials charged him with the attempted rape of Mary Warner in 1808, did not raise the issue of a minor female's competence as a witness at his original trial despite the fact that the file identified Mary as under the age of eight. Notably, nothing in the Superior Court record identified the youth as a minor himself; only on the face of the indictment did the magistrate note that he had appointed Mr. Goddard as guardian to the boy for the legal process. Though Deming pleaded not guilty, the Court found him guilty based on the young girl's testimony and sentenced him to a seven-year term at Newgate Prison. The fact that the jury assigned a sentence of seven years rather than the maximum sentence of life in prison for an attempted rape may have reflected the Court's concern over the reliability of Mary's testimony. Apparently the issue of the competence of the girl as a witness became a factor three years later when Deming petitioned the General Assembly for an early release from prison. As did other minors, he noted his own youth in the petition, but he also referred to the "peculiar circumstances under which he was convicted." This may have been a reference to the questionable veracity of the girl's testimony. The General Assembly record did not include a record of any discussion of this petition, making it impossible to determine what swayed the legislators, but they did vote to release the teen from prison.[16]

In 1813 the state apparently considered ten-year-old Polly Brown of New London a competent witness in the trial of Araunah Randall of New London on charges that he had attempted to rape her. The charges also included the accusation that Randall had cruelly wounded and injured Polly while trying to rape her though no other witnesses attested to the actual assault. Randall pleaded not guilty to the charges but did not challenge the reliability of evidence provided by the ten-year-old. The jury found Randall guilty and sentenced him to seven years in Newgate. The length of the sentence again reflected the discretion granted to the Superior Court and may have revealed the jury's reluctance to send a man to prison for life on the testimony of a ten-year-old girl.[17]

No such reluctance marked the ruling of the Superior Court in 1815 when it imposed a life sentence on Edward Green, a transient black man, for the attempted rape of fifteen-year-old Sally Wright of Norwich. Though the attempted assault took place on the public highway where Green threw Sally to the ground with great violence in his attempt to commit the rape, the court did not provide any witnesses to the assault other than the victim herself. Nevertheless, the fact that Sally was, at fifteen, over the age of discretion may have given the jurors confidence in her version of the story. However, the fact that Green was a transient black man may have been equally responsible for his receiving the maximum term allowed for attempted rape.[18]

In 1821 a change in the Connecticut statute imposing the punishment for rape and attempted rape probably reflected the concern lawmakers had with sentencing a man to death or even life in prison on the uncorroborated testimony of a young girl. Although as Zephaniah Swift had pointed out thirty years earlier, sexual concourse with a female under ten was rape under the common law, hereafter the state differentiated between the rape of a girl under age ten and the rape of other females, thus codifying the common law crime cited by Swift. The death sentence remained in force for those who committed rape of any female who was ten or older, but the new law directed that anyone who "shall carnally know and abuse any female child under 10 years" was to be sentenced to life in Newgate Prison "or for such other term as the court shall determine." The same revision of the criminal laws also gave jurors discretion in sentencing those convicted of attempted rape. Though the new law did not create a different level of sentencing for attempted rapes of girls under ten, it did provide broad choice in the sentencing guidelines. Courts could sentence those convicted of attempted rape to life or to any other term thought suitable. Such broad powers could accommodate wide differences in circumstances and evidence, especially when conviction depended on the testimony of a young girl.[19]

Even with this new option for a reduced sentence, an 1824 case seemed to bear out the reluctance of juries to convict a man of rape or attempted rape on the uncorroborated testimony of a young female. The initial charge, issued in April of 1824, accused Thomas Freeman, a black man from Montville, of sexual assault and asserted that he "wickedly, unlawfully, and feloniously carnally" knew Hannah Fargo, a four-year-old girl. The state also claimed that Thomas had beaten and wounded the girl. Though Thomas was himself a minor, the New London County Court did not take notice that he was under age twenty-one and ordered him held over twenty-four weeks for trial at the Superior Court, probably because he was unable to post a surety bond for his appearance at the trial. Not until the Superior Court heard the case was did it assign Isiah Isham as guardian to defend the youth. The jury heard the evidence against Thomas, who pleaded not guilty. Despite the inclusion of the separate charge of physical assault that the child's parents could have corroborated, the Superior Court dropped all charges in the case, freeing Thomas. Even though the file did not contain depositions from either the victim or her family that might have revealed the quality of the child's testimony, it seems clear that the jury dismissed the evidence, since rape prosecutions against men of color more often resulted in convictions.[20]

The presumed competency of a minor victim who was over the age of ten was probably a factor in the conviction of another black youth charged with attempted rape in 1828. In this situation, the justice of the peace hearing the charges immediately identified Albert Brown of Colchester as under the age of twenty-one and assigned a Mr. Brown as his guardian. The justice then found sufficient cause to hold Albert for the attempted rape of fourteen-year-old Lucinda Kellogg, also of Colchester. At the Superior Court trial, the judge replaced Brown and assigned E. A. Bulkely as guardian to defend the black youth but rejected his plea of not guilty. Though Lucinda was the only witness against Albert, the judge sentenced him to five years at the new Connecticut State Prison at Wethersfield.[21]

That the state would protect black girls from sexual assault as well as white girls was apparent just a year later, in 1829. A black adult male attempted to commit a rape, this time against a thirteen-year-old black girl, but surprisingly the case files did not identify the race of either the accused or the victim. The sentence for the crime was identical to the sentence assigned to Albert Brown for his attempt on Lucinda. The State's Attorney charged that Simon Whip of Lyme seized, beat, and wounded Mary Ann Olney of Lyme, endangering her life in an attempt to rape her. Whip, who was so destitute that the state had to provide him suitable clothing for his court appearance, pleaded not guilty at the justice court, but the justice of the peace jailed him for failure to provide sureties for his appearance at the Superior Court. Again at the Superior Court Whip pleaded not guilty. Nevertheless, based on the evidence of the thirteen-year-old, the jury convicted Whip and sentenced him to five years at the State Prison.[22]

A further change in the laws against rape and attempted rape in 1830 may have been another attempt to resolve the struggle jurors had had in accepting the testimony of girls under the age of ten, especially when determining the length of a prison sentence. The new law set a mandatory life sentence for rape of any female over the age of ten, a reduction from the prior death sentence, but reduced the potential penalty for the rape of a child under ten to a sentence of seven to ten years, thus removing the potential of a life sentence. The new law also changed the term for an attempted rape to a sentence of three to ten years, no matter what the age of the victim. The legislators may have hoped that the greater leniency and discretion provided to the judge when he sentenced men convicted of the rape of very young girls would keep jurors from discounting the testimony of those under the age of discretion.[23]

Ironically, a case decided just prior to the passage of the new law may have been a harbinger of the change. In January of 1830 the State of Connecticut accused twenty-two-year-old Erastus Clark of Lyme of an assault with the intent to commit a rape on nine-year-old Mercy Shipman, daughter of Elisha Shipman of Lyme. Clark pleaded not guilty to the charge, but the jury found him guilty. Yet, perhaps indicating misgivings over the veracity or reliability of the child's testimony, the judge sentenced Clark to only one year at the State Prison plus a fine of $300 though he could still have sentenced him to a life sentence under the existing statute. Fifteen months later, in 1831, Ashel Clark, father of Erastus, petitioned the Connecticut General Assembly to release his son from prison. His petition asserted that when the State's Attorney had tried his son for the attempted rape the young man had still been living at home with him and that neither of them had money for a defense. He also claimed that not only had the neighbors of the

Shipmans doubted Mercy's evidence, but that even her own father had not believed her. The elder Clark complained that his son had served the twelve months of his term but was still in prison because he had no money to pay the fine. His plea to the General Assembly was that it must either cancel the fine or allow Erastus Clark to sign a note for the amount, guaranteed by his father. The Assembly voted to release the young man as soon as he signed a note for the fine and court costs, but since the committee members did not comment on the father's challenge to Mercy's testimony, their reasons for allowing the release were not clear.[24]

A second case in 1830 revealed the continued concern over the reliability of the testimony of minor females in cases of rape, in this case despite the fact that the assailant was African-American. The state charged Mystic native Thomas Wesley with the rape of thirteen-year-old Lydia Saunders of Lyme. At the initial indictment at the justice court in Lyme, the justice of the peace identified Thomas as a "person of color" and ordered him held in jail pending a trial at the Superior Court, but he did not identify the accused as under age, though Thomas was just twenty years old. Not until the Superior Court trial did the judge appoint Mr. Isham as guardian to represent the youth, who by that time had spent 37 weeks in jail awaiting trial. The first time the Superior Court heard the evidence, it convicted Thomas of rape and sentenced him to be hanged. In response, Isham made a motion for a new trial, which the judge denied. Nevertheless, after a number of petitions seeking clemency for the youth reached the General Assembly, in May of 1830 the Assembly commuted the minor's death sentence to a sentence of life in prison. Then, in September of 1830 the Superior Court seemed to reverse itself, granting a new trial for Thomas on the grounds that Lydia's "story was improbable and she might not recollect with accuracy." Despite this apparent concern over the reliability of the sole witness, the jury at the retrial again found Thomas guilty and reaffirmed his life sentence. While the commutation of the death sentence represented the hesitancy of members of the General Assembly to sentence a youth to death on the uncorroborated testimony of a girl, this confirmation of the youth's guilt on retrial "protected" the victim but may also have been racially motivated because Lydia was white while Thomas was black.[25]

Although his victim was under the prescribed age of ten, concerns over the believability of the girl's testimony did not result in a lesser sentence for the charge against Theophilus Fletcher. Here again race was probably the deciding factor in the severity of the 1831 sentence against Fletcher when the Superior Court convicted the thirty-six-year-old attempting to rape Almira Yeoman of Griswold, a girl under the age of ten. Identified as "a person of color," Fletcher, actually an Oneida Indian, pleaded not guilty to the charges of attempted rape and assault. The indictment asserted that Fletcher had done the child a real injury in his attempt to rape her. Despite the sentencing guidelines that directed a sentence of between two to seven years because the victim was under the age of ten, the jury found Fletcher guilty and imposed a sentence of eight years. Though the State's Attorney did not prosecute a separate charge of physical assault against the defendant, the harshness of the sentence probably reflected the jury's knowledge of the girl's injuries and the fact of his race. Ironically, Fletcher never served a day in prison, escaping from the sheriff who was delivering him to the State Prison to serve his sentence.[26]

An 1838 change in the statutes concerning rape reduced the potential punishment for attempted rape while retaining the lesser punishment for the rape of a girl under age ten. The change is puzzling because the sentence for the actual rape of a girl under the age of ten remained at seven to ten years in the state prison, but the punishment for assault with the intent to rape any female changed from a maximum of life to a determinate sentence of three to ten years in prison, a potentially equal sentence for a lesser crime. The concern over the veracity of a child's testimony on a rape did not seem to extend to her testimony over an attempted rape. A possible explanation for the inconsistency might be that a child who succeeded in fending off a sexual attack would have physical injuries to provide supporting proof of her allegations.[27]

Prior to the change in the law, the question of proof had also plagued the prosecutions of those who raped adult females. In 1835 the New London County Court tried Lester H. Maynard of Waterford on a charge of rape. Yet, surprisingly, after finding Maynard guilty of having "carnal knowledge of the body of Mahala Brook, wife of Hugh Brook, by force and arms," the court imposed a sentence of only two years, despite the fact that the maximum punishment for rape was still a life sentence. The reason for such leniency could be found in the prior case that had found Mahala herself guilty of bigamy for having consensual sex with Joshua Beckwith of Waterford. Protecting the morals of a convicted adulteress apparently didn't carry much weight with Connecticut jurors. As Zephaniah Swift had said, the credibility of the victim "must be judged."[28]

Despite, or perhaps as a result of the change in the law, those accused of rape or attempted rape of minor females continued to question the reliability of the testimony of young girls since none of the cases provided independent verification that a rape had actually occurred. In 1840 the New Haven County Court convicted John Bagshaw of attempting to rape Elizabeth Stanley, a girl under the age of eight. Sentenced to a four-year term,

Bagshaw sought early release from prison in 1842. Petitioning the General Assembly for clemency, he wrote that he had never had any other feelings for Emily than those of kindness and affection since she was living in his house as his adopted child. He claimed that the girl had not suffered any injury and that the only evidence offered against him at his trial had been Emily's testimony. He challenged the truth of that testimony saying that since the girl was under the age of eight she did not understand the nature of an oath. More to the point, he accused "persons unfriendly to him" of having directed the girl's statement so the "her mind was unfairly biased against him." Though the committee of the General Assembly could have accepted Bagshaw's challenge to Emily's testimony, especially since she was at seven under the age of discretion, the members reaffirmed the sentence and voted to keep him in prison for his full term.[29]

Others accused of the rape or attempted rape of girls under ten fared better. In 1846 New London resident John Morris faced a charge of raping seven-year-old Mary A. Durfee. Despite John's claim that he was innocent of the charge, at the justice court the justice of the peace found him guilty of rape and bound him over for trial at the Superior Court, then jailed him for his inability to provide surety. Not until the Superior Court trial did the judge identify John himself as a minor and assign H. Willey as his guardian and counsel. John again pleaded not guilty; the jury agreed and freed the youth, probably because of concerns about the reliability of the evidence from a girl of seven. In the same year the justice court at Stonington found Nathan Wilcox, Jr. guilty of the rape of five-year-old Harriet M. Davis, designated a "woman child" in the court documents, and set his bond at $1,000. When this case came before the Superior Court, the State's Attorney dropped the prosecution. In 1853 John Wood of Colchester faced charges that he assaulted and raped Mary Ann Sullivan, a four-year-old girl from Colchester. At the justice court hearing the only witness against the accused was young Mary Ann; John Wood pleaded not guilty, but the justice of the peace found probable cause to hold him for trial at the Superior Court, setting a bond of $2,000. Only at the Superior Court did the State identify John as a minor, assigning him Hiram Willey as guardian *ad litem*. John again pleaded not guilty to the charge of attempted rape; disagreeing with the findings of the justice of the peace, the jury agreed with his plea and brought in a verdict of not guilty.[30] In all of these cases juries and judges obviously were hesitant to send men to prison based on the uncorroborated testimony of young girls.

In contrast to the refusal to convict to Morris, Wilcox, and Wood on the testimony of very young girls, a number of prosecutions in the New London Superior Court for rape or attempted rape of girls over seven did result in convictions. This revealed that jurors would punish men who sexually assaulted girls when the girls' testimony was more reliable. In 1848 the state accused Henry Lawrence of Stonington, "a man of color," with both the attempted rape and the attempted murder of Stonington resident Ellen M. Holmes, "a female infant (a term still applied to those under the age of twenty-one) of the tender age of fifteen years." The jury dismissed the attempted murder charge but found Lawrence guilty of the attempted rape, sentencing him to ten years at the State Prison, the maximum allowable term. In 1849 the state charged Delino White of Thompson with attempted rape. The indictment claimed he "with a wicked, abandoned, and licentious mind wantonly and brutally" beat eight-year-old Phebe Whipple with the "intent to ravish and carnally know" the female child. Because the wounds from the beating were so serious that the girl's life was in danger, the physical evidence of the assault might have helped sway a jury's decision when faced with testimony from an eight-year-old. However, the fact that White pleaded guilty to the charge of attempted rape was far more likely the explanation of the jury's sentence of four years at the State Prison.[31]

Clearly in cases of rape, Connecticut juries were willing to sentence men for sexual assaults on children when they believed they could rely on the children's testimony. Nevertheless, as discussed in the analysis of crimes against public order, throughout the first half of the nineteenth century, convicts serving sentences for sexual assault or rape continued to challenge the veracity and believability of the testimony of their young victims.

SEDUCTION OF A MINOR: CONSENT TO SEXUAL ABUSE?

That the intent of the parties was critical to the criminal status of an individual was clear in 1847 with the passage of a new law prohibiting the seduction of minor females. Distinct from prosecutions for rape, which carried the implication of a man forcibly assaulting a girl or woman, the new statute made consensual sex with a female under the age of twenty-one a criminal act on the part of the male but apparently exempted the female from prosecution on charges of fornication or prostitution. The law directed punishment of up to a year in the county jail and a fine not to exceed $1,000 for "every person who shall seduce and commit fornication with any female under twenty-one or who shall entice and take away any such female" from her parent, guardian, or residence. The law may have set the age for the girls at twenty-one rather than at eighteen because under Connecticut civil law, girls under twenty-one still needed the consent of their parents to marry. They were also legally incapable of entering into contracts prior to reaching twenty-one. Perhaps recognizing the wiles of a seducer were more dangerous the second time around, legislators set the penalty for a second offense under the new law at a term of up to three years at the State Prison and a fine of up to $2,000. In addition, the law reflected the continuing interest of a girl's parent or guardian in her well being because it directed that the parent or guardian of the victim of seduction could bring a lawsuit for damages against the seducer for "loss of services or for such aggravation as may have attended the commission of the injury." This law clearly reflected the rise in the late eighteenth and nineteenth-century of middle-class morality that had carved out a separate sphere for New England women, viewing them as guardians of the morals of their families. Writing in 1797, Zephaniah Swift had raised the issue of protecting the virtue of middling (perhaps all) women. "Purity of manners," he wrote, "must depend upon principles instilled in the minds of youth by education." According to Swift, parents had an obligation "to impress on the minds of their female children these all-important truths: that chastity is the particular ornament of the sex." Apparently Connecticut residents did not find a legal way to protect the chastity of their daughters until the passage of the new law.[32]

The application of the new statute was apparent in a case just six months after its passage when a jury convicted an adult male of the crime of soliciting a minor to commit the act of fornication. According to the New London County Court records, James Guy of Norwich did "unlawfully, wrongfully, and maliciously solicit and entice" sixteen-year-old Emma Tillotson "to commit with him the act of fornication." This was not a rape charge; it was a charge of the seduction of a minor. The files indicated that Guy lured Emma "from the service of her parent to reside with him in habits of illicit intercourse." Guy even offered to set Emma up in New York City and provide for her as long as she lived "to induce her to live as a common prostitute." The specific charge against Guy at his original justice court hearing was that he "corrupted the morals and effected the ruin of Emma, a virgin." Though the jury found Guy guilty, because he defaulted before sentencing by fleeing the court's jurisdiction, the judge did not impose a specific sentence, making it difficult to determine how harshly juries and judges would apply the law. In contrast to the prostitution cases against minor females discussed in an earlier chapter, the justice of the peace did not charge Emma with any crime at all, though it seemed clear from the files that the girl had been living "as a common prostitute."[33]

In a similar case the following year, the State's Attorney brought charges of seducing a minor against Alonzo Frisby of Groton. According to four witnesses from the village of Noank, the accused, "wholly lost to all sense of decency and morality and intending to incite lewd, unchaste, and licentious desires" in Caroline Ashley, seduced the girl, "to her great disgrace." The witnesses testified that eighteen-year-old Caroline had been living in Groton with her parents but willingly joined with Frisby in the act of fornication. The charge did not allege Frisby had raped the girl. Though the Court found Frisby guilty of seducing a minor and sentenced him to serve three months in the common jail and imposed a $100 fine, it did not charge Caroline with any crime at all, reflecting the change from the eighteenth-century practice of holding minor females equally responsible for their sexual activity.[34]

The pattern of excusing minor females from the consequences of being sexually active continued. Again in 1848 an adult male enticed a girl away from her parents to commit fornication. Once again only the man faced prosecution for a crime. The justice court claimed that Frank Joseph of New London had enticed and taken away "an infant female child under the age of twenty-one years, to wit of the age of fifteen years," one Eliza Stanton, to induce her to commit fornication. As in the prior cases, the State's Attorney brought no criminal charges against the minor female even though the file asserted that the girl did commit fornication with Joseph. After posting surety to appear at the County Court, Joseph skipped town, forfeiting his bond, making it difficult to determine the severity of punishments juries would choose.[35]

Skipping bond to avoid the consequences of his actions also was the choice for another seducer of a minor. In 1850 at a hearing at a justice court Alexander Comstock of Norwich faced charges of enticing seventeen-year-old Mary Elizabeth Bradbury from her parents and her residence in Norwich for the purpose of fornication. The justice of the peace convicted Comstock for seducing the girl and committing fornication "to the great corruption of her morals" and bound him over to the Superior Court for trial and determination of punishment. Apparently unwilling to take a chance with justice at the Superior Court, Comstock defaulted, forfeited his $1,000 bond, and probably fled New London County. As in previous cases, neither the justice of the peace nor the Superior Court charged Mary Ann with any offense.[36] These cases all reflect a change in the standard implemented to protect underage females from sexual activity if not sexual abuse.

INCEST: ABUSE WITHIN THE BONDS OF FAMILY

Incest cases involved a distinct form of sexual abuse of children. What complicated the issue of incest was that colonial society both expected and directed that children obey their parents. The law against stubborn children directed that any children who were stubborn or rebellious against their parents faced a potential sentence of "hard labor and severe punishment" if the magistrates found them guilty. As a result, the question of what constituted proper obedience clouded the issue of coercion in cases of incest. Thus, most charges of incest in the early years of the colony did not allege that a father had actually raped his daughter. The punishment assigned for incest revealed that distinction. The law in the early eighteenth century did not mandate the death penalty for incest as it did for rape and adultery but instead imposed public humiliation. Any man or woman who married or had sexual relations with anyone within the prohibited degrees of relationship, which included children and grandchildren, had to sit on the gallows an hour, suffered a whipping of not more than forty stripes, and had to wear a capital letter I two inches high sewn on his or her outer garments, "for everafter." The law also sought to prevent incestuous marriages by listing the degree of relationships within which a man could not marry.[37]

A 1725 case of incest against nineteen-year-old Sarah Perkins of New Haven illustrated the difficulty Connecticut's colonial courts had in resolving such examples of the sexual abuse or exploitation of minors by their fathers. In March of 1725 the New Haven Superior Court found both Sarah and her father guilty of incest. Their punishment for incest seemed to presume the lack of force by the adult because rather than punishing her father for rape, the judge ordered both to sit on the gallows, suffer a whipping, and wear a letter I attached to their clothing. In May of the same year Sarah petitioned the General Assembly pleading for clemency, in effect claiming that she was not guilty of incest because, "she was unnaturally as it were, forced thereto by her father's sovereign authority." In her petition she noted that she had confessed her transgression and had shown great sorrow and repentance. Assembly members voted to release Sarah from her punishment because it was clear to the Assembly that she "was grossly ignorant not only of the heinous nature of the crime laid to her charge, but also of the paternal authority of her said father over her." The Assembly appeared to recognize that Sarah lacked the understanding of exactly what she owed her father under the guise of obedience and when she had the right to disobey his commands.[38]

Although the law against incest remained in force, prosecutions for incest were rare, probably reflecting the reluctance of daughters to accuse their fathers of sexually inappropriate behavior and the reluctance of families to expose their problems to the rest of the community, a conspiracy of silence that surrounded incest. Not until the nineteenth century did the New London County courts have to deal with such charges concerning minor children. In April of 1812 New London Justice of the Peace William P. Cleaveland charged that fellow New Londoner Daniel Hull had committed incest with his nineteen-year-old daughter Esther. Cleaveland's indictment said that Hull had "conducted himself in a most lascivious and carnal manner" with Esther and had been found in bed with her. Unlike in rape prosecutions, Cleaveland heard a number of witnesses who testified to the consensual nature of the sexual activity between father and daughter. Though the justice carefully noted the names of the witnesses, he did not include the age of Hull's daughter, making it appear that age was not relevant to the charges. Because Hull could not provide bond for his appearance at the New London County Court trial, Cleaveland jailed him until the September hearing. At the Superior Court for New London County, in *State v. Daniel Hull,* the State's Attorney alleged that the incest had gone on for over eighteen months, during which time Hull had often gotten into bed with his own daughter and had carnal knowledge of her. Clearly, with eyewitnesses testifying to the sexual activity, young Esther had had the opportunity to cry out against her father but apparently had not. Because Hull's wife, who was also named Esther, was still living, the court also claimed that he was guilty of adultery as well but did not prosecute the charge separately. Though Hull pleaded not guilty, the jury convicted him and sentenced him to sit for one hour on the gallows with a rope around his neck, to be whipped twenty-five stripes, and to wear the letter I on his outer garments in open view. He also had to wear the rope around his neck so long as he lived in the state. In addition Hull had to pay $77.04 to the state for the cost of his own prosecution. This case differed from the Perkins case in that the state did not charge Esther Hull with the crime of incest even though there was apparently no testimony that Hull had abused his parental authority over the girl to convince her to comply with his wishes.[39]

In contrast in 1813 the state initially charged Ezekial Ball of Woodbridge with incest but eventually convicted him of attempted rape of his daughter, "then of tender years." Conviction on the more severe charge must have reflected the age of the girl and the non-consensual nature of the crime. Sentenced to life in prison, Ball petitioned the Connecticut General Assembly for release from prison in 1825, but notably did not assert his innocence of the original charges. The committee reviewing the petition took note of the fact that Ball had attempted carnal knowledge of one of his own daughters, an eight or ten-year-old. Though Ball had forty-seven New Haven residents submit two separate petitions in support of his effort to gain release from prison, the committee rejected the plea for clemency, saying the "enormity and brutal nature of the offense" did not justify releasing Ball.

The decision almost certainly reflected the influence of a counter petition submitted by Ball's former wife and children who wrote that he was a "monster and hard-hearted wretch" who had blamed his wife and father-in-law for his conviction and who had threatened the life of his mother-in-law. They also pleaded that the committee could not know "the feelings of an afflicted child" or the time spent in mourning over the inhuman deed of such a wretch. The language of this opposing petition revealed the divisive nature of the act of incest on a family. Despite the initial rejection of Ball's plea for release, in 1829 the General Assembly did vote to release him from prison after he had served sixteen years for his crime.[40]

In a number of cases in the 1830s, the state continued to treat incest with younger girls as similar to rape. In these cases the original charges usually included an accusation of incest, but the prosecution and sentencing were actually for the crime of rape or attempted rape. In 1835 the state accused Joseph Slate of incest and the rape of his seven-year-old daughter Angelina, asserting he had carnally known his own daughter. The girl appeared as the only witness in the case. Though Slate claimed he was innocent, he did not challenge the admissibility of his daughter's testimony. The jury found him guilty, but sentenced him to only four years in prison. Since sentencing guidelines for the rape of a child under ten dictated a term of seven to ten years, the lesser sentence may have reflected the jury's concern with the accuracy of testimony from a child under the age of discretion.[41]

In a case from 1836, the state accused Archibald Hall of New London with four counts of incest and the rape of his eleven-year-old stepdaughter Amelia Goodwin. The question of consent by the child was not an issue since the state also alleged that Hall had assaulted and beaten the girl with the intent to ravish her. As with the prosecution of Slate, the charge of incest appeared largely irrelevant; the jury convicted Hall of rape and sentenced him to six years at the State Prison, apparently giving full weight to the testimony of the eleven-year-old.[42]

In contrast, the question of the reliability of a young girl's testimony eventually resulted in the reversal of the 1837 attempted rape conviction of Fairfield resident Beal Bunnell. At the Fairfield County Court in Danbury, a jury found Bunnell guilty of the assault and attempted rape of his two daughters, twelve-year-old Harriet and eight-year-old Elizabeth. Because he supposedly sexually abused both girls, the jury sentenced him to two consecutive eight-year terms at the State Prison. At the trial, in his defense Bunnell did not raise the issue of the reliability of the children's evidence. Nevertheless, in 1840 sixty Fairfield residents signed a petition to the Connecticut General Assembly requesting it release Bunnell because

Bunnell's wife had poisoned the girls' minds against him and suborned their testimony. According to the petitioners, Bunnell's wife Anna hated him and wanted to get rid of him. The girls, asserted the petitioners, were both illiterate and were liable to be led by their "wicked and corrupt" mother; they had been the only witnesses against their father at his trial. Anna had supposedly "instilled a feeling of inveterate hatred" against Bunnell in the girls. Furthermore, claimed Bunnell's supporters, Anna's own character for veracity was bad. The General Assembly voted to release Bunnell, apparently accepting the petition's claims concerning the unreliability of the young children as witnesses.[43]

In contrast to the favorable outcome for Beal Bunnell's appeal, when George Paine of Newton used similar arguments to discredit the testimony of his eleven-year-old daughter Emeline, the General Assembly refused to shorten his sentence. Paine, convicted of incest and rape against Emeline in 1850, had received a sentence of twenty-two years in prison. In 1853 Paine himself asked the Assembly for release from his sentence, calling the evidence used to convict him "slight and negligible." He asserted that Emeline had been the only witness against him and her testimony was not corroborated. Furthermore, he claimed his daughter was very illiterate and was "entirely under the pernicious influence of her mother who had rendered his life wretched and unhappy." To emphasize the malignant influence of his wife, he claimed she had had two illegitimate children during the three years he had been in prison. The Assembly refused to consider the petition. A year later a number of Newtown citizens submitted their own petitions asking the General Assembly to release Paine. Harry Platt wrote that the girl's grandmother was hostile to Paine. Aaron Sanford wrote that Paine had become a drunkard because of difficulties with his wife and her family and that the girl's grandmother, Sally Crofeet, had influenced her testimony. William Beard claimed that "because of the age of the girl and all the circumstances of the case" Paine had suffered all the punishment he ought to have. This may have been a reference to his perception that the girl's testimony was unreliable because she was under the influence of a hostile parent. According to William Platt, public opinion held that the grandmother had wrongly influenced the child. William Andruss said that he knew Emeline Paine and that her testimony was false because "she was apt to tell wrong stories." Paine reissued his own petition, saying this time that his wife and mother-in-law had incited Emeline to accuse him of the incest. However, Paine may have undercut his own appeal by adding: "if he was guilty he had no remembrance because he was under the influence of intoxicating drink taken to drown his troubles." Even with that proviso, he asserted that he had been entirely lacking in the necessary intent to commit the "horrible crime." Despite the number of people who challenged the value of testimony by an eleven-year-old, the General Assembly again refused to release Paine from his sentence.[44]

Rarely in the nineteenth century did the state convict a minor child of participating in the crime of incest, but the language used in a case in 1848 alleging a daughter willingly had sexual relations with her father revealed broad condemnation of such behavior. Unlike the incest case in the eighteenth century when Sarah Perkins had pleaded coercion on the part of her father, the arrest warrant for Mary Maynard of Waterford alleged she was "a most corrupt, licentious, and abandoned person" when she had carnal knowledge of her father David Maynard. The justice court writ identified Mary as a minor, the legitimate daughter of David, and named Charles Daniels of Waterford to serve as her guardian for the trial. Unable to post bond after the justice court found her guilty, Mary remained in jail until the Superior Court trial. At that trial the state assigned Hiram Willey, Esq. to serve as the girl's guardian *ad litem*. Though Willey entered a not-guilty plea for her, he made no claim that the father had forced the girl into committing the crime. Calling the girl "wholly lost to all sense of decency, morality, and virtue," the jury found her guilty and sentenced her to a two-year sentence to be served at the New London County jail. In comparison, when the jury found her father guilty, they sent him to the State Prison at Wethersfield for a term of five years. The reason for the difference in the length of the sentence was not clear, but jurors may have assumed Maynard's culpability was greater than his daughter's because he was in a position of power over her.[45]

The relative paucity of cases involving the sexual abuse of children, especially in the case of incest, may have reflected a public unwillingness to air the "dirty laundry" of the sexual exploitation of children. Nevertheless, those cases that appeared on the record did reveal that, as in other areas of the criminal law, the courts and juries had to struggle with issues of the reliability of underage testimony while still trying to protect under-age victims of sexual assault. The law prohibiting the seduction of minors provided the clearest signal, however, that the legal system had established a different expectation for women under twenty-one, at least when they came from respectable homes.

Chapter Six

From Retribution to Rehabilitation: Children and the Criminal Law in the 19th Century

> The great man of public criminals becomes so through a regular process of education and an early course of tuition in a common jail is generally one of the most important elements of this education.
>
> —Dr. Charles Albany "Report to the Connecticut General Assembly," 1853

> It must be apparent to everyone that the common jail is not the place for boys.
>
> —*The Hartford Courant,* August 20, 1853

As can be seen in the various categories of criminal prosecution, in the several decades before the American Revolution, the criminal law in Connecticut revealed a gradual shift to the recognition that individuals under twenty-one needed different treatment than adults when they broke the law. A primary problem from the 1640s on had been determining the criminal responsibility of minors, initially based on the common law doctrine that malice could supply the want of age in deciding whether or not to hold a child responsible for his or her actions.[1] Thus a recognizably evil child, such as Jonathan Stoddard, was fully responsible for murdering his brother and his neighbors. Nevertheless, because Connecticut statutes mandated that minors could neither initiate nor defend lawsuits, nor serve in nearly any official capacity, officials had developed both civil and criminal procedures that served to provide a form of legal representation for children. Yet the initial focus of these procedural and substantive changes had not been on the legal rights of the children but on protecting the property of the adults responsible for minors facing legal charges because the adults were responsible for the financial liability for any fines or court fees the magistrate assessed against the child. Magistrates had to notify parents, guardians, or masters of any criminal charges against children in their care. Though such notification had first appeared early in the eighteenth century, failure to notify a responsible adult had not fatally impaired the state's case in many proceedings, as seen in the case of William Harris's lewd, lascivious, and naked dancing. In a number of such cases, minors went through indictment, trial, and sentencing without any apparent legal notice to responsible adults.

In many instances in the eighteenth century the children who did not obtain proper advice or notification of their right to some form of representation were often either members of poor families or were African American or Native American. As Nina Dayton asserts, this lack of legal protection could reflect a biased, racist society that sheltered minors from affluent families while exposing other children to the full force of the law.[2] The failure could equally be a result of poor or minority parents who lacked experience with the legal culture. They might not have known what protections Connecticut mandated for their children and thus did not challenge the legality of the outcome. A further explanation could lie in the immaturity of the legal system itself because many members of the bar and most of those who served as justices of the peace, as magistrates, or as jurors lacked adequate formal legal training. They, too, clearly did not always recognize that children required special treatment before the law.

One of the prime reasons for requiring notification of parents, guardians, or masters concerning pending legal action was that Connecticut law held the adults in charge of children responsible for any fines incurred by those children. As a result, the rather relaxed language of a typical summons to adults that, "they be notified to appear if they saw cause to assist and defend the accused," masked the reality that, upon the conviction of a minor, the responsible adult had to bear the financial consequences. In such a situation, most adults chose to appear to protect their own assets. As discussed in cases of breach of the peace, when Stonington Justice of the Peace Nathaniel Minor arrested nine teenagers in 1783 for breach of the peace, he specifically noted in the writ that any execution of damages or fines was to go forth not against the defendants, but against their parents, guardians, or masters, citing the relevant Connecticut statute to bolster his case. He carefully notified the fathers and the masters of the white youths. He also provided legal notice to the masters of the three black teenage defendants. What is not clear from the case record is whether or not the adults did appear to represent their children. All nine defendants pleaded guilty; Minor assessed a fine of three shillings and court costs for each. Someone paid for the white boys, but the fines and costs remained unpaid for the black youths. Obviously, whether or not the adults represented their children in court, Minor gave them legal notice of their fiscal responsibility, rather than depending on the minors for payment.[3]

The period after the American Revolution was notable for vast changes in American law. Between the 1780s and the 1850s Connecticut law regarding juvenile criminals underwent a fundamental transformation. First, attitudes toward the criminal responsibility of children began to deviate from the common law doctrine that malice could supply the want of age in determining whether or not to hold a child responsible for his or her actions. Adults began to believe instead that a lack of a moral upbringing and education rather than malice lay behind many criminal acts by children. Correspondingly, people started to question whether it was fair to punish children for factors beyond their control. In addition, the treatment of children, once convicted, eventually diverged from the punishments meted out to adult criminals. By the 1820s and 1830s both juries and the members of the Connecticut General Assembly were more open to the idea that youthful high jinks and thoughtless petty crimes should not land a child in prison. A major breakthrough came in 1843 when the state passed a discretionary sentencing law that provided the option of different sentencing guidelines for those under seventeen convicted of most categories of crimes. By 1853 the reforming impulse culminated in the creation of the State Reform School for Boys that separated juvenile criminals from the adult penal system and mandated the elimination of a child's criminal record upon successful completion of his sentence. The goal of the reform was to treat children who broke the law as patients in need of treatment rather than as criminals, children who could be rescued and educated to become upstanding citizens. The change was the result of an ongoing struggle to reconcile an increasing demand for the maintenance of law and order with a growing willingness to view children as essentially different than adults.

THE CONTEXT OF THE TRANSFORMATION

The changes in the treatment of children before the criminal law were products of a gradual alteration. Several factors propelled the transformation in the way in which the Connecticut legal system dealt with minors: changes in the criminal law, especially in sentencing, a shift in attitudes toward children themselves, and the rise of the middle-class ante bellum reform movements. An important factor was that the criminal law itself became more uniform. With the opening of the Connecticut state prison known as the Newgate

Prison in the former copper mine in Granby in the 1780s, fixed terms of imprisonment for crimes against public order and crimes against property replaced the former loose system of fines and corporal punishment that had existed throughout the colonial period. Under the colonial system, children who broke the law, except those in capital cases and those deemed incorrigible, had rarely faced long-term imprisonment. Adam Hirsch has even made a valid claim that throughout the colonial period imprisonment was part of a system to coerce payment of fines and relevant court costs rather than a form of punishment. Since both colonial and later state laws directed that parents and guardians had to pay the fines incurred by minors as punishment for the children breaking the law, adults were the ones who faced imprisonment for failure to pay. Those same parents and guardians were most often the people who imposed direct punishment on children convicted of criminal actions. Even when the statutes had set specific physical punishments of whipping or sitting in the stocks for certain crimes, changing attitudes toward physical punishment following the Enlightenment ideas of Cesare Beccaria on prison reform may have influenced Connecticut's phasing out of physical retribution and replacing it with fixed terms of imprisonment, set by state statutes. Beccaria's reforms reflected the belief that replacing physical punishment with imprisonment was both more rational and more humane. As early as 1764 Beccaria had advocated replacing punishment based on "gross and capricious terror" with more lenient but more predictable punishments such as prison sentences.[4] Though such a reform may have eased punishments for adults, for children in Connecticut the new system was far more onerous than what it replaced because it eliminated judicial discretion in the determination of the punishment.

The fact that minors could now face lengthy incarceration in the dreadful conditions of the old copper mine could have influenced the increasingly formal treatment of their rights to ensure some form of legal protection or representation. Zephaniah Swift writing in 1795 asserted that the laws of the state vested all Connecticut residents with equal rights, including the right to security and protection. Since youths, he said, were incapable of either prosecuting or defending against legal actions because of their age and inexperience, he advocated the extension of a special protection. Under his category of the guarantee of security and protection, he claimed parents owed to their children the duty of aiding and assisting them in all legal actions. Furthermore, Swift claimed that Connecticut practice by 1795 mandated that if a child had no parent, guardian, or master able or willing to assist in his or her defense, the state courts had to appoint a guardian to protect the child for the duration of the legal action. Failure by a magistrate or judge to appoint such a guardian would automatically result in the reversal of any judgment against the child, according to Swift.[5]

Despite Swift's formal assertion of such protections afforded to minors and despite the existence of an established group of lawyers who practiced in the county courts, it took considerable time before magistrates were consistent in providing that protection for all minors charged under the criminal laws of the state. Beginning in the early 1800s Connecticut courts did begin to offer more formal protection for minors under indictment for breaking the law. Rather than the prior rather cavalier notice to parents to "appear if they saw cause," magistrates initiated the practice of formally appointing temporary guardians, often choosing lawyers who practiced in the county, who would represent and protect the interests of the child during the trial, even if the child had parents who could assist him or her. These guardians *ad litem* stood to gain financially from their duties because fees for their services were usually part of the court costs assessed against the defendant. Yet despite an increasingly professional bar membership and the lure of additional income, the appointment of guardians *ad litem* was not apparent in every case involving children. Furthermore, when such protection was lacking, the courts did not automatically dismiss charges against children. As previously cited cases in the various categories of criminal prosecutions have made clear, poor children and children of color often did not receive the mandated legal representation. This may have been because of the reluctance of attorneys to take on cases that did not promise payment or the lack of experience such families had with the vagaries of the court system in Connecticut.

That the lack of attention to the legal rights afforded to minors was not entirely due to considerations of race or gender was clear in the assault case against Azariah Beebe, Jr. of Waterford. In 1804, "regardless of the filial duty of a son towards a father," Beebe struck his father with a club, knocking him to the ground. He then seized a large stone and beat his father, fracturing his skull and nearly killing him. The writ in the case, which originated at the justice court, did not identify Beebe as a minor. Beebe, without legal representation, admitted the facts of the case, and because he was unable to post bond for his appearance at the Superior Court, he went to jail. Charged with assault with the intent to kill his father (rather than under the stubborn-child law), Beebe again pleaded guilty at his Superior Court trial. The ourt sentenced him to a three-year term at Newgate Prison. Although the vital records of the town of Waterford reveal that Azariah was under the age of twenty-one both at the time of the crime and at his Superior Court trial, neither he nor the State's Attorney raised the issue of his underage status, nor did the youth file a later appeal to overturn his conviction.[6] His failure to pursue legal challenges to his conviction based on his age might have been because knowledge of the protections afforded to minors was not widespread or because his father did not wish to stay the punishment afforded by the law, even if it affected him financially.

Even as the state formally mandated that minors obtain proper legal protection or representation, the authorities still believed in holding children responsible if they broke the law. Nevertheless, the issue of criminal liability became more shaded by the end of the eighteenth century. Writing in 1795, Zephaniah Swift had summarized the official attitude toward the accountability of minors. He asserted that lawmakers believed children under the age of seven were incapable of criminal actions because of a child's immature understanding. Crime, according to Swift, required that a person commit an unlawful act in league with a vicious will; this, he claimed, was entirely lacking in those under the age of seven. In Swift's judgment, under Connecticut laws the presumption of criminal intent for children between the ages of seven and fourteen was also absent in many cases. Nevertheless, he labeled that age span the "doubtful period," writing that if a child between seven and fourteen "appears to have a mischievous disposition and to have conducted himself in such a manner as to show himself possessed of discretion, he may be considered guilty of a crime." This willingness to hold young children accountable may have been a remnant of the old Puritan belief in the innate evil in the heart of all people. This rule of responsibility depended not exclusively on the child's age but on his or her understanding of wrongdoing and the parallel capacity to understand the difference between good and evil. To illustrate his conclusions, Swift enumerated a number of cases of children under fourteen executed by the colony or state for capital crimes. Included in this group were a thirteen-year-old girl who murdered her mistress, a nine-year-old boy who killed his playmate, a ten-year-old boy who murdered a companion, and an eight-year-old boy who had burned two houses and a barn, showing "malice, cunning, and revenge." Swift himself recognized that an evil intent could overcome the assumed innocence of youth.[7] Yet in none of the cases cited did Swift deal with the issue of whether responsible adults had taught the children to discern the difference between good and evil, a question that actually drove the reform attempts in the next century.

That race and class or the paucity of a child's moral instruction could also influence the treatment of minors facing the criminal laws of Connecticut was sometimes apparent in the General Assembly's treatment of petitions for clemency or pardons. Though Hannah Occush's youth and ignorance had not saved her from execution, in the 1790s minors and the adults representing them began the practice of pleading their youth and inexperience to win reductions of their prison sentences at Newgate Prison.

EDUCATION AND THE ISSUE OF CRIMINAL RESPONSIBILITY

In the opening decades of the nineteenth century a greater number of petitions for clemency did cite the youth of the criminals as a reason to reduce their sentences, and many increasingly stressed the lack of educational opportunities for youth in prison, but the response of the Connecticut General Assembly was mixed. Some youthful felons remained incarcerated for their full terms; others did succeed in having their terms converted to periods of indentured service. Between 1810 and 1830 of twenty petitions by minors for clemency, only nine succeeded, though that was a higher success rate than petitions by adults for pardons or early release. Of those petitions that achieved success, many included a direct or veiled reference to the poor quality of the child's previous moral instruction or education. In the 1790s, petitions to the General Assembly for early release or commutation of minors' sentences of imprisonment most often were a simple plea for mercy, saying the child could not survive the hardships of incarceration. After 1810, such petitions increasingly stressed new issues. Some claimed that the child's lack of education and proper experiences had led him or her into the commission of the crime. Other youthful petitioners pleaded for mercy because while in prison they would have no way to gain an education and would thus be unable to play a useful role in society upon completion of their sentences. A few of the petitions attacked the very conditions of the prison environment itself, saying that Newgate was not "a seminary the best calculated for science or the sacred principles of morals and religion." This line of attack stressed the polluting influence of experienced criminals.[8]

Although the ultimate reform of the criminal was not one of the original goals of creating a state prison, new ideas about the importance of education, influenced by the writings of Locke, and later Rousseau and Pestalozzi, may have had an impact on Connecticut state legislators. Enlightened adults gradually came to view children as beings whose early experiences could, and should, have an impact on the kind of adults they would become. Since changes in sentences creating a mandate for incarceration at Newgate meant a greater possibility that children would go to prison if they broke the state's laws, in the 1790s Connecticut legislators had passed a law to provide a modicum of protection for minors. The statute directed the warden to classify all prisoners at the State Prison at Newgate by both age and criminal experience and to keep them separate to prevent the demoralizing and corrupting influence of hardened offenders on those who were yet young in crime. The palliative impulse had little impact because the prison was unable to enforce such segregation since no guards supervised the prisoners at night in the caverns of the former copper mine. Furthermore, with all the criminals congregated in a single chamber sixty feet below the ground, the result was there no way for children in the prison to avoid coming into contact with adult criminals.[9]

One enterprising prisoner attempted to exploit that shortcoming and obtain an early release from his prison sentence. In 1833 Wheeler Morgan, a career criminal at the State Prison at Wethersfield, petitioned the Connecticut General Assembly for an early release from his current sentence. Unlike many adults and children who utilized the language of reformation and redemption in their attempts to gain clemency from the Assembly, Morgan attacked the system of imprisonment itself. He blamed the state's inability or unwillingness to segregate young prisoners from old for his descent into a life of crime. He said that when he was first at Newgate in 1820, he was but twenty years old. There fellow prisoners who had committed every crime known to mankind corrupted him, subjecting him to the "midnight ramblings" of robbers, counterfeiters, forgers, swindlers, thieves, pick pockets, adulterers, fornicators, assassins, and drunkards. Morgan claimed his initiation into a life of crime was entirely the fault of the state for sending him to prison but failing to divide experienced criminals from the novices in crime. Boldly, Morgan claimed monetary damages for his first three-year term: a dollar for the first day in prison, doubled each day thereafter for all 1004 days of his original sentence. Rather than demanding the cash, Morgan said he would instead accept release from his current term of imprisonment for burglary. Notably, he expressed no remorse for his criminal actions. Though the General Assembly rejected Morgan's plea for clemency, it revealed a problem the state had had to deal with since the opening of Newgate: the corrupting influence of practiced felons on children sent to prison.[10]

Perhaps what triggered Morgan's unique appeal was that by the 1820s, much of the rhetoric behind the effort to close Newgate Prison and replace it with a modern reformatory had stressed the dangers of incarcerating youthful law breakers with more experienced criminals. In 1825 the General Assembly Committee on the State Prison criticized the current system, writing that "rather than a school for reformation it is a seminary of vice." The Prison Overseers' report that same year called the prison "rotten to the core" and decried the continued practice of placing all the criminals in a single vault at night "where the novice in crime is deeply instructed in the whole art and mystery of crime. It is a nursery of crime." That report went so far as to claim that even segregating the prisoners at Newgate by age would not solve the problem because, "There is many a veteran of crime who is in the greenness of his days."[11] Clearly, Connecticut lawmakers were concerned about the impact of imprisonment on the young, especially in company with experienced felons.

Although in the 1790s neither state nor prison officials linked the abortive attempt to prevent negative influences on young criminals with a parallel attempt to provide the young lawbreakers with appropriate education while they were incarcerated, efforts to provide education for children in prison were at the heart of attempts to alter the treatment of children under the criminal law in Connecticut in the nineteenth century. Many educational reformers stressed the importance of education in molding new citizens for the Republic. Obviously, children imprisoned underground or working twelve-hour days in prison workshops with adult criminals could not easily become model citizens. Books on educational reform increasingly stressed nurture over nature in developing the character of children. No longer did all adults view children as inherently evil, but rather as specimens of Locke's *tabula rasa,* blank slates subject to influence for good or evil depending on their education and experiences or as Rousseau's inherently good beings, subject to ruin by the wrong type of education or experience. Education was particularly important to nineteenth-century American reformers who believed that the nation needed to be improved to meet the promise of the new republic.[12] In cases where family, or especially maternal, influence was lacking, Connecticut reformers often advocated that the state assume the role of instilling values of obedience, industry, and piety. Moreover, the idea of the state's responsibility for imparting moral values was not new in the nineteenth century. Since the seventeenth century Connecticut town selectmen had had the right to remove children from parents deemed unfit fit by the selectmen. The law allowed and even directed the selectmen to place such children in apprenticeships where they could learn both industry and morality. Such direct intervention was still permissible in the towns of nineteenth-century Connecticut. Reformers even argued as early as the 1820s that if the towns had a responsibility to protect and educate the children of habitually neglectful parents, the state had an even greater responsibility to educate and reform the children under its direct custody in the state's jails and prison.[13]

General ideas about education in the nineteenth century blended with Connecticut's long tradition of requiring education for those children between the ages of four and sixteen and made their way into Connecticut's criminal laws concerning juveniles. Witness, for example, the attitudes toward the need to educate children that appeared in petitions to the court for clemency for minors. When Eliakim Peck asked the General Assembly in 1810 to release his seventeen-year-old son Raymond, serving a sentence at Newgate Prison for passing counterfeit notes, he stressed the boy's lack of understanding. The petition said that poor Raymond was "altogether unacquainted" with the world, business, money, or the laws of the state. Being in prison would not alter that ignorance. Jenny Freeman went further in her petition for her thirteen-year-old daughter Anna in 1813, seeking Anna's release from a seven-year jail term for arson. She alleged the girl had been ignorant of "the enormity of the crime or its consequences" and prayed that the Assembly "take Anna's tender age into consideration and her inability to obtain instruction in her present situation which will render her useful when she is discharged." In 1815 fifteen-year-old Joshua Chapman asked for clemency from his one-year sentence to Newgate for horse theft. He admitted the crime but said that he had never been "blessed with instruction in morals, letters, or religion commensurate to youth of his age." His petition added that he had been advised that Newgate was not the place to obtain such instruction.[14] While none of the teens obtained their freedom, their stress on the need for education and their inability to obtain that education in jail or prison was a new feature in attempts to gain clemency.

More liberal views of the purposes of education coupled with Enlightenment notions of reform no doubt help explain the gradual changes in the treatment of child criminals. More to the point, the harshness, brutality, and consistency of the laws themselves provided the true impetus for the transformation. In 1795, Zephaniah Swift in his examination of the laws of Connecticut called for a time in which the betterment of society would secure "mild and humane treatment" for children in all cases before the courts. Though he addressed most of his concern to restraining or amending laws to prohibit the permitted use of what he viewed as cruel physical punishment by parents and masters against children, as noted earlier he had also criticized the Connecticut system responsible for executing children as young as eight years old.[15]

Furthermore, though the Connecticut legal system had adopted the use of guardians appointed by the courts to advise and represent children accused of crime, the use of such guardians was inconsistent and often ineffective. In the first several decades of the nineteenth century court dockets revealed numerous trials of children facing charges of crimes against property, and even capital crimes, without the benefit of such guardians. Similar to the contemporary situation of over-worked legal-aid attorneys, even when guardians *ad litem* assisted children in their defense, the limit of that assistance was often to urge the youths to plead guilty, even in some cases where later evidence proved the child's innocence. Adding the potential for further injustice was a conspicuous class and racial bias, and sometimes even a gender bias in the application of Connecticut criminal law for juveniles. Children of affluent parents were rarely without a guardian to represent them in court whereas orphans without property, poor children, and children of color often lacked guardians appointed by the courts.

THE START OF REFORM

Interest in educational reform and new ideas about penitentiaries as opposed to old-fashioned prisons coupled with the negative experiences of convicted underage criminals came into sharp focus with the opening of Connecticut's modern prison in Wethersfield in 1828. Solitary confinement in the cells every night and a rule of silence for the prisoners in the prison workshops during the day would, reformers argued, protect youthful criminals from the contamination and corruption of exposure to more seasoned lawbreakers while they served their sentences. Supporters of the new system of incarceration also passed laws that increased the number of crimes punishable by terms in the state prison, rather than in the county jails, since they believed the prison would more effectively reform and rehabilitate criminals of any age. Laws now mandated that anyone, including children and women, convicted of a crime that would have resulted in a sentence to Newgate now had to serve the sentence at the new state prison. Prior to 1828, state law had directed that women who had committed crimes punishable by a sentence at Newgate would serve the sentence at the county jail "to be kept with none but females," but no such softening had formally applied to children sentenced to serve at the old prison.[16] As a result the opening of the new prison resulted in a greater number of minors being sent to prison by the local courts because magistrates lost the discretionary power to fine and whip minors or to send them to county jails or workhouses as punishment for certain relatively minor crimes. In 1811 only eight of the forty-six Newgate inmates had been under twenty-one. In 1830, three years after the opening of the new prison, the prison population of 167 included twenty-three children under age twenty. In another four years the number of youthful offenders reached twenty-eight, including a thirteen-year-old boy sentenced to a four-year term for burglary.[17]

To achieve the lofty goal of changing criminal behavior, the prison chaplain sought an uplifting reform almost as soon as the prison opened its doors. In his first annual report to the General Assembly he called for funds for the purchase of books to be used to educate the criminals in his care, especially the young. In that report he provided statistics that illustrated that few of the convicts under twenty-one had had adequate schooling and that many could not read at all. He asserted that education prevented crime and claimed that not one of the convicts currently in the prison had obtained a full course of what he designated a liberal education. The chaplain also described his creation of a Sabbath school in the prison for those under age twenty, about nine percent of the prison population, to teach them basic literacy and Christian morality. He further asserted that because of the rigid separation and isolation of the convicts the new prison was fulfilling its mission to prevent the contamination of younger criminals by the older and more experienced felons.[18]

From the moment of its opening the State Prison at Wethersfield became a model held up to the county jails in the state. Praising the benefits of the new system of prison isolation in his Prison Director's Report of 1834, Amos Pillsbury, warden of the prison, directed criticism at the old-style county jails that continued the old system of keeping criminals in common cells. In hostility that mirrored earlier attacks on Newgate by reformers, Pillsbury said youths who first broke the law and revealed their "thievish propensity" often spent their sentences in county jails with accomplished villains so that the jails became "schools of crime." Such an association, he lamented, threatened what little virtue the child might still have and impeded any efforts at reformation. His recommendation was that the legislature enact a law to require the updating of the county jail system to copy the prison system of isolation and discipline. In addition, Pillsbury praised his prison's rule of silence, claiming it helped prevent the young offenders from becoming familiar with the arts and experiences of hardened criminals. By implication, even the youngest lawbreakers had a better chance of reform under Pillsbury's modern supervision than in the antiquated county jails.[19]

Nevertheless, visibly disagreeing with the warden's optimistic assessment of the virtues inherent in the new state prison, minors and their parents and guardians continued their attempts to escape the confines of sentences at the Wethersfield. In the decade of the 1830s twenty-two petitions for the early release of juvenile offenders from the prison reached the Connecticut General Assembly; nine were successful.[20] A new element in the language of the petitions after 1830 was an attempt to attribute the lawless acts of youthful criminals to improper influences as well as poor education, perhaps implying that neither prison nor jail could protect children against additional poor examples. This also may have a reflected a decline in the Calvinistic view of children as inherently evil, since many now saw children through Rousseau's lens as born good but polluted by contact with the world. In what seems to have been a contradiction of Zephaniah Swift's assertion that possession of a mischievous spirit made minors responsible for their crimes, these nineteenth-century petitions cited high spirits, impulsiveness, and thoughtlessness as mitigating rather than incriminating factors.[21]

Friends of eighteen-year-old Abby Reed focused on her impulsiveness in their petition for a pardon in 1833. The girl was serving a four-year sentence at the prison for the attempted murder of a New Haven man; she had thrown a rock at the man, striking him on the temple and nearly killing him. The petitioners wrote that Abby was in the bloom of her youth and had only been defending her father who had been brawling with another drunkard. Seeing no way to break up the fight, the "young and heedless girl" impulsively threw a large rock at her father's assailant, not intending to hurt the man but motivated by her love for her father, or so claimed the sympathetic petitioners. Not only did the petitioners believe the girl probably should not have faced a prison sentence for protecting her father; the petition also revealed a special gender bias in the girl's favor. Supporters claimed that since Abby was but a girl, the circumstances of her intent to kill were clearly in doubt since she could not have thrown the rock with any accuracy and it must have hit the victim on the temple by random chance. Furthermore, the girl's advocates wrote that imprisonment at the state prison was excruciating for a female of her age. She was not a "character hardened and impenitent . . . and still might make a useful woman" if protected from the negative influences at the prison.[22]

The combination of mitigating circumstances and the negative atmosphere of the prison might have not have been sufficient to sway the legislative committee hearing Abby's petition for freedom. Fortunately for the girl, additional factors may have influenced the committee's positive evaluation of the girl's plea. Abby Reed was also the heroine responsible for blocking a major escape attempt by desperate criminals in the prison. When five prisoners broke out of their cells in 1833 and murdered the guard on duty, preliminary to escaping through the prison kitchen, Abby was alone in a cell beyond the door dividing the men from the women in prison. Instead of waiting for the men to break through that door or assisting them in their escape, which would have allowed her to escape as well, Abby instead woke the prison matron and alerted her to the escape attempt. This action, wrote the Committee on the State Prison, "deserved the humane consideration" of the whole Assembly on her behalf. In response, the General Assembly voted not only to release the girl from prison but also granted her a full pardon. Was this clemency or gratitude? In the same legislative session the Assembly denied the clemency petition of Julia Stedman (identified by the Assembly as a "colored" woman jailed for assault with intent to kill) who also helped in forestalling the prison break. Possibly Abby's race as well as her youth and heedlessness were factors in determining her early release.[23]

Implementing Warden Pillsbury's criticism of the antiquated county jail system, the legislature pushed the modernization of the county jails, opening new facilities in Hartford and New Haven, modeled on the system of discipline and separation of prisoners found at Wethersfield. In his 1837 report, Pillsbury praised the new jails and added the claim that the prevention of new crimes depended on the proper education of the young. With modern jails, children could be restrained from committing crimes without "being contaminated by the evil minds of others," and they could continue their education since teachers had easier access to children incarcerated in jail rather than in the state prison. Pillsbury even suggested that children convicted of crime ought to be treated as patients in need of a cure rather than as criminals deserving punishment.[24]

CHILDREN AS VICTIMS RATHER THAN VILLAINS

Providing education and moral instruction for the juvenile prisoners in the county jails did not solve the problem of what to do with children who ended up in the state prison. Within ten years of the opening of the state prison in Wethersfield, not only reformers but the prison warden and prison chaplain themselves admitted that the prison could not meet the needs of society in reducing the crimes committed by minors or in rehabilitating child criminals to become useful members of society upon their release from prison. In 1838 the Committee on the State Prison recommended that the "young in crime" be completely separated from older and more hardened criminals, even in the workshops. Even supporters of the existing system at the prison admitted that it could not prevent children from being contaminated by their proximity to adepts in crime. Reports to the General Assembly concerning repeat offenders revealed that many had first served sentences in prison for relatively petty crimes and had graduated to more serious crimes as adults once they had completed their initial sentences in Wethersfield. The warden, revealing his conversion to the idea that prisons should do more than merely confine prisoners, asserted that children needed to be treated differently when they broke the law because prisons could not do a proper job of reforming them. Saying that the mandated hours of labor were too long and harsh for children, the warden appealed to the legislators to require less bodily labor of children and to provide more time for their intellectual and moral development. At the time of that recommendation, the youngest prisoner under his care was only eleven years old. The General Assembly took no action. By 1840 a crisis atmosphere loomed. Both the warden's annual report and the General Assembly's prison committee reports recommended removing children from the state prison and wholly separating them from the contamination of the career criminals. The committee even went so far as to recommend that the state appropriate $1,000 of the prison surplus for the continued upgrading of the county jail system to provide a less onerous incarceration for children. This time, obviously influenced by the concerns of both the warden and the committee, the Assembly passed the appropriation.[25]

Despite the increased appropriation, the prison remained a dreadful place for children. The chaplain's report in 1842 made it clear that little improvement had occurred. He noted a recent increase in the number of children confined in the state prison, despite the amelioration of conditions in the county jails. Since the first opening of the prison, minors had accounted for nearly one fifth of the prisoners. The chaplain asserted that that figure had climbed in the most recent two years to one quarter or greater. He said this increase placed a difficult burden on him. Though he did not venture any theory on why the number of youths had increased, the hard times of the Depression of 1837 could have had a ripple effect, increasing hardship for the poor and forcing their children into lives of crime. He did mention that out of all the 169 prisoners, 92 had lost both their parents before they reached age twenty-one. He also noted that nearly one quarter of the inmates were Black or Indian, leading him to advocate increased education for both races before they ended up in prison. The increased burden clearly overwhelmed the chaplain. Even in prior years children had gotten insufficient education because they had to work the same hours as the adults in prison, six days a week. With an increase in the number of juvenile criminals, the chaplain now said that he could not meet their educational needs and fulfill his other duties at the prison. He pleaded with the General Assembly for additional funding for "my young charges, some of them just entering their teens." After considering a resolution that would have reduced the children's daily labor by two hours "so that they may receive instruction," the Assembly refused to order any reform and denied his request for additional money. Continuing to try to meet the needs of minor criminals despite his failure to gain additional funding, in 1843 the chaplain reported that he had formed two classes of juvenile convicts to teach them to spell and read. Perhaps still trying to elicit support from the General Assembly, he asserted that the nearly thirty children were doing well and seemed to appreciate the privilege of getting an education.[26]

Although these pleas for reform did not open the state's coffers to assist youthful criminals, nevertheless these reports by the warden and the chaplain signaled the beginning of a new approach by the early 1840s when an atmosphere of confusion afflicted the issue of what to do about juvenile criminals. Throughout the state the reform rhetoric that castigated the prison as a college of crime responsible for destroying the moral fiber and future potential of the children incarcerated there began to influence jurors at all levels. Many juries regularly found children not guilty rather than sentencing them to terms in the state prison. This, in turn, created another problem affecting the moral upbringing of children. A Connecticut General Assembly Committee on the Prison reported in 1843 that more and more children were breaking the laws of the state with impunity because they were aware of the "general repugnance" to send them to prison. Jurors supposedly suffered juvenile offenders to go at large or sentenced them to relatively short terms, allowing the children freedom to return to society and contaminate their fellows with their "corrupting influence." The committee members forcefully asserted that children who broke the law required a different system of punishment and reformation than could be adopted in either the state prison or the county jails. The report pointed to the hundred children committed to either the Hartford or New Haven county jails in 1843 alone and the twelve children newly-sentenced to the state prison to emphasize the magnitude of the problem. Members asserted that those numbers did not reveal the totality of the problem of youthful lawbreaking because the number accounted for did not include "those whose crimes are overlooked by the humanity of the public who are unwilling to send them to our prison."[27]

Marking a shift in attitudes toward children who broke the law, that same report blamed lack of parental guidance and control for the children's criminal conduct rather than complaining abut the youths' "innate vicious propensities," a change from the prior common-law view of a child's criminal responsibility. Claiming that children who broke the law were of equal intelligence and had no worse dispositions than other children, the committee recommended that the state remove youthful criminals from the evil example of both their parents and adult convicts. All that was needed to make juvenile delinquents valued members of society, said the report, was proper restraint and a good moral education. The report proposed that such children have the benefit of moral and religious instruction of a kindly, cheerful, and parental character and that the method of restraint and reform should allow them to learn a trade that would permit the youths to fulfill a useful role in society at the end of their sentences. What the committee members recommended, in effect, was that the state should undertake the role of providing a replacement family for children who broke the law.[28]

This proposal fit neatly with the nineteenth-century reforming impulses seeking to remold American society to the ideals of middle-class ante bellum reformers. Since many of the children who appeared in the Connecticut court system in the 1830s and 1840s were the offspring of recent immigrants, transients, the poor, or people of color, reforms directed at turning them into responsible citizens were particularly important in the eyes of middle-class advocates of reform. Providing a model and a precursor for such social reform, in the 1830s a number of groups in the state had obtained charters from the Assembly to create orphanages or schools for pauper children. Lydia H. Sigourney best expressed the goals of the various incorporators in her proposal for a school for the education of poor children of color: "In consequence of the ignorance or poverty or idleness of their parents, many children of this description are in danger of being educated to a life of idleness, vice, and misery." Sigourney wanted the state to allow her to "take such female children as they may judge suitable objects of charity" and to terminate parental rights. Her object, she asserted, was to rescue such children from the influence of bad example. Those in the General Assembly who sought prison reform for minors were seeking the same goal. Committee proponents of the benevolent rehabilitation cited existing Connecticut reform efforts for the benefit of the deaf, the blind, and the insane poor; they asserted that children who broke the state's laws because of neglectful parents had just as much right to the state's benevolence as had those other unfortunate groups of people and advocated the creation of a state reform school for juvenile criminals. The lofty goal of such a school would be to turn all recipients of the state's humanitarian efforts into useful, virtuous members of the middle class. The issue was whether "hundreds of ignorant children shall be abandoned to ignorance and crime or be trained up in usefulness and virtue." To those Assembly members worried about the cost of such a reform attempt, the committee report cited the current cost to Connecticut society from the crimes themselves, the costs of trying the criminals, and the ensuing costs of incarcerating the convicts and strongly recommended the creation of a juvenile reform system in the state. As an alternative, the report fell back on the proposal that the state return discretionary sentencing to the county courts so that humane jurors would not be tempted to release young criminals from the consequences of their crime if they had an alternative to sending the children to serve their terms at the Wethersfield prison.[29]

THE FAILURE OF DISCRETIONARY SENTENCING

Whether concerned about the cost of establishing a separate penal system for young offenders or worried that such a system would not protect society from the current or future depredations of youthful criminals, the Connecticut General Assembly ignored the Prison Committee's major recommendation. Instead, members focused on the suggestion concerning discretionary sentencing because that reform could provide some form of education for young lawbreakers that would not be at the expense of state taxpayers. In 1843 the Assembly passed a law permitting discretionary sentencing for those under age seventeen who had committed crimes. This new law permitted the county courts the option of sentencing boys and girls under seventeen to equivalent length sentences at county jails rather than at the state prison. The apparent reasoning behind the change in the law was that being imprisoned closer to home would permit youngsters to receive an education at the county jails, if, of course, their parents had sufficient money to hire private teachers for their children. Yet, because many of the children convicted of crimes came from families that had already failed to recognize the need for education, such "permission" had little impact on solving the problem of educating or reforming young criminals. A secondary, yet perhaps more compelling, reason for the introduction of discretionary sentencing might have been that imprisonment closer to home and family would mitigate the perceived harshness of a sentence of incarceration and thus induce soft-hearted jurors to convict children rather than to find them not guilty.[30] Thus, the change would restore the lagging respect for the law, control poorly-supervised children, and protect society from further crimes against property and the public order such children might commit.

Unfortunately, discretionary sentencing satisfied neither the reformers nor the supporters of law and order; it did not solve the problem of how to reform children who broke the law but merely kept them closer to home. In 1845 and 1846 at the Hartford County jail, those under the age of twenty-one accounted for 29% of commitments. In 1850 the number was equally as great. Yet juveniles continued to comprise fourteen percent of the state prison population, a figure equal to the period prior to the advent of discretionary sentencing.[31]

Since the duration of sentences remained identical whether served at Wethersfield or in a county jail, imprisonment for children remained a preposterous punishment in the eyes of many, especially among those who petitioned for pardons for children in the 1840s. Because state sentencing guidelines rejected consideration of mitigating circumstances, many children served what appeared to be excessively harsh sentences in jail for what seemed to be crimes of youthful disobedience or heedlessness. One fourteen-year-old boy stole a basket of walnuts and, in his shame at being in jail, compounded his crime by trying to escape. His combined sentence for the two crimes was six years in the county jail. Fourteen-year-old Nelson Pooshe, the "Huck Finn" of Manchester, committed four minor thefts over a two-year period. Because of the low value of the items stolen, none of the thefts, considered on its own merits, would have resulted in more than a fifteen-day jail sentence. However, because state law mandated a term in the state prison for a third conviction for theft, the judge sentenced the child to four years imprisonment; under the terms of the discretionary sentencing act Nelson served his time in the county jail. After failing to obtain clemency at the original sentencing, the boy's mother petitioned the General Assembly for his release after he had served two years, claiming that the child's crimes resulted from "a spirit of childish and boyish mischief, and not out of any uncommon and unnatural depravity of the heart." The clemency order for Nelson put the General Assembly on the side of those who did not believe youthful minor crimes deserved stiff sentences whether in jail or in the state prison. The Assembly voted to release the lad to a special guardian who was to apprentice the boy into a proper trade. The trade off for Nelson was a five-year apprenticeship rather than two more years in jail, but an apprenticeship would provide a positive vocational education lacking in jail. Yet the solution revealed the legislators' concerns with the problem of youthful lawbreakers: the law must prevent novice felons from breaking the law while training them in habits of morality and industry that would turn them from a life of crime.[32]

Clearly, harsh, predetermined sentences such as that imposed on young Nelson could make it difficult to convince many jurors to convict children. Petitioners regularly complained to the General Assembly that many children continued to commit crimes with impunity, apparently secure in the knowledge that kindly jurors would not expose them to the hardship and contamination of the county jails even when that was the alternative to the harsher climate at the state prison. This revealed the fallacy of the legislators' express belief that discretionary sentencing would restore respect for the law. Furthermore, many petitions for pardon or early release from the county jails criticized conditions in the jails using the same language directed against the inequities of the state prison, emphasizing that the lack of instruction in the county penal system destroyed any hope a child might have of becoming a useful citizen. In 1846 thirty citizens of Manchester sought an early release for fourteen-year-old Elihu Stillman Squires, serving two years at the Hartford County Jail. They asserted that the boy had "made little progress in the rudiments of education and in jail his chance for education would cease." Only release from jail could return the child "to steady habits and save him to his community."[33]

THE FINAL STEPS TO THE STATE REFORM SCHOOL FOR BOYS

The culminating shift in the treatment of juvenile criminals in Connecticut was obviously the result of dual reform impulses, both what David Rothman has identified as the need to control society and also the broader drive to improve it. Beginning in the late 1840s hundreds of humanitarian-minded individuals besieged the Connecticut General Assembly with petitions, initially calling for state charters to open privately-funded houses of refuge for wayward youths and eventually seeking a state-operated, state-funded reform school for boys. Most of the petitions pointed out the complex nature of the problem of punishing children for their crimes, the complexity first delineated in the committee report of 1843. First, those in authority often justifiably overlooked petty offenses committed by boys who were not under the proper control of parents or suitable guardians, because, as the petitioners claimed, sending such children to jail usually did them more harm than good by removing them from any possibility of education and by exposing them to the corrupting habits and influences of hardened criminals. The second dilemma was that the realization of their relative impunity from prosecution engendered in the youths disrespect for the law. Third, and seemingly of the most importance to many of the petitioners, the future welfare of Connecticut society demanded a means to remove children who broke the law from the temptation of committing more crimes and to educate such youths in habits of virtue, piety, and industry. Yet despite the forceful arguments supporting the petitions from dozens of towns, for several years the General Assembly took no action to respond to the requests for state intervention to rehabilitate the lives of juvenile criminals. The prison director at Wethersfield even joined the fray in 1849, claiming that the prison itself had a greater effect in reforming prisoners than the jails. Perhaps more to the point he also asserted he could do the job at a lower cost to the state since it cost two dollars a day to incarcerate a prisoner in a county jail whereas he could provide for prisoners at only fifty cents a day. Nevertheless, the warden strongly supported the creation of a separate institution for youths who had broken the law.[34]

Success appeared imminent in 1850. Finally the Assembly accepted a petition spearheaded by Theodore Woolsey, president of Yale College, and

Benjamin Silliman, also of Yale, combining it with dozens of similar petitions and referring all the requests to a special legislative committee to study the feasibility of creating a state reform school for boys. When the special committee made its report to the members of the General Assembly at its May 1850 session, the committee members reiterated in even stronger language the arguments previously presented by the petitioners. First, a great number of young lawbreakers escaped punishment entirely because of the very great reluctance of prosecutors, juries, and judges to impose existing laws and punishments "with all their force on persons so young, so neglected, and so ignorant." Committee members accepted the reasoning put forth by the petitioners: failure to punish youthful lawbreakers did "induce boldness and hardiness in guilt" among the delinquents and contribute to additional crimes, but incarceration of young felons with more experienced convicts was an even greater cause of crime. In contrast, the committee asserted that opening a reform school for boys would ensure not only a greater certainty of punishment, because jurors would not hesitate to convict out of a misplaced sense of kindness, but would also lead to a greater respect for the law among the young. Furthermore, a reform school would provide both the moral training and vocational instruction demanded by reformers at the same time as it restrained young felons from the commission of more serious crimes. To buttress their arguments, the committee members warned that many of the criminals currently serving life sentences at the Wethersfield prison had begun their lives in crime as petty thieves and vagrants. Creation of a reform school would reduce the potential future aggravated offenses of the current generation of vagrant, thieving boys. The special committee was especially interested in securing an immediate passage of a bill for the reform school because Woolsey and Silliman had offered $10,000 in private donations to assist the state in establishing such a school. Nevertheless, despite the strong arguments of the committee and the numerous supporting petitions, the legislature tabled the recommendation.[35]

In 1851 Connecticut's governor Thomas Seymour took up the cry for the reform effort, issuing a special message to the Assembly that called for the establishment of a school that would eradicate the evil propensities of youthful criminals because for children prison was a place that concealed rather than destroyed "the germs of vice." Seymour called for a less degrading place for youthful offenders, saying that no matter how good a job the prison or the county jails might do in disciplining children, a term in either hardened "the heart in crime instead of suppressing the growth of evil passions and inclinations. To the mind of youth, the penitentiary becomes the grave of reputation and a bar to the return to any path of virtue."[36]

Apparently after neither the offer of a $10,000 private subsidy nor the Governor's outspoken support swayed the careful legislators in the General Assembly, supporters of the reform plan brought in an outside "expert" to address the Assembly with the latest reform rhetoric. Dr. Charles Albany summarized the feelings of all those who had been advocating reform for the prior ten years, pointing out the modern changes in attitudes toward the criminal responsibility of children and the need for education to eradicate crime. Improperly raised children were no more culpable for turning to crime, Albany said, than a crab apple tree should be blamed for producing bitter fruit. These were children exposed as soon as they could walk to a sort of infant school of crime on the streets where they lived. Sending such poorly raised, badly educated boys to prison only added to their criminal potential, Albany claimed, giving them the benefit of instruction from professors of the most advanced universities of criminal learning. When such a child finished his term at the prison and returned to the streets, his sojourn behind bars, Albany said, raised the lad to higher respect in his criminal community, competent to teach his companions all he had learned in prison.[37]

Having condemned the current system of rehabilitation, Albany presented the alternative to the legislators if they authorized the creation of a reform school "where the welfare of society is best served by the reform of the criminals." The school would raise a child from the gutter, clean him, clothe him, and feed him. "It is a new thing for him to be free of bodily suffering, to be sure of food when he is hungry." In Albany's idealized view, such a child would learn gratitude, would strive to win the approval and affection of those caring for him, and would end up becoming a better person. According to Albany, if the state established a reform school, within just a generation or two there would be only one fifth or one tenth the number of criminals in the state's jails and prisons because "the fountain of supply would be effectively cut off." Albany went on to praise the shrewdness, energy, and courage of boys who managed to survive on the streets, living by their wits, neglected by both their families and society. He capped his plea for a favorable response to the reform school by asserting that if Connecticut authorities could direct those positive traits into proper channels by education and firm discipline, such boys would become "noble leaders of men."[38] Here was the middle-class reformer's goal: take children who threatened the order of society and reform them to play a vital role in that same society.

Whether swayed by Albany's eloquence or determined to secure the funding from Woolsey and Silliman, in 1851 the Connecticut General Assembly finally authorized the creation of the State Reform School for Boys. In the bill to create the new institution, the legislators proclaimed that the school would not only remove children from the invidious influence of the streets, their families, and their criminal comrades; it would transform the boys into responsible contributors to society: pious, moral, and educated. The school would treat the youths not harshly as criminals, but tenderly as objects of sympathy. However, a close look at the bill reveals the potential for sentences at the new school to be even more severe than at the state's prisons and jails, at least for minor crimes. The law allowed county courts to send any boy under the age of sixteen to the new reform school in lieu of sentencing him to the mandated term under existing criminal statutes. The school could keep a child until it succeeded in reforming him, it could bind him out as an apprentice until the age of twenty-one, or it could remand him to the state prison if the boy proved to be incorrigible. In theory, a child who under the old system would have spent thirty days in jail for a minor theft could remain at the state reform school until the age of twenty-one. The only protection against excessive and arbitrary terms offered to a boy was that the school could not keep him for more than ninety days under an order of the justice of the peace without the approval of the board of selectmen in the child's town. Within that rather unlimited grant of control over the destiny of children in the reform school, the statute ordered that the school's director was to instruct the youths in piety and morality and to provide such education as was best suited to their ages or intellectual capacities. The boys were also to learn a trade while at the school, working at jobs that matched their strength and disposition. To keep the expense to the state as low as possible, the act also directed that the respective counties sending the children would bear the cost of maintaining boys at the new school, at a cost of one dollar per child per week. Thus the new school answered the concerns of not only the humanitarian reformers and the advocates of law and order, but also insulated some state citizens from the costs inherent in that reform. Residents of relatively crime-free rural districts would not have to bear the cost of reforming the paupers and delinquents of the crowded cities.[39]

Unwillingness by Connecticut's legislators to meet the total cost of fulfilling the mandate to reform youthful criminals elicited more reform rhetoric even before the school opened in 1853. Governor Seymour continued his support, calling for an increased appropriation of $25,000 by the lawmakers to be added to the $29,500 already spent. Resorting to the now familiar language of redemption, he claimed the new institution would save from "utter ruin that class of youthful offenders who, cast off from moral restraint and groping in ignorance or inflamed by angry passions, ripen early for crime and set public opinion at defiance." The newly-appointed trustees of the school added their pleas for additional funding claiming that the original amount contributed by the state and by private donations had not been sufficient to complete the entire building as originally planned. Without more money the school would be seriously overcrowded, impeding its reform mission.[40] The *Hartford Courant* weighed in on the side of adequate spending for the reform as well, mirroring the prior decade of reform rhetoric:

> It must be apparent to everyone that the common jail is not the place for boys, to say nothing of the danger of contamination from older criminals, the entire absence of all reformatory or educational influences together with the loss of self respect and regard for character.
>
> Multitudes of idle and vicious boys are now allowed to infest our cities and larger towns, corrupting our children, stealing our property, burdening the night with their profanity and obscenity, training themselves and their companions for a life of crime and perhaps a death of infamy, who are not arrested, simply because the officers of the law know that an arrest and commitment to the common jail would only make them worse.
>
> A nobler enterprise, or one more imperatively demanded in the State of Connecticut, has never been undertaken by our legislature.41

In what became a litany that would be familiar to modern observers of state institutions, the reform school continued to struggle for funding. In 1854, Seymour asked for an additional $22,000 because the budget-minded legislators had appropriated only $12,000 of the prior request. He also estimated that another $15,000 would be necessary to finish the original plan of the building to house up to 350 youths. At that time the school held one hundred and forty boys, children "not confined as criminals upon whom the deep mark of infamy should remain stamped . . . but their minds and morals cared for and their reformation attempted." Even as the number of minors at the state prison remained at about twelve percent of the prison population and comprised twenty-two percent of the new commitments to the Hartford County jail, Governor Seymour could optimistically predict that "the object of punishment is the prevention of crime, and no more certain means can be devised to prevent crime, than the reformation of the offender." Since the state reform school would rehabilitate young criminals, Seymour believed it was accomplishing a positive role not only for the children but also for all the citizens of the state.[42]

Despite continued problems with state funding, the school's trustees pledged to fulfill their responsibility to prepare the vagrant youths under their stewardship for lives as good citizens and valued members of society. The 1855 school report to the legislature bemoaned the paucity of resources that had resulted in overcrowded rooms and workshops and "consequent deficiencies of proper discipline, education, and employment." Nevertheless, in an effort to elicit continued legislative support, the trustees offered letters from some of the boys as evidence of the reformation and rehabilitation accomplished at the reform school. One boy wrote that he was glad he had been sent to the school because "if I had run in the streets of Boston and New York as I used to, I should never have been a man." Another wrote his mother to tell her that the school had provided him the encouragement to become a man, and he urged his mother to have his younger brothers profit from his misadventures by telling them to go to school, be good boys, and "to never take anything which did not belong to them." Other letters praised the education provided by the school and the opportunity to make something of previously wasted lives.[43] Such success stories represented all that the reformers were trying to achieve.

Thus by the mid-nineteenth century the humanitarian view of children as essentially good beings in need of the proper experiences and influences replaced the seventeenth-century vision of children as the equivalent of adults, subject to the same restraints and punishments. The opening of the State Reform School in Meriden in 1853 marked the merger of two reforming impulses in one institution. It provided a setting in which reformers could attempt to make good citizens out of potentially poor ones, and it also created a humane way to ensure increased social control for a potentially dangerous segment of the population, an important secondary goal for middle-class citizens who felt threatened by disorder in mid-nineteenth century America. The unspoken premise behind this legal solution to the dual problem, an idea that anticipated late-nineteenth-century sociological jurisprudence, was that the law could shape society as well as react to it.

Notes

NOTES TO THE INTRODUCTION

1. Not only were all Americans once children themselves; at times the majority of Americans were under the age of twenty-one. Figures from a colonial Connecticut census in 1774 revealed that 56.7 % of Connecticut residents were under the age of twenty-one. In the 1800 Federal census the median age was sixteen. *Public Records of the Colony of Connecticut*, vol. XIV, Charles J. Hoadly, ed. (Hartford: Case, Lockwood, & Brainard Company, 1887), 491.
2. David J. Rothman, "Documents in Search of a Historian: Toward a History of Childhood and Youth in America," *Journal of Interdisciplinary History*, 2, no. 2 (Autumn 1971), 374.
3. Lewis Mumford, *The Culture of the Cities* (New York: Harcourt, 1938), 430–31; Philippe Aries, *Centuries of Childhood: A Social History of Family Life* (New York: Vintage Books, 1962), 33.
4. John Demos, "Developmental Perspectives on the History of Childhood," *Journal of Interdisciplinary History*, vol. 2, no. 2, (Autumn 1971), 315; John Demos, *A Little Commonwealth* (New York: Oxford University Press, 1970), 57, 182; Bernard Faber, *Guardians of Virtue: Salem Families in 1800* (New York: Basic Books, 1972), 4; Ross W. Beales, Jr., "In Search of the Historical Child: Miniature Adulthood and Youth in Colonial New England, *American Quarterly* 27 (October 1975), 379, 392; Michael Zuckerman, *Peaceable Kingdoms: New England Towns in the 18th* Century (New York: Alfred A. Knopf, 1970), 73; Constance B. Schulz, "Children and Childhood in the Eighteenth Century," *American Childhood, A Research Guide and Historical Handbook (*Westport, CT: Greenwood Press, 1985), 65; Christine Stansell, *City of Women: Sex and Class in New York, 1789- 1860* (New York: Alfred A. Knopf, 1986), 214.
5. Schulz, 64; Linda Pollack, *Forgotten Children* (Cambridge: Cambridge University Press, 1983), 271; Holly Brewer argues that Locke's ideas on responsibility helped create a separate status for children at the time of the Revolution because of the belief that those in positions of responsibility should base their authority on "virtue and reason, attributes that came only with age." This rebounded on the concept of childhood, thus viewing it as a distinct period and status. Holly Brewer, "Age of Reason? Children,

Testimony, and Consent in Early America," *The Many Legalities of Early America,* Christopher Tomlins and Bruce H. Mann, eds. (Chapel Hill: University of North Carolina Press, 2001), 293, 331.

6. Schulz, "Children and Childhood," 58.
7. George Lee Haskins, *Law and Authority in Early Massachusetts: A Study in Tradition and Design* (New York: The Macmillan Company, 1960), 82.
8. Michael Grossberg, *Governing the Hearth: Law and the Family in Nineteenth-Century America* (Chapel Hill: University of North Carolina Press, 1985), 235–36, 301; Joseph M. Hawes, *The Children's Rights Movement: A History of Advocacy and Protection* (Boston: Twayne Publishers, 1991), 2. Hawes argues that the concept of *parens patriae* is the legal basis for all intervention on behalf of minors to this day.
9. Haskins, 82.
10. Everett C. Goodwin, *The Magistracy Rediscovered: Connecticut, 1636–1818* (Ann Arbor: UMI Research Press, 1981), 3.
11. Howard Cohen, *Equal Rights for Children* (Totowa, NY: Littlefield, Adams, & Co., 1980), vii.
12. Cornelia Hughes Dayton, *Women Before the Bar: Gender, Law, and Society in Connecticut: 1639–1789* (Chapel Hill: University of North Carolina Press, 1995), 11–12.
13. Ibid., 12–13.
14. Bruce H. Mann, *Neighbors and Strangers: Law and Community in Early Connecticut* (Chapel Hill: University of North Carolina Press, 1987), 2–6.
15. Frances M. Caulkins, *History of New London, Connecticut* (New London: H. D. Utley, 1895), 142, 341; New London County Court "Trials," vol. 1, June 1677, 90; 97; New London County Court, "Trials," vol. 3, Sept. 1673, 62, June 1674, 68; Barbour files, CSL.
16. Dayton, 4.
17. Mann, 6; Stansell, 215; Schulz, 64. While Mann argues that law in the colonial period was not static, both Stansell and Schulz maintain that the law is essentially conservative, often, as Schulz writes, "the last to conform to change."
18. Zephaniah Swift, *A System of the Laws of the State of Connecticut,* vol. I (Windham, CT: John Byrne, 1795), 1; *The Code of 1650,* (Hartford: Silas Andrus, publisher, 1830), 38–39, 96, 29.
19. Charles M. Andrews, *The Colonial Period of American History* Vol. II (New Haven: Yale University Press, 1936); Goodwin, 3, 13–14.
20. *The Code of 1650,* 28, 29.
21. Michael Zuckerman, *Peaceable Kingdoms,* numerous.
22. Arthur Calhoun claimed that Locke was popular in New England, basing his conclusions on library lists, book collections, and the use of quotations from Locke in almanacs. In contrast Philip Greven, Jr. denied that Locke had a wide audience, saying his works were only accessible to educated men with personal libraries. Arthur W. Calhoun, *A Social History of the American Family,* vol. 1 (New York: Barnes & Noble, 1945), 119; Philip J. Greven, Jr., *Child-Rearing Concepts, 1628–1861* (Itasca, IL: F. E. Peacock Publishers, Inc., 1973), 15.

23. Albert E. Van Dusen, *Connecticut* (New York: Random House, 1961), 23–24, 41. Van Dusen noted that the clarity and brevity of Connecticut's new government reflected the drafting skills of the young colony's only trained lawyer, Windsor resident Roger Ludlow.
24. Van Dusen, 41, 42, 70; Adam Hirsch discussed a similar limitation on law-making imposed on the Massachusetts Bay colony by its charter but asserted that early laws, especially on theft and punishment, reflected the Puritan outlook rather than the English one. Adam J. Hirsch, *The Rise of the Penitentiary: Prisons and Punishment in Early America* (Chelsea, MI: Book Crafters, Inc., 1992), 4.
25. George Haskins has claimed the courts in Massachusetts played a similar role in the maintenance of order. George Lee Haskins, *Law and Authority in Early Massachusetts* (New York: The Macmillan Company, 1960), 84; Goodwin, 35; *Records of the Particular Court of Connecticut: 1639–1663* (Hartford: The Connecticut Historical Society, 1928), 10,16,31,33,97, 258, 262–63.
26. Van Dusen, 65; *The Code of 1650* (Hartford: Silas Andrus, publisher, 1830), 20, 28, 38, 39, 65, 70–74. The various statutes in the new legal code referred to children in a number of ways, as minors, children, infants, or as persons who were not of full age. The terms appear to have been interchangeable.
27. Edmund S. Morgan, *The Puritan Family* (New York: Harper & Row, 1966), 6.
28. *The Code of 1650,* 39, 60–63.
29. John Thomas Farrell, "The Administration of Justice in Connecticut" (Yale University dissertation, 1939), 131.
30. *Colonial Records of Connecticut,* vol. IV, Charles V. Hoadly, ed. (Hartford: Case, Lockwood and Brainard, 1868), 235–36, 312, 346–348. The importance of the new office of justice of the peace to keeping order was apparent in the jurisdiction they gained over anyone who used "threatening words, turbulent behavior, or actual violence," and over anyone who "shall terrify and disquiet any of the King's people."
31. *Colonial Records of Connecticut,* vol. V, Charles V. Hoadly, ed. (Hartford: Case, Lockwood, & Brainard, 1870), 48; New London County, County Court files, Box 233, Feb. 1774.
32. Haskins, 207. That tendency towards leniency for those who repented their evil ways long continued to be a factor in Connecticut's criminal justice system. Petitions for clemency to the General Assembly routinely expressed sorrow and remorse. Letters from children held at the Reform School for Boys in the 1850s also included regrets and apologies for their lawlessness. Adam Hirsch noted the same melding of punishment and mercy in early Massachusetts when malefactors confessed their wrongs. Hirsch, 9–10.
33. Haskins, 84.

NOTES TO CHAPTER ONE

1. *The Code of 1650* (Hartford: Silas Andrus, 1830), 20–21; Zephaniah Swift, *A System of the Laws of the State of Connecticut,* vol. 1 (Windham, CT: John Byrne, 1795), 206.

2. *The Code of 1650,* 80–81; *State Records of Connecticut,* vol. 2, Charles J. Hoadly, editor, 258–59; *Connecticut Public Acts, 1849–1854,* chapters 47, 51.
3. *The Code of 1650,* 64, 96; *The Public Records of the Colony of Connecticut,* Benjamin Trumbull, ed., vol. I, 139, vol. II (Hartford: F. A. Brown, 1850), 50; *Acts and Laws of His Majesties Colony of Connecticut* (Boston: Bartholomew Green, 1702,) 19, 49, 76–77; *Acts and Laws of His Majesties Colony of Connecticut,* 1716–1749 (Hartford: reissued in facsimile by Albert C. Bates, 1919), 495.
4. *The Code of 1650,* 2; *Acts and Laws of His Majesties Colony of Connecticut,* 1702, 1; *Public Records of the Colony of Connecticut,* vol. I, Benjamin Trumbull, ed., 558; *Public Records of the Colony of Connecticut,* vol. IV, Charles J. Hoadly, ed., 438.
5. Lois Forer, "Rights of Children: The Legal Vacuum," in *The Rights of Children: Emergent Concepts in Law and Society,* Albert E. Wilkerson, editor (Philadelphia: Temple University Press, 1973), 29; *The Code of 1650,* 64–65.
6. Swift, *A System of the Laws of the State of Connecticut,* vol. 2 (Windham, CT: John Byrne, 1796), 335–6.
7. *The Code of 1650,* 26–27; *Public Records of the Colony of Connecticut,* vol. VIII, Charles J. Hoadly, editor, 138.
8. John Thomas Farrell, "Administration of Justice in Connecticut" (Yale University dissertation, 1937), 126; *The Records of the Particular Court of the Colony of Connecticut* (Hartford: Connecticut Historical Society, 1928), 19, 29, 74; *The Public Records of the Colony of Connecticut,* vol. I, 82.
9. *Records of the Particular Court,* 217; New London County Court Records, Vol. 3, # 93, Sept. 1676.
10. Connecticut Superior Court, New London County, Files, Box 7, March 1727, case 36.
11. Connecticut Superior Court, New London County, Files, Box 9, Sept. 1741, case 37; Barbour files, CSL.
12. New London County, "County Court Trials and Dockets," vol. 22, Nov. 1755, case 192; New London County, County Court files, Box 202, June 1755, case 192.
13. Hartford County, "County Court Records," vol. 19, June 1773, case 26, 58 and Feb. 1774, 144–45.
14. New London County, "County Court Trials and Dockets" vol. 26, Nov. 1786, case 186; New London County, County Court files, Box 246, Nov. 1786, case 186;
15. Connecticut Court Records, Justice Courts, Box 554, Lyme, Records of William Noyes, 1790–1806, August 1793.
16. Connecticut Court Records, Justice Courts, Box 554, Lyme, Records of William Noyes, Justice of the Peace, Oct. 1798, 79.
17. *Records of the Colony of Connecticut,* vol. IV (Hartford: Case, Lockwood, and Brainard, 1868), 235–36.
18. Connecticut Superior Court, New London County, "Records of Trials," April 1810, case 2, case 9; Richard H. Phelps, *Newgate of Connecticut*

(Camden, ME: Picton Press, 1996), 94. The Newgate Prison records note in 1811 that Jack Clark was black but that he was from Portugal.

19. Connecticut Superior Court, New London County, "Records of Trials," Oct. 1822, case 99; Connecticut Superior Court, New London County, files, Oct. 1822, case 99; Phelps, 102. George was still in prison more than two years later, perhaps because he was unable to pay court costs of his prosecution.
20. New London County, "County Court Records, Trials," March 1826, case 223; New London County, County Court files, Box 312, Mar. 1826, case 223; Phelps, 114.
21. Connecticut Superior Court, New London County, files, Box 50, Oct. 1828, case 93, 94.
22. New London County, "County Court Records of Trials," vol. 33, Feb. 1834, case 302; New London County, County Court files, Box 321, Feb. 1834, case 302; New London County, "County Court Records of Trials." vol. 33, Nov. 1834, case 319.
23. New London County, "County Court Records," vol. 33, Feb. 1837, case 209, June 1837, case 330; New London County, County Court files, Box 326, Feb. 1837, case 209, Box 327, June 1837, case 330; Connecticut Superior Court, New London County, files, Box 55, Sept. 1837, case 274, 275.
24. Connecticut General Assembly, Rejected Bills, Box 10, folder 57, 1835, #60.
25. Connecticut Court Records, Justice Courts, Box 579, Stonington, Francis P. Sheffield, Justice of the Peace, August 1848, 6.
26. Connecticut General Assembly, Rejected Bills, 1834–45, Box 10, folder 51, 1834, #100.
27. Connecticut General Assembly Papers, CSL, Box 25, 1837, Petitions granted, #121A.
28. Connecticut General Assembly Papers, CSL, Box 25, 1837, Petitions granted, #121a, 122, 123b, 124. In 1841 Oliver, still under twenty-one, supposedly burglarized the store of Timothy Turner of Montville, stealing goods and $10.50 in cash. Though the court provided George Hill, Esq. as Oliver's guardian *ad litem,* the jury found the youth guilty and sentenced him to a six-year term at the State Prison as a repeat offender. Hill did not raise the issue that the earlier conviction was imposed illegally. Doing so might have resulted in a reduction in his client's sentence. Connecticut Superior Court, "New London County Record of Trials," vol. 7, Sept. 1841, case 191.
29. New London County, County Court files, Box 334, Nov. 1842, case 205, 217; New London County, "County Court Records of Trials," vol. 34, June 1843, case 180; New London County, County Court files, Box 335, June 1843, case 180; Connecticut Superior Court, New London County files, Box 61, March 1844, case 730; Connecticut Superior Court, New London County files, Box 63, March 1848, case 572, 585.
30. Connecticut General Assembly Papers, CSL, Box 32. 1840 cont. Reports 1–36, #36; Connecticut General Assembly Papers, CSL, Box 36, 1843 Reports 1–76, 17A; Connecticut General Assembly Reports, CSL, Box 36,

1843, Juvenile, Miscellaneous Resolves, #73 a-d; *Public Acts of the State of Connecticut, 1839–1843,* Chapter 91, page 97.

31. *Public Statute Laws of the State of Connecticut* (Hartford: S. G. Goodrich, 1821), 152; Connecticut General Assembly Papers, CSL, Box 3, 1823 Acts and Resolves 1–50; Connecticut General Assembly Papers, Box 6, 1825 Reports and Miscellaneous, cont. 1–29, #8B; Connecticut General Assembly Reports, CSL, 1845–46, Box 42, Public Acts 1A-56B, 41A; *Connecticut Public Acts, 1849–1854,* 14–15.
32. Connecticut General Assembly Papers, Box 38, 1843–44 Petitions Accompanying Resolutions, 1–118, #101.
33. New London County, "County Court Records," vol. 34, Nov. 1844, case 155, 60; Connecticut Superior Court, "New London County Trials," vol. 8, March 1845, case 892, 58; Connecticut Superior Court, New London County files, Box 61, March 1845, case 892.
34. Connecticut Court Records, Justice Courts, Box 566, New London, John Grace, Justice of the Peace, July, 1847; Connecticut General Assembly Papers, CSL, Box 44, 1847, Boroughs and Cities, #80, 81.
35. Connecticut General Assembly Papers, Box 48, 1848, State Prisons and Jails 1–113, #18, 19.
36. New London County, "County Court Records." vol. 34, June 1849, case 358, 442; New London County, County Court files, Box 341, June 1849, case 358.
37. Connecticut Superior Court, "New London County Trials," vol. 8, March 1850, case 422; Connecticut Superior Court, New London County files, Box 65, March 1850, cases 421, 422.
38. Connecticut Superior Court, " New London County Trials," vol., 8, Sept. 1850, case 493, 547; Connecticut Superior Court, New London County files, Box 66, Sept. 1850, case 493.
39. Connecticut Superior Court, "New London County Record," vol. 9, Sept. 1853, case 219, 83 and case 220, 84.
40. Connecticut General Assembly Papers, Box 36, 1843 Reports, #46B, Box 40, 1845 Reports, #25; Box 52, 1850 Reports, #2; Box 53, 1851 Reports, #1 and #6D; Box 60, 1853 Reports, #8.
41. Connecticut General Assembly Papers, Box 53, 1851 Reports 35–91, #79 A-D.
42. Connecticut General Assembly Papers, Box 66, 1855, Reports to the General Assembly, #A, School Chaplain's Report, #13 A, 13 C, 14 E.
43. *Acts and Laws of His Majesties Colony of Connecticut in New* England (New London: Timothy Green, 1715), 13; Swift, vol. 2, 368.
44. *Acts and Laws of His Majesties Colony of Connecticut in New England* (New London: 1715), 13; New London County, "County Court Trials and Dockets," vol. 21, June 1744, case 168; New London County, County Court files, Box 190, Nov. 1744; Barbour files, CSL.
45. *Acts and Laws of the State of Connecticut,* 1796 - 1808, 1795, 182; *Records of the State of Connecticut,* vol. 7, Leonard Labaree, ed., 494.
46. Preston, Connecticut Town Papers, CSL, Sept. 1798, #121.

47. *Acts and Laws of the State of Connecticut, 1796–1808,* 1801, 566; *Public Statutes of the State of Connecticut* revised 1821, Title 22: section 19, 154–55.
48. New London County, Superior Court "Record of Trials," vol. 1, Sept. 1801, case 6/146, CSL; New London County, Superior Court files, Box 32, Sept. 1801, case 6/146, CSL.
49. New London County, Superior Court "Record of Trials," vol. 2, Sept. 1804, case 106, CSL; New London County, Superior Court files, Box 35, Sept. 1804, case 106, CSL.
50. Phelps, 97, 99, 107; New London County, "County Court Records of Trials," vol. 33, Nov. 1838, case 271; New London County, County Court files, Box 329, Nov. 1838, case 271.
51. Connecticut General Assembly Papers, Box 5, 1825 Petitions and Resolves 1–49, #22; New London County, "County Court Records of Trials," vol. 34, Nov. 1845, 190, case 570; New London County, County Court files, Box 337, Nov. 1845, case 570; Connecticut General Assembly Papers, Box 45, 1847 Burroughs, Cities, and Towns 1–130B, # 74, 75; Connecticut Superior Court, "New London County Record of Trials," vol. 9, Dec. 1853, 121, case 176; Connecticut Superior Court, New London County files, Box 68, Dec. 1853, case 167, 176.
52. Connecticut Court Records, Justice Courts, Box 579, Stonington, Francis Sheffield, Justice of the Peace, Dec. 1851, 61, 63.
53. Connecticut General Assembly Papers, Box 60, 1853 Engrossed bills 1–125, #65.
54. Connecticut General Assembly Papers, Box 60, 1853 Engrossed bills, #54.

NOTES TO CHAPTER TWO

1. Everett C. Goodwin, *The Magistracy Reconsidered* (Ann Arbor: UMI Research Press, 1981), 11; Hugh Campbell Black, *Black's Law Dictionary,* 6th edition (St. Paul, MN: West Publishing Co., 1990), 114; Zephaniah Swift, *A System of the Laws of the State of Connecticut,* vol. 2 (Windham, CT: John Byrne, 1796), 24.
2. Zephaniah Swift, *A System of the Laws of the State of Connecticut,* vol. 1 (Windham, CT: John Byrne, 1795), 217–218; Henry A. Dutton, *A Revision of Swift's Digest of the Laws of Connecticut* (New Haven: Henry M. Peck, 1884), 61.
3. New London County, "County Court Records," vol. 3, June 1680, 142; Frances M. Caulkins, *A History of New London* (Hartford, CT: The Press of Case, Tiffany, & Co., 1852), 253.
4. New London County, "County Court Records," vol. 8, June 1714, case 202; Barbour files, CSL; New London County, "County Court Records," vol. 9, Aug. 1715, case 25; Barbour files, CSL.
5. New London County, "County Court Records," vol. 13, June 1721, case 106; New London County, County Court files, Box 163, file 106; Barbour files, CSL.

6. New London County, County Court files, Box 204, Nov. 1756, case 174; New London County, "County Court Trials and Dockets," vol. 22, Nov. 1756, case 174; Barbour files, CSL.
7. Swift, vol. 1, 205. Swift discussed the case of a father whose son had been beaten by another boy. The man, to revenge the quarrel, "went near a mile and beat the other boy so much that he died; this was called manslaughter only, and not murder."
8. Hartford County, "County Court Records," vol. 18, June 1772, case 89, 252; Barbour files, CSL.
9. Connecticut Superior Court, New London County files, Box 21, Sept. 1780, case 41.
10. New London County, County Court files, Box 235, Feb. 1782, case 162.
11. Connecticut Superior Court, New London County files, Box 23, March 1784, case 73.
12. New London County, "County Court Trials and Dockets," vol. 26, Nov. 1786, case 141; New London County, County Court files, Box 246, Nov. 1786, case 141; Connecticut Superior Court, New London County files, Box 25, Mar. 1787, case 40; Barbour Files, CSL.
13. New London County, "County Court Trial and Dockets," vol. 26, Dec. 1788, case 228; New London County, County Court files, Box 251, Dec. 1788, case 288; Connecticut Superior Court, New London County files, Box 27, March 1789, case 17; New London County, "County Court Trials and Dockets," vol. 27, Dec. 1789, case 310; New London County, County Court files, Box 252, Dec. 1789, case 310; New London County, "County Court Trials and Dockets," vol. 27, Nov. 1793, case 29.
14. Connecticut Superior Court, New London County files, Box 27, Sept. 1789, case 4.
15. Connecticut Court Records, Justice Court, Box 554, Lyme, William Noyes, Justice of the Peace, 1790–1806, May 1792, 15.
16. Connecticut Court Records, Justice Court, "Records of William Noyes," Lyme, Sept. 1799, 84.
17. Richard H. Phelps, *Newgate of Connecticut* (Camden, ME: Picton Press, 1996), 96–117; Connecticut General Assembly Papers, Box 22, Reports 1834, folder 2, 1–36, #36 D, pages 8–12.
18. New London County, "County Court Trials and Dockets," vol. 28, Feb., 1800, case 42; New London County, County Court files, Box 268, Feb. 1800, case 42. The files identified George Reed of Lyme as the boy's legal guardian, yet Smith, his master, represented him in court.
19. Connecticut Court Records, Justice Court, Box 569, New London, Josiah Isham, Justice of the Peace, Oct. 1809; Barbour Files, CSL.
20. New London County, "County Court Records," vol. 29, Dec. 1801, case 66.
21. Connecticut Court Records, Justice Courts, Box 568, New London, Edward Learned, Justice of the Peace, June, 1825; Box 566, New London, William P. Cleaveland, Jr., Justice of the Peace, April 1827; Box 568, New London, William P. Cleaveland, Justice of the Peace, August 1827; Box 570, New London, William P. Cleaveland, Justice of the Peace, March 1829; Barbara

W. Brown & James M. Rose, *Black Roots in Southeastern Connecticut* (Detroit: Gail Research Co., 1980), 209, 211.

22. New London County, "County Court Records, Trials and Dockets," vol. 30, June 1814, case 252; New London County, County Court files, Box 292, June 1814, case 252; Barbour files, CSL.
23. New London County, County Court files, Box 317, Mar. 1839, case 80.
24. Connecticut Court Records, Justice Court, Box 569, New London, William P. Cleaveland, Jr., Justice of the Peace, May 1830; New London County, "County Court Records," vol. 32, June 1830, case 375; New London County, County Court files, Box 317, June 1830, case 375.
25. Connecticut Court Records, Justice Courts, Box 569, New London, William F. Brainard, Justice of the Peace, Oct. 1831; Barber files, CSL.
26. Connecticut General Assembly Papers, Box 52, 1850 Reports 1–66, #2 Report on County Jails; Connecticut General Assembly Papers, Box 53,1851 Reports 1–34, #1, Report of Hartford County jailer; Connecticut General Assembly Papers, Box 66, 1855 Reports to the General Assembly 1–33B, #19A, State Prison Warden's Report; New London County, "County Court Records of Trials," vol. 33, Nov. 1841, case 236; New London County, County Court files, Box 333, Nov. 1841, case 236; New London County, "County Court Records of Trials," vol. 33, Nov. 1842, case 204; New London County, County Court files, Box 334, Nov. 1842, case 204.
27. Connecticut Court Records, Justice Courts, Box 569, New London, Henry Douglas, Justice of the Peace, Oct. 1843; New London County, "County Court Records of Trials," vol. 34, June 1849, case 385; New London County, County Court files, Box 341, June 1849, case 385; Connecticut Superior Court, "New London County Records," vol. 19, Aug. 1855, case 228/436; Connecticut Superior Court, New London County files, Box 70, Aug. 1855, case 436.
28. Connecticut General Assembly Papers, Box 66, 1855 Reports to the General Assembly 1–33B, 15G, Reform School Superintendent's report.
29. *The Code of 1650* (Hartford: Silas Andrus, 1830), 64–65.
30. Swift, vol. 2, 368.
31. Crimes and Misdemeanors, Series I, Vol. 1, part 1, Connecticut archives, 104–105.
32. Crimes and Misdemeanors, Series I, Vol. 1, part 1, Connecticut archives, 104–105.
33. Crimes and Misdemeanors, Series 1, Vol. 1, part 1, Connecticut archives, 108.
34. Crimes and Misdemeanors, Series 1, Vol. 1, part 1, Connecticut archives, 107.
35. Crimes and Misdemeanors, Series 1, Vol. 1, part 1, Connecticut archives, 109a; New London County, "County Court Records," vol. III, Sept. 1676. #86.
36. Crimes and Misdemeanors, Series 1, Vol. 1, part 1, Connecticut archives, 109 a.
37. Ibid., 109a, 109b, 110.

38. Ibid., 112a.
39. Crimes and Misdemeanors, Series 1, Vol. 1, part 1, 110.
40. Crimes and Misdemeanors, Series 1, vol. 1, part 1, 114; New London County, County Court Records, vol. 1, #53, #62; Caulkins, 369.
41. Connecticut Superior Court, New London County files, CSL, Box 21, March 1780, case 34; Brown and Rose, 275; *The Connecticut Courant,* July 31, 1786; Connecticut Superior Court New London County files, CSL, Box 25, Sept. 1786, case 74.
42. Connecticut Superior Court New London County files, CSL, Box 25, Sept. 1786, case 74; *The Connecticut Courant,* Oct. 9, 1786 and Oct. 30, 1786. Thank you to Denise Grosskoph for directing my attention to the newspaper articles on this case.
43. Connecticut General Assembly Papers, 1786, Petitions, Resolves, 306.
44. *The Connecticut Courant,* Dec. 25, 1786.
45. Daniel Cohen, *Pillars of Salt, Monuments of Grace* (Oxford: Oxford University Press, 1993), 90–93.
46. Frances M. Caulkins, *History of New London, Connecticut* (New London, CT: H. D. Utley, 1895), 576–77.
47. New London County Superior Court, Papers by Subject, Box 134, Inquests, 1711–1870 A-M, May 23, 1810.
48. Connecticut Superior Court, New London County, "Records of Trials," vol. 3, Jan. 1816, case 50; Brown and Rose, 15; Connecticut Superior Court, New London County files, Box 42, Jan. 1816, case 50.
49. Connecticut Court Records, Justice Courts, Box 569, New London, Josiah Isham, Justice of the Peace, Sept. 1828.
50. Connecticut Superior Court, New London County, "Record of Trials," vol. 5, Oct. 1828, case 96; Connecticut Superior Court, New London County files, Box 50, Oct. 1828, case 96.
51. Connecticut General Assembly Papers, Box 18, 1833 continued Petitions and Resolves, 1–45, #5A, 9A.
52. Ibid. It is notable that at the original trial neither John nor anyone else raised the question of parental abuse to explain or justify John's action.
53. Connecticut General Assembly Papers, Box 18, 1833 continued Petitions and Resolves, 1–45, #5A, 9A.
54. Connecticut General Assembly, Rejected Bills, Box 21, folder 131, 1846, #86.
55. Connecticut General Assembly, Rejected Bills, Box 26, folder 173, 1851, #51.
56. *The Hartford Courant,* vol. XVII, no. 165, July 26, 1853, 2; Connecticut General Assembly Rejected Bills 1853–54, Box 29, folder 195, 1854, # 68 G-H.
57. *The Hartford Courant,* vol. XVII, no. 165, July 26, 1853, 2.
58. Connecticut General Assembly, Rejected Bills 1853–54, Box 29, folder 195, 1854, #68 A.
59. New Haven County, "Superior Court Docket," from October 1852 to April 1855, October term for 1853, case 5 and January term for 1854, case 1; Connecticut General Assembly, Rejected Bills 1853–54, Box 29, folder 195, 1854, #68 A.

60. *The Hartford Courant,* July 26, 1853, 2–3; *The Hartford Courant,* "The value of circumstantial evidence," August 4, 1853, 2; Connecticut General Assembly Rejected Bills 1853–54, Box 29, folder 195, # 68 G-H.
61. Connecticut General Assembly Rejected Bills 1853–54, Box 29, folder 195, #70 A-C, 71–80.
62. Ibid., #68 A.
63. Ibid., #69 A-D.
64. Connecticut General Assembly Rejected Bills 1853–54, Box 29, folder 195, 1854, #69 D; *The Hartford Courant,* August 20, 1853, 2; New Haven County, "Superior Court Docket," from October 1852 to April 1855, October term for 1853, case 5 and January term for 1854, case 1. Included with the files for this case was a note from Leander Parmalee, jailer at the New Haven County Jail, that he had called out eighteen policemen and the military, including a captain, three lieutenants, and thirty-eight privates to attend Michael's hanging. Considering the outpouring of support for Michael from the Irish community in New Haven, he might have been anticipating a public challenge to the execution.

NOTES TO CHAPTER THREE

1. Everett C. Goodwin, *The Magistracy Rediscovered: Connecticut: 1636–1818* (Ann Arbor: UMI Research Press, 1981), 3; Bruce H. Mann, *Neighbors and Strangers: Law and Community in Early Connecticut* (Chapel Hill, NC: University of North Carolina Press, 1987), 5.
2. *The American Puritans: Their Prose and Poetry,* Perry Miller, ed. (Garden City, NY: Anchor Books, 1956), 90 - 91.
3. Edmund S. Morgan, *The Puritan Family: Religion and Domestic Relations in Seventeenth-Century New England* (New York: Harper & Row Publishers, Inc., 1966), 2–7.
4. Morgan, *90–92; The Code of 1650* (Hartford: Silas Andrus, 1830), 11–12, 38–39; *The Public Records of the Colony of Connecticut,* vol. I, Benjamin Trumbull, ed. *(Hartford: F .A Brown, 1850), 521;* Eva Butler, "Transcripts of New London Town Meetings," vol. V, June 1662, 13.
5. *Acts and Laws of His Majesties Colony of Connecticut,* 1702 (Boston: Bartholomew Green & John Allen, 1702), 59; *Public Records of the Colony of Connecticut,* vol. V, Charles Hoadly, ed. (Hartford: Case, Lockwood, & Brainard, 1870), 382–83; *Acts and Laws of His Majesties Colony of Connecticut* (New London, CT: Timothy Green, 1715), 207; *Acts and Laws of His Majesties Colony of Connecticut, 1716–1749* (Hartford, CT: reissued in facsimile by Albert C. Bates, 1919), 280.
6. *Public Statutes of the State of Connecticut,* revised: 1821 (Hartford, CT: S. G. Goodrich, 1821), 169–170; *Public Statutes of the State of Connecticut,* 1838, Title 105: section 3, 595; *Connecticut Public Acts, 1849–1854,* chapter 49, 95.
7. *The Code of 1650, 43–44.*
8. *Acts and Laws of His Majesties Colony of Connecticut* (1702), 98, 104; *Acts and Laws of His Majesties Colony of Connecticut* (1715), 68, 106;

Acts and Laws of His Majesties Colony of Connecticut (1716–1749), 1721, 261–262. In none of the cases of Sabbath breaking reported by the justices of the peace did they ever invoke the penalty against parents or guardians. Adults clearly accepted responsibility for this type of misbehavior by their children.

9. *Acts and Laws of the State of Connecticut, 1796–1808,* 1795, 370.
10. New London County, "County Court Records," vol. 16, June 1727, case 243; New London County, County Court files, Box 167, June 1727; Barbour files, CSL.
11. New London County, "County Court Records," vol. 13, Feb. 1722/23, case 243; New London County, County Court files, Box 103, Feb. 1722/23, case 69.
12. New London County, Justice Court Records, Box 565, New London, John Hempsted, Justice of the Peace, Nov. 1773; Barbour files, CSL; Norwich, CT Justice Court, Richard Hide, Justice of the Peace, Sept. 1774, CSL; New London County, Justice Court Records, Box 565, New London, John Hempsted, Justice of the Peace, July 1778; Barbour files, CSL.
13. Zephaniah Swift, *A System of the Laws of the State of Connecticut,* vol. 2 (Windham, CT: John Byrne, 1796), 326.
14. *Acts and Laws of the State of Connecticut,* 1796 - 1808, 1795, 370; Connecticut Court Records, Justice Courts, Box 554, Lyme, CT, William Noyes, Justice of the Peace, April 1796; Justice Court Records, Lyme, CT, Moses Warren Collection, July 1800.
15. Connecticut Court Records, Justice Court, Box 553, Goshen, Theodore Norton, Justice of the Peace, Aug. 1815, files 211, 212, 213, 214.
16. Connecticut Court Records, Justice Courts, Box 553, Goshen, Theodore North, Justice of the Peace, Aug. 1819, file 264.
17. Connecticut Court Records, Justice Courts, Box 568, New London, William P. Cleaveland, Jr., Justice of the Peace, April 1826; Barbara W. Brown & James M. Rose, *Black Roots in Southeastern Connecticut* (Detroit: Gail Research Co., 1980), 209.
18. Connecticut General Assembly Papers, Box 66, 1855 Reports to the General Assembly, 1–33 B, #15 G, "Reform School Superintendent's Report," #13 A, "Reform School Chaplain's Report," #14 B "Letters from boys at the Reform School."
19. George Lee Haskins, *Law and Authority in Early Massachusetts* (New York: The Macmillan Company, 1960), 82; *The Code of 1650, 65.*
20. *Records of the Particular Court of Connecticut,* 1639–1663 (Hartford, CT: The Connecticut Historical Society, 1928), March 7, 1650/51, 97; New London County, "County Court Records," vol. 3, June 1, 1680, 142.
21. *Acts and Laws of His Majesty's Colony of Connecticut* (1702), 85; New London County, "County Court Records," vol. III, 114, 115.
22. *Public Records of the Colony of Connecticut,* vol. V, Hoadly, ed., 317.
23. New London County, "County Court Records," vol. 3, 211, New London County, County Court Files, Box 158, 1713; Barbour Collection, CSL. While the colony had laws against disorderly conduct in general, none specifically prohibited adults from meeting together in the houses of fellow residents either during the day or evening.

24. *Acts and Laws of His Majesties Colony of Connecticut in New England* (New London: 1715), 86, 149; *Public Records of the Colony of Connecticut,* vol. V, Hoadly, ed., 130, 531.
25. *The Public Records of the Colony of Connecticut,* vol. VI, Hoadly, ed. (Hartford: Case, Lockwood, & Brainard, 1872), 166, 171, 290; New London County, "County Court Trials," vol. 12, 119–120, cases 88, 89, 123; New London County, County Court files, Box 162, June, 1720, cases 88, 89.
26. *Acts and Laws of His Majesties Colony of Connecticut,* 1715, 158; Zephaniah Swift, *A System of the Laws of the State of Connecticut,* vol. I (Windham, CT: John Byrne, 1795), 217–18; New London County, "County Court Trials and Dockets," vol. 21, Aug. 1748, case 72.
27. *The Public Records of the Colony of Connecticut,* vol. X, Charles J. Hoadly, ed. (Hartford: Case, Lockwood, & Brainard, 1877), 557–559; New London County, "County Court Trials and Dockets, " vol. 22, Feb. 1757, case 161; New London County, County Court files, Box 205, Nov. 1757, case 161; New London County, "County Court Trials and Dockets, " vol. 22, June 1758, case 5; New London County, "County Court Trials and Dockets," vol. 23, Feb. 1759, case 129; Barbour files, CSL.
28. *The Public Records of the Colony of Connecticut,* vol. X, 558; vol. XI, 256–57.
29. New London County, "County Court Trials and Dockets," vol. 22, June 1758, case 144; New London County, County Court files, Box 206, Nov. 1758, case 28; Barbour files, CSL; Frances M. Caulkins, *History of New London, Connecticut* (New London, CT: H. D. Utley, 1895), 512.
30. New London County, "County Court Trials and Dockets," vol. 23, Feb. 1760, case 19; New London County, County Court files, Box 207, Feb. 1760, case 19; Barbour files, CSL.
31. Connecticut Court Records, Justice Courts, Box 579, Stonington, Nathaniel Minor, Justice of the Peace, Feb. and March 1783.
32. New London County, "County Court Trials and Dockets," vol. 26, Nov. 1784, case 221; New London County, County Court files, Box 241, Nov. 1784, case 221.
33. *Acts and Laws of Connecticut,* 1796–1808, 326.
34. Connecticut Court Records, Justice Courts, New London, Box 567, Josiah Isham, Justice of the Peace, Feb. 1810.
35. Connecticut Court Records, Justice Courts, New London, Box 568, William P. Cleaveland, Jr., Justice of the Peace, Jan. 1813.
36. Hugh Campbell Black, *Black's Law Dictionary,* sixth edition (St. Paul, MN: West Publishing Co., 1990), 1327; Albert E. Van Dusen, *Connecticut* (New York: Random House, 1961), 182–184; Connecticut Superior Court, "New London County Record of Trials." vol. 3, Sept. 1814, case 35.
37. Connecticut Superior Court, "New London County Record of Trials," vol. 3, Sept. 1814, case 18; Connecticut Superior Court, New London County files, Box 41, Sept. 1814, case 18.
38. Connecticut Court Records, Justice Courts, Box 566, New London, Eben Learned, Justice of the Peace, Jan. 1814.

39. Connecticut Court Records, Justice Courts, New London, Box 567, William P. Cleaveland, Jr., Justice of the Peace, Sept. 1825.
40. Connecticut Court Records, Justice Courts, Box 566, William P. Cleaveland, Jr., Justice of the Peace, July 1827; Brown and Rose, 209.
41. Connecticut Court Records, Justice Courts, Box 568, New London, Henry Douglas, Justice of the Peace, Sept. 1842.
42. Connecticut General Assembly Papers, Box 66, 1855, Reports to the General Assembly 1–33B, 15G Reform School Superintendent's Report, 13C-E, Reform School Chaplain's Report.
43. New London County, County Court files, Box 321, June 1833, case 253.
44. New London County, "County Court Record of Trials." vol. 33, Feb. 1834, case 317; New London County, County Court files, Box 321, Feb. 1834, case 317.
45. New London County, "County Court Records of Trials," vol. 33, Nov. 1837, case 322; New London County, County Court files, Box 327, Nov. 1837, case 322.
46. New London County, "County Court Record of Trials," vol. 33, Feb. 1839, case 236.
47. New London County, "County Court Records," vol. 34, Nov. 1843, case 216; New London County, County Court files, Box 335, Nov. 1843, case 216.
48. Connecticut Court Records, Justice Courts, Box 566, New London, John Grace, Justice of the Peace, July, 1844.
49. Connecticut General Assembly Papers, Box 57, 1852, Acts, document 18.
50. New London County Court, "County Court Record of Trials," vol. 34, Nov. 1847, 341, case 579; New London County Court, County Court Files, Box 339, Nov. 1847, case 579; Brown and Rose, 30.
51. New London County, "County Court Record of Trials," vol. 34, Nov. 1848, 421, case 1012; New London County, County Court files, Box 340, Nov. 1848, case 1012.
52. *The Code of 1650,* 29–30.
53. *The Code of 1650,* 103.
54. *Records of the Particular Court,* 33.
55. *Colonial Records of the Colony of Connecticut,* Vol. 1, 124; Caulkins (1895), 250; New London County Court, County Court Records, Vol. 3, 53, 59.
56. *Acts and Laws of His Majesties Colony of Connecticut* (1716–1749), 1727, 344.
57. New London County, "County Court Trials and Dockets," vol. 17, June 1733, case 236; New London County, County Court files, Box 172, June 1733, case 236; Barbour files, CSL.
58. Ibid.
59. *Public Statutes of the State of Connecticut,* revised 1821, note 5, 177; Swift, vol. 1, 221.
60. Connecticut Superior Court, "New London County Record of Trials," vol. 2, Jan. 1804, case 118; Connecticut Superior Court, New London County files, Box 34, Jan. 1804, case 118; Barbour files, CSL.

61. *Records of the State of Connecticut,* vol. 10, 1800–1801, Albert E. Van Dusen, editor, 34n; *Public Statutes of the State of Connecticut,* revised 1821, 107, 177.
62. Connecticut Court Records, Justice Courts, Box 569, New London, John Grace, Justice of the Peace, Dec. 1844; Connecticut Court Records, Justice Courts, Box 579, Stonington, Frances Sheffield, Justice of the Peace, Jan. 1848.
63. Connecticut General Assembly Papers, Box 66, 1855 Reports to the General Assembly, 1–33B, 15G Reform School Superintendent's Report, 13D-E Reform School Chaplain's Report.
64. *The Public Records of the Colony of Connecticut,* vol. 1, Trumbull, editor, 527; *The Code of 1650,* 48; *Acts and Laws of His Majesties Colony of Connecticut* (1702), 7.
65. New London County, "County Court Trials," vol. 2, Sept. 14, 1668, 13; New London County, "County Court Records," vol. 7, June, 1702, 347; New London County, County Court files, Box 153, June 1702.
66. New London County, "County Court Records," vol. 12, 1719–1720, June 1720, case 74; New London County, County Court files, Box 162, June 1720, case 74.
67. New London County, "County Court Trials and Dockets," vol. 17, Nov. 1732, case 277; New London County, County Court files, Box 171, Nov. 1732, case 277.
68. New London County, County Court files, Box 180, Nov. 1739, case 28, case 30.
69. New London County, "County Court Trials and Dockets," vol. 21, June 1749, case 111; New London County, County Court files, Box 194, June 1749, case 111.
70. New London County, "County Court Trials and Dockets," vol. 21, Nov. 1750, case 13; New London County, County Court files, Box 194, case 13.
71. New London County, "County Court Trials and Dockets," vol. 21, Nov. 1751, case 16.
72. New London County, "County Court Trials and Dockets," vol. 23, Nov. 1762, case 59; New London County, "County Court Trials and Dockets," vol. 24, Nov. 1763, case 62; New London County, County Court files, Nov. 1763, case 62; Barbour files, CSL.
73. Haskins, *Law and Authority in Early Massachusetts* (New York: The Macmillan Company, 1960), 147; *The Code of 1650, 29; Acts and Laws of His Majesties Colony of Connecticut in New England* (1702), *12; Acts and Laws of the State of Connecticut,* 1796–1808, 186, 349.
74. Richard H. Phelps, *Newgate of Connecticut: Its Origin and Early History* (Camden, ME: Picton Press, 1996), 92.
75. Connecticut General Assembly Papers, Box 5, 1825 Petitions and Resolves 1–50, # 1 A-D, 3, 4.
76. Connecticut General Assembly Papers, Box 7, Rejected Bills 1827–1829, folder 27, 1828–1829, #57.

77. Connecticut General Assembly Papers, Box 7, Rejected Bills, 1827–1829, folder 27, 1828–1829, #67; Connecticut General Assembly Papers, Box 11, 1829 Petitions and Resolves 1–34, #24A, 24B; Phelps, 112.
78. Connecticut General Assembly Papers, Box 12, 1830 Petitions and Resolves 1–39, # 32A, 33A.
79. Connecticut General Assembly Papers, Box 19, 1834 Petitions Granted 72–149, #112 A. The issue of sexual capability was a factor in the 1831 clemency petition of David Jackson, imprisoned for life in 1824 on charges of bestiality. At the time of the trial the petition claimed that the boy was under the age of fourteen and "had not attained to years of puberty." The trial judge had accepted the state attorney's objection to evidence of the boy's age. The boy was not yet twenty-one at the time of the petition. The Assembly ordered his freedom. General Assembly Rejected Bills, Box 9, 1831–34, folder 39, 1831–32, #56.
80. New Haven County Superior Court files, Box 600, 1828–1830, Jan. 1829, *State v. Joel Doolittle;* Connecticut General Assembly Rejected Bills, Box 9, 1833, folder 43; Connecticut General Assembly Papers, Box 22, 1835 Reports, folder 2, 1–26, # 36D, page 8, Prison Warden's Report; Box 22, 1835 cont., Petitions Granted.
81. Connecticut General Assembly Papers, Box 44, 1846, Towns and Boroughs, 1–122, #52–52.
82. Litchfield County Superior Court Dockets, vol. 3, 1833–1841, Feb. 1841, #158; Connecticut General Assembly Papers, Box 48, 1848, State Prison and Jails 1–113, #7.
83. Connecticut General Assembly Rejected Bills, Box 26, 1851, folder 174, #82A.
84. Connecticut General Assembly Rejected Bills, Box 9, folder 39, 1831–31, #62.
85. *Acts and Laws of His Majesties Colony of Connecticut* (1716–1749), 1717, 225.
86. Connecticut General Assembly papers, Box 30, 1839, Resolutions with petitions, #33 a, c.
87. A number of eighteenth-century prosecutions for lascivious carriage appeared to concern attempted rape or attempted rape, as in 1750 when forty-eight-year-old Nathaniel Post of Norwich tipped over Lydia Williams and, "exposed her most private parts, taking out his most private part." The New London County Court found Post guilty only of lascivious carriage but fined him the punitive sum of eighty pounds with thirty-nine pounds in court costs. New London County, "County Court Trials and Dockets," vol. 21, Nov. 1750, case 149; files, Box 196, case 149.
88. Connecticut Court Records, Justice Courts, Box 570, New London, William P. Cleaveland, Jr., Justice of the Peace, Feb. 1822; Connecticut Court Records, Justice Courts, Box 569, New London, William P. Cleaveland, Jr., Justice of the Peace, July 1828, Sept. 1828.
89. New London County, "County Court Record of Trials," vol. 34, Feb. 1848, cases 668, 670, 671; New London County, County Court files, Box 339, Feb. 1848, case 671; Brown and Rose, 129, 343, 360.

90. *The Code of 1650,* 28; *Records of the Particular Court of Connecticut, 1639–1663,* 3, 13, 48.
91. Connecticut Superior Court, New London County, files, Box 17, Sept. 1767, case 51.
92. New London County, County Court files, Box 226, June 1770, case 106.
93. New London County, "County Court Record of Trials," vol. 32, Dec. 1817, case 456; New London County, County Court files, Box 298, Dec. 1817, case 456; Barbour files, CSL.
94. *Public Statutes of the State of Connecticut,* revised 1821, Title 22, page 163, section 61; Connecticut General Assembly, Rejected Bills, 1831–34, Box 9, folder 39, # 56, 58. Ironically under civil law, minors were still not able to sign notes or enter into contracts, yet the Assembly required as a condition of the boy's release that he obligate himself for payment of the costs of his prosecution and appeal.
95. Connecticut General Assembly Papers, Box 63, 1854 Governor's Messages, 1–16, # 4 O-P.

NOTES TO CHAPTER FOUR

1. *The Code of* 1650 (Hartford: Silas Andrus, 1830), 38–39, 42; Philip J. Greven, *Child-Rearing Concepts, 1628–1861: Historical Sources* (Itasca, IL: F. E. Peacock Publishers, Inc., 1973), 14.
2. John Locke, *Second Treatise of Government,* edited by C. B. Macpherson (Indianapolis, IN: Hackett Publishing Co., Inc., 1980), 32; Greven, 29, 44, 89, 125.
3. Howard Cohen, *Equal Rights for Children* (Totowa, NY: Littlefield, Adams, & Co., 1980), vii; George Lee Haskins, *Law and Authority in Early Massachusetts (New York: The Macmillan Company, 1960),* 82; Michael Grossberg, *Governing the Hearth* (Chapel Hill, NC: University of North Carolina Press, 1985), 236.
4. Joseph M. Hawes, *The Children's Rights Movement* (Boston: Twayne Publishers, 1991), 2; *The Code of 1650, 38–39.*
5. Hawes, 4–5; *Public Records of the Colony of Connecticut,* vol. I, Benjamin Trumbull, ed. (Hartford: F. A. Brown, 1850), 515; *Acts and Laws of His Majesties Colony of Connecticut* (Boston: Bartholomew Green & John Allen, 1702), 98.
6. *The Code of 1650,* 66; *Acts and Laws of His Majesties Colony of Connecticut* (1702), 75.
7. Zephaniah Swift, *A System of the Laws of the State of Connecticut,* vol. 1, (Windham, CT: John Byrne, 1795), 221–222; vol. 2, 28, 302.
8. New London County Superior Court Records, Papers by Subject: Inquests 1711–1870, A-M, Box 134, Sept. 23, 1717, October 14, 1779, April 8, 1781; Inquests 1711–1870, N-Z, Box 135, July 2, 1743, October 1786. The two cases involving Native-American children at the end of the eighteenth century did not include Native Americans in the jury of inquest, reflecting how the state had marginalized its Native-American population.

9. Jean Jacques Rousseau, *Emile* (New York: Dutton, 1962); Peter Gregg Slater, *Children in the New England Mind in Death and in Life* (Hamden, CT: Archon Books, 1977), 9.
10. New London County Superior Court, Papers by Subject: Inquests 1711–1870, A-M, October 3, 1834, March 30, 1841, March 1854.
11. William J. Frost, *Connecticut Education* (Chester, CT: Pequot Press, 1974), 49–50; *Acts and Laws of His Majesties Colony of Connecticut,* 1702, 95; *Public Statutes of the State of Connecticut* revised 1821 (Hartford: S. G. Goodrich et al., 1821), 319.
12. Charles Manwaring, *A Digest of Early Connecticut Probate Records,* vol. 1, 1635–1700 (Baltimore, MD: Genealogical Publishing Co., Inc., 1995, c1904), 114; *Records of the Particular Court* (Hartford: The Connecticut Historical Society, 1928), 243; Eva Butler transcripts, CSL, New London town meeting records vol. X, April 1, 1662, 48.
13. New London Town Papers, 1674–1925, Bonds and Indentures, 1728–1850, Box 3, April 1750; Eva Butler transcripts, New London miscellaneous records, 1778–1779.
14. Connecticut Court Records, CSL, Coddington Billings Collection 1743–1844, Box 7, Waterford, CT, August, 1820; Lyme Town Papers, March 21, 1825 (located in the Lyme Town Hall attic); East Haddam, CT Bigelow Collection, July 1, 1842, #228. Though the indenture promised William training as a farmer, town records from 1854 identified the then 21-year-old as a factory operative.
15. *Acts and Laws of the State of Connecticut, 1796–1808,* 293 (A problem with this safety valve for abused children was that if the courts did not uphold their claims of abuse, the children had to serve triple the time they had been absent from their employer's service.); *Public Records of the Colony of Connecticut,* vol. IV, Charles J. Hoadly, ed. (Hartford: 1868), 310; Swift, vol. 1, 222.
16. *Public Statutes of the State of Connecticut,* revised 1821, 319, section 6.
17. *Records of the Particular Court,* 21, 119, 203; Swift, vol. 1, 222.
18. Manwaring, vol. 1, 524.
19. New London County Court, County Court files, Box 154, July 26, 1703.
20. Ibid.
21. Ibid.
22. Ibid., Sept. 21, 1703.
23. Ibid. Despite being in an adversarial role in the case concerning Martha Tomson, William Borden later served as guardian to Temperance, the youngest daughter of Jonathan and Mary Tilison, after Jonathan's death in 1719. New London Probate Records, #615–616 microfilm 1135, Sept. 29, 1719.
24. New London County, County Court files, Box 159, Nov. 1716.
25. New London County, County Court files, Box 163, case 111, Nov. 1720.
26. Ibid.
27. New London County, "County Court Records," vol. 12, case 111, Nov. 1720, 186.

28. New London County, "County Court Records," vol. 13, June 1723, case 94, 280; New London County, County Court files, Box 164, Feb. 1722 - Nov. 1723. Connecticut had passed a law in 1702 directing that no apprentice bound for learning a trade could be assigned to another master for more than one year without the consent of some authority authorized by the Court. This was the law under which Thomas sought protection, but the court ignored his plea to review the legality of his current indenture. *Acts and Laws* (1702), 75.
29. New London County, "County Court Records," vol. 13, case 95, June 1723, 280; New London County, County Court files, Box 164, case 95, June 1723.
30. New London County, County Court files, Box 190, June 1744, case 204.
31. New London County Superior Court Papers by Subject, Inquests, 1711–1870, A - M, Box 134, Jan. 14, 1750/51; Connecticut Superior Court, New London County files, Box 12, Sept. 1751, case 7.
32. New London County, "County Court Trials and Dockets," vol. 22, June 1754, case 68.
33. New London County, County Court files, Box 201, Feb. 1755, case 50.
34. New London County, "County Court Trials and Dockets," vol. 26, Feb. 1787, case 244. This case may also have been notable because Freeman was a common surname used by freed slaves in Groton. The Court extended its protection to her perhaps in spite of her race.
35. Connecticut Superior Court, New London County files, Box 22, March 1781, case 10.
36. New London County, "County Court Trial and Dockets," vol. 27, Feb. 1796, case 42.
37. Connecticut Superior Court, New London County, "Records of Trials," vol. 1, Mar. 1800, case 67 (1/62); Connecticut Superior Court, New London County files, Box 31, Mar. 1800, case 67.
38. Ibid.
39. Connecticut Court Records, Justice Courts, Box 579 Stonington, Elijah Palmer, Justice of the Peace, June 1801.
40. New London County, "County Court Trials and Dockets," vol. 29, Nov. 1805, case 33; Barbour files, CSL. In a second case Nathan sued the master of the ship for $70 for unpaid wages for the same voyage on the *Favorite* from Norwich to South Carolina. When he failed to appear in the New London County Court to prosecute the case, the Court found in favor of Stanton. New London County, County Court files, Box 277, Nov. 1805, case 32.
41. Connecticut Superior Court, New London County, "Records of Trials," vol. 5, Sept. 1832, case 24.
42. Connecticut Superior Court, New London County, files, Box 52, Sept. 1832, case 24.
43. Connecticut Superior Court, New London County, "Trials," vol. 8, Mar. 1850, case 60, 486; Connecticut Superior Court, New London County, files, Box 65, Mar. 1850, case 60.

44. New London County Court, "County Court Records," vol. 33, Nov. 1838, case 246; New London County, County Court files, Box 329, Nov. 1838, case 246.
45. New London County, "County Court Records," vol. 33, Nov. 1839, case 51; New London County, County Court files, box 330, Nov., 1839, case 51.
46. *The Code of 1650,* 39; Swift, vol. II, 28.
47. New London County, "County Court Records," vol. 33, Feb. 1836, case 225; New London County, County Court files, Box 325, Feb. 1836, case 325.
48. Connecticut Superior Court, New London County, "Record of Trials," vol. 7, Mar. 1842, case 27; Connecticut Superior Court, New London County, files, Box 59, Mar. 1842, case 27.
49. Tapping Reeve, *Law of Baron and Femme, of Parent and Child, of Guardian and Ward* (New Haven: Oliver Steele, 1816), 288.
50. *Public Records of the Colony of Connecticut,* vol. IV, 285; Connecticut Superior Court, New London County files, Box 7, Sept. 1737, case 62; Barbara W. Brown and James M. Rose, *Black Roots in Southeastern Connecticut: 1650–1900* (Detroit: Gail Research Co., 1980), 158.
51. Connecticut Superior Court, New London County files, Box 10, Mar. 1747, case 28.
52. Connecticut Superior Court, New London County files, Box 11, Sept. 1750.
53. Connecticut Superior Court, New London County files, Box 12, Mar. 1753, case 13; Box 7, Sept. 1853, case 35.
54. Connecticut Superior Court, New London County files, Box 14, Sept. 1759, case 36, Sept. 1760, case 41; Connecticut Superior Court, New London County files, Box 23, Sept. 1784, case 165.
55. *Connecticut State Records,* vol. 14, Arnold, ed., May 1808, 36; *Public Statutes of Connecticut,* revised 1821, Title 22, 153.
56. Cornelia Hughes Dayton, *Women Before the Bar: Gender, Law and Society in Connecticut, 1639–1789* (Chapel Hill, NC: University of North Carolina Press, 1995), 12; Connecticut Superior Court, New London County "Records of Trials," vol. 2, Jan. 1808, case 123; Connecticut Superior Court, New London County files, Box 37, Jan. 1808, case 123; Brown & Rose, 279.
57. Connecticut Superior Court, New London County files, Box 52, Sept. 1832, case 70 and 102; New London County, Superior Court Letters by Subject, Inquests, 1711–1875, N - Z, Box 135, Sept. 17, 1832.
58. Connecticut Court Records, Justice Courts, Box 554, Lyme, "Records of William Noyes, 1790–1806," Jan. 1801, 101. At the same justice court session Noyes heard charges of lascivious carriage against Munsel and Anna Simons of Lyme. While he found the writ insufficient in law and dismissed the charge, the case may have provided an explanation of the tension between father and daughter.
59. Connecticut Superior Court, New London County, "Record of Trials," vol. 1, Jan. 1803, case 14/129; Connecticut Superior Court, New London County files, Box 33, Jan. 1803, case 14/129; Swift, vol. 2, 302.
60. New London County, County Court files, Box 227, Nov. 1805, case 52.

61. Connecticut Superior Court, New London County, "Records of Trials," vol. 3, Jan. 1815, 48; Connecticut Superior Court, New London County files, Box 41, Jan. 1815, case 47; Brown & Rose, 96; Phelps, 93, 98–101.
62. Connecticut Court Records, Coddington Billings Collection 1743–1844, Box 7, Stonington, May 1815, CSL.
63. New London County, "County Court Record of Trials," vol. 33, Feb. 1834, case 303; New London County, County Court files, Box 321, Feb. 1834, case 303.
64. Connecticut Superior Court, New London County, "Record of Trials," vol. 6, Mar. 1835, case 88; Connecticut Superior Court, New London County files, Box 53, Mar. 1835, cases 88, 90. Matilda Davis was also known as Matilda Tuma. Despite the damning evidence against her, the State did not even arrest her for the death of Jane until March of 1835. Also notable in this case was the failure of witnesses to intervene to protect the girl from the abuse.
65. Connecticut Superior Court, New London County, "Record of Trials," vol. 6, Mar. 1837, case 222; Connecticut Superior Court, New London County files, Box 55, Mar. 1837, cases 221, 222; New London County, County Court "Record of Trials," vol. 34, Nov. 1846, page 247, case 922; New London County, County Court files, Box 338, Nov. 1846, case 922; Connecticut Superior Court, New London County, "Trials," vol. 8, Aug. 1851, page 606, case 694; Connecticut Superior Court, New London County files, Box 66, Aug. 1851, case 694.
66. New London County Superior Court, Papers by Subject, Inquests, 1711–1870 A - M, Box 135, Oct. 30, 1842; Connecticut Superior Court, New London County, "Record of Trials," vol. 7, Mar. 1843, case 522; Connecticut Superior Court, New London County files, Box 60, Mar. 1843, case 521, 522.
67. Connecticut Superior Court, New London County, "Record of Trials," vol. 6, Sept. 1837, case 265; Connecticut Superior Court, New London County files, Box 55, Sept. 1837, case 264, 265; Connecticut General Assembly Papers, 1840, cont., Reports 1–36, Box 32, 36 Q.
68. *Statutes of Connecticut,* 1838, Title 20, Crimes and Punishments, 147.

NOTES TO CHAPTER FIVE

1. Zephaniah Swift, *A System of the Laws of Connecticut,* vol. 2 (Windham, CT: John Byrne, 1796), 237.
2. Cornelia Hughes Dayton, *Women Before the Bar: Gender, Law, and Society in Connecticut, 1639–1789* (Chapel Hill: University of North Carolina Press, 1995), 12.
3. *The Code of 1650* (Hartford: Silas Andrus, 1830), 28, 30, 48; *Records of the Particular Court of* Connecticut (Hartford: The Connecticut Historical Society, 1928), 3, 10, 31, 35; Acts *and Laws of His Majesties Colony of Connecticut* (Boston: Bartholomew Green & John Allen, 1702), 63; Swift, vol. 2, 333.
4. Swift, vol. 2, 308–309. Swift noted in 1797 that carnal knowledge of a female under the age of ten, whether against her consent or not, was consid-

ered a rape under the common law. Connecticut did not pass a statute specifically addressing this issue until 1821. At that time though punishment for rape was the death penalty, the new law directed only life imprisonment for those who raped girls under ten.

5. Connecticut "Crimes and Misdemeanors," Series I, vol. 1, part 1, May 14, 1677, 87–89, 102.
6. New London County, County Court files, Box 175, June 1736, case 370; Judson Keith Deming, *Genealogy of John Deming* (Dubuque, Iowa: The Press of Mathis-Mets Co., 1904), 29; "Lyme Land Records," vol. 4, Feb. 6, 1722/23, 91. In 1723 Greenfield sold his house and 4 acres in Lyme for 50 pounds and bought it back three years later for just 32 pounds; in 1726 Deming, newly arrived in Lyme, purchased a house and 60 acres for 550 pounds, "Lyme Land Records," vol. 4, page 226.
7. New London County, County Court files, Box 175, June 1736, case 370.
8. Ibid.
9. New London County, County Court, "Trials and Dockets," vol. 18, June 1736, case 370; Bruce P. Stark, *Lyme, Connecticut: From Founding to Independence* (self-published, 1976), 9; *The Diary of Joshua Hempstead, 1711–1758* (New London, CT: New London County Historical Society, 1901), 304.
10. "Old Lyme 1st Congregational Church Records," vol. 1, 65, CSL Microfilm, reel 74.
11. "Old Lyme 1st Congregational Church Records," vol. 1, 30, 66, CSL Microfilm, reel 74.
12. *The Code of 1650*, 29.
13. Connecticut "Crimes and Misdemeanors," 1702 - 1703, I: 322 - 331; New London County, County Court files, Box 154, Sept. 1703.
14. Connecticut Superior Court, New London County files, Box 13, Sept. 1756, case 30; Barbara W. Brown & James S. Rose, *Black Roots in Southeastern Connecticut* (Detroit: Gail Research Co., 1980), 469; Swift, vol. 2, 308 - 309.
15. Zephaniah Swift, *A System of the Laws of Connecticut,* vol. 1 (Windham, CT: John Byrne, 1795), 444 - 445.
16. Connecticut Superior Court, New London County "Records of Trials," vol. 2, Jan. 1809, case 83; Connecticut Superior Court, New London County files, Box 38, Jan. 1809, case 83; Richard H. Phelps, *Newgate of Connecticut* (Camden, ME: Picton Press, 1996), 92 -93; *Connecticut State Records,* vol. 15, Arnold, editor, May 1811, 223. The state-mandated sentence for attempted rape had been set at a life by the General Assembly in 1795, but the law allowed the Superior Court the discretion to shorten the sentence. *Acts and Laws of the State of Connecticut, 1796 - 1808,* Public Acts, 186.
17. Connecticut Superior Court, New London County "Record of Trials," vol. 3, Sept. 1813, case 55; Connecticut Superior Court, New London County files, Box 41, Sept. 1813, case 55.
18. Connecticut Superior Court, New London County "Record of Trials," vol. 3, Jan. 1815, case 46; Connecticut Superior Court, New London files, Box 41, Jan. 1815, case 46; Brown and Rose, 164.

19. *Public Statute Laws of the State of Connecticut,* revised 1821 (Hartford: S. G. Goodrich et al., 1821), 152, section 12; Swift, vol. 2, 308.
20. Connecticut Superior Court, New London County "Record of Trials," vol. 4, Oct. 1824, case 74; Connecticut Superior Court, New London County files, Box 47, Oct. 1824, case 74.
21. Connecticut Superior Court, New London County "Record of Trials," vol. 5, Oct. 1828, case 97; Connecticut Superior Court, New London County files, Box 50, Oct. 1828, case 97; *Black Roots in Southeastern Connecticut,* (43) identified Albert Brown as a black "feebleminded" farm hand, but there was no evidence in the file of the trial that the Court took Albert's mental state into consideration when assigning the less than maximum sentence for the crime.
22. Connecticut Superior Court, New London County "Record of Trials," vol. 5, Jan. 1829, case 99; Connecticut Superior Court, New London County files, Box 50, Jan. 1829, case 99. In the case files, the Superior Court identified Mary Ann merely as a single woman between the age of thirteen and fourteen years. *Black Roots in Southeastern Connecticut* identified both Whip and Olney as African Americans, 437.
23. *The Norwich Courier,* vol. IX, No. 13, June 23, 1830, XXXIII, no. 1666, "laws of Connecticut passed in A. D. 1830."
24. Connecticut Superior Court, New London "Record of Trials," vol. 5, Jan. 1830, case 34; Connecticut General Assembly, Rejected Bills, Box 9, folder 39, 1831 - 1832, # 65, 66.
25. Connecticut Superior Court, New London County "Record of Trials," vol. 5, Sept. 1830, case 4; Connecticut Superior Court, New London County files, Box 51, Sept. 1830, case 4, Connecticut General Assembly Papers, Box 22, Reports, Folder 2, 1–36, #36 D, page 9; Brown and Rose,, 434.
26. Connecticut Superior Court, New London County "Record of Trials," vol. 5, Sept. 1831, case 69; Connecticut Superior Court, New London County files, Box 52, Sept. 1831, case 69; Brown and Rose, 127; *Connecticut Gazette,* 28 September, 1831.
27. *Statutes of Connecticut* (1838), Title 20: section 10, 11, and 12, 145.
28. New London County Court, "County Court Trials and Dockets," vol. 33, June 1835, cases 283 and 284; Swift, vol. 2, 308–309.
29. Connecticut General Assembly Rejected Bills, Box 17, 1842, folder 105, #100A.
30. Connecticut Superior Court, New London County "Trials," vol. 8, Sept. 1846, cases 196 & 197, page 176, case 205, page 178; Connecticut Superior Court, New London County files, Box 62, Sept. 1846, case 197, 205; Connecticut Superior Court, New London County "Record of Trials," vol. 9, Sept. 1853, case 209, page 78; Connecticut Superior Court, New London County files, Box 68, Sept. 1853, case 209.
31. Connecticut Superior Court, New London County "Trials," vol. 8, Mar. 1848, case 580; Connecticut Superior Court, New London County files, Box 63, Mar. 1848, cases 539, 580, 581.
32. *Public Acts of the State of Connecticut,* 1836–1850, May session 1847, Chapter 27, page 27; Swift, vol. 2, 333. The records did not include suffi-

cient evidence to determine the class status of the victims of seduction, but notably, none of the victims was African American, perhaps implying that the law only protected the morals of white females.

33. New London County, "County Court Record of Trials," vol. 34, Nov. 1847, 337, case 543; New London County, County Court files, Box 339, Nov. 1847, case 543.
34. New London County, "County Court Record of Trials," vol. 34, Feb. 1848, 359, case 662; New London County, County Court files, Box 339, Feb. 1848, case 662.
35. New London County, "County Court Record of Trials," vol. 34, Nov. 1848, 413, case 968; New London County, County Court files, Box 340, Nov. 1848, case 968.
36. Connecticut Superior Court, New London County, "Trials," vol. 18, Sept. 1850, case 413, page 546; Connecticut Superior Court, New London County files, Box 65, Mar. 1850, case 413.
37. *The Code of 1650,* 30; Acts *and Laws of His Majesties Colony of Connecticut* (1702), 72–73.
38. *Public Records of the Colony of Connecticut,* vol. VI, Charles J. Hoadly, ed. (Hartford: Case, Lockwood, & Brainard, 1872), 526; "New Haven Vital Records," vol. 1, 148, CSL.
39. Connecticut Court Records, Justice Courts, Box 567, New London, William P. Cleaveland, J. P., April, 1812; Connecticut Superior Court, New London County "Record of Trials," vol. 3, Sept. 1812, case 108; Connecticut Superior Court, New London County files, Box 40, Sept. 1812, case 108; Barbour files, CSL.
40. Connecticut General Assembly, Rejected Bills 1824 - 1827, Box 6, folder 11, 1824, #145; folder 13, 1825, #108, 109, 110, and 112A; Phelps, 100, 112.
41. New London County, County Court files, Box 324, June 1835, case 277.
42. New London County, County Court files, Box 326, June 1836, case 234.
43. Connecticut General Assembly Papers, Box 31, 1840 Petitions Granted 87 - 141, #112 a.
44. Connecticut General Assembly, Rejected Bills, Box 29, folder 194, 1853, #48 a; Box 30, folder 200, 1854, #52 A &54 A.
45. Connecticut Superior Court, New London County "Trials," vol. 8, Sept. 1848, case 693, page 373; Connecticut Superior Court, New London County files, Box 64, Sept. 1848, case 693, 695.

NOTES TO CHAPTER SIX

1. Zephaniah Swift, *A System of the Laws of the State of Connecticut,* vol. 2 (Windham, CT: John Byrne, publisher, 1796), 368.
2. Cornelia Hughes Dayton, *Women Before the Bar: Gender, Law, and Society in Connecticut, 1639–1789* (Chapel Hill, NC: University of North Carolina Press, 1995), 11–12.
3. Connecticut Court Records, CSL, Justice Courts, Box 579, Stonington, Nathaniel Minor, Justice of the Peace, Feb. 1783.

4. Adam J. Hirsch, *The Rise of the Penitentiary* (Chelsea, MI: Bookcrafters, Inc., 1992), 7; Douglas Hay et al., *Albion's Fatal Tree: Crime and Society in Eighteenth-Century England* (London: Pantheon Books, 1975), 23–24.
5. Zephaniah Swift, *A System of the Laws of the State of Connecticut,* vol. 1 (Windham, CT: John Byrne, publisher, 1795), 205, 217.
6. New London County, Superior Court "Record of Trials'" vol. 2, Jan. 1804, case 118, CSL; New London County, Superior Court files, Box 34, Jan. 1804, case 118, CSL; Barbour Files, CSL.
7. Swift, vol. 2, 367–368.
8. State of Connecticut, *Crimes and Misdemeanors,* 2nd series, V 134, IV 157–58, II 131–2, V 10–12, 15,16, 49–50; Connecticut General Assembly Rejected Bills, CSL, Box 1, 1810 Committees, S-Z, #4, Box 2, 1813 Committees M-Z, folder 22, #31, Box 3, 1815, folder 4, # 110.
9. David J. Rothman, *The Discovery of the Asylum: Social Order and Disorder in the New Republic* (Boston: Little, Brown, 1971), 62; Connecticut General Assembly Rejected Bills, Connecticut State Library, Box 9, folder 43, #86.
10. Connecticut General Assembly Papers, Rejected Bills, 1833, Box 9, folder 43, #86.
11. Connecticut General Assembly Papers, Box 6, 1825, Reports and Misc. #2 A, cont. #7 M, 8 B, 8 J
12. Peter Gregg Slater, *Children in the New England Mind in Life and Death* (Hamden, CT: Archon Books, 1977), 72, 110, 148; Abigail Adams wrote to Mercy Otis Warren in 1773 quoting a poem that said the goal of parental education was to control "boisterious passion" and "humanize the soul." Warren's response was that she believed, "attention to fix a sacred regard to veracity in the bosom of youth the surest guard to virtue." L. H. Butterfield, editor, *Adams Family Correspondence,* 1773 (New York: Atheneum, 1965), 85, 87.
13. *The Code of 1650* (Hartford, CT: Silas Andrus, publisher, 1830), 39; Swift, vol. 1, 219.
14. Connecticut General Assembly, Rejected Bills, 1808–1810, Box 1, Committees S-Z, folder # 4; Connecticut General Assembly, Rejected Bills, 1811–1814, Box 2, Committees M-Z, folder 22, # 31; Connecticut General Assembly, Rejected Bills, 1815, Box 3, folder 4, # 110.
15. Swift, vol. 1, 222.
16. Swift, vol. 2, 319; *Acts and Laws of the State of Connecticut* (Hartford: Hudson & Goodwin, 1796), 186.
17. Richard H. Phelps, *Newgate of Connecticut: Its Origin and Early History* (Camden, ME: Picton Press, 1996), 92–95; Connecticut General Assembly Papers, Box 13, 1830 Reports, #34 D, Box 22, 1834 Reports, folder 2, #36 D, 8–12.
18. Connecticut General Assembly Papers, Box 13, 1835, Reports, number 2, #38 A.
19. Ibid., Reports #38 N.
20. Connecticut General Assembly Papers, Boxes 12–29, CSL.
21. Slater, 72.

22. Connecticut General Assembly Papers, Box 17, 1833 Public Acts and Resolutions, #23, CSL.
23. Connecticut General Assembly Papers, Box 17, 1833 Public Acts and Resolutions, #23, CSL; General Assembly Rejected Bills, Box 9, 1833, Folder 43, # 93.
24. Connecticut General Assembly Papers, CSL, Box 26, 1837 cont., Reports, Banks, #36 D.
25. Connecticut General Assembly Papers, CSL, Box 27, 1838 Reports, #66 d, Box 31, 1840 Reports, #26 A.
26. Connecticut General Assembly Papers, CSL, Box 35, 1842 Reports, #2b; Connecticut General Assembly Papers, CSL, Box 1, folder 105, Rejected Bills, #71; Connecticut General Papers, Box 36, 1843 Reports, 1–176, Prison Chaplain's report, 20.
27. Connecticut General Assembly Reports, CSL, Box 36, 1843, Juvenile, Miscellaneous, Resolves, #73 a.
28. Ibid., # 73 b.
29. Connecticut General Assembly Papers, CSL, Box 30, 1839, Rejected Bills, Resolutions with petitions, folder 63, 1836, #137; Connecticut General Assembly Reports, CSL, Box 36, 1843, Juvenile, Miscellaneous, Resolves, #73 C-D. Sigourney made it clear in her petition that she intended to train girls at her school in the domestic arts to enable them to find employment as maids, cooks, and laundresses.
30. Connecticut General Assembly Papers, CSL, Box 36, 1833, File 1–116, #47.
31. Connecticut General Assembly Papers, CSL, Box 40, 1845 Reports, #25; Box 52, 1850 Reports, #2.
32. Hartford County Superior Court files, CSL, Box 101, Jan. 1845; Connecticut General Assembly Papers, CSL, Box 44, 1847, Boroughs and Cities, #80, 81.
33. Connecticut General Assembly Papers, CSL, Box 21, Rejected Bills 1846–47, folder 131, #78.
34. Rothman, 62; Connecticut General Assembly Rejected Bills, CSL, Box 24, folder 156, #7; Connecticut General Assembly Papers, Box 50, 1849 Reports, #36C.
35. Connecticut General Assembly Papers, CSL, Box 53, 1851 Reports, #79 A-D.
36. Connecticut General Assembly Papers, CSL, Box 54, 1851, Messages and Proclamations, #43 H.
37. Connecticut General Assembly Papers, CSL, Box 63, 1854, Messages of Governors, # 4 G through Q.
38. Ibid.
39. Connecticut General Assembly Papers, CSL, Box 55, Public Acts, # 3 A-G.
40. Connecticut General Assembly Papers, CSL, Box 58, Proclamations, #40 H.
41. *The Hartford Courant,* vol. XVII, no. 187, August 20, 1853, 2.
42. Connecticut General Assembly Papers, CSL, Box 63, Governor's Messages, #40, Box 65, Military Commissions, #81 L.
43. Connecticut General Assembly Papers, CSL, Box 66, 1855 Reports to the General Assembly, #12 A, E, 1855 Reports, #14 C.

Bibliography

MANUSCRIPT SOURCES

Connecticut State Library, State Archives, Hartford, CT.
Barbour Collection of Connecticut Vital Records.
Connecticut Archives. Microfilm.
Crimes and Misdemeanors, Series 1 (1662–1789), Series 2, (1671–1820).
Old Lyme 1st Congregational Church Records. vol. 1.
Probate Records.
Court Records.
Coddington Billings Collection 1743–1844.
Hartford County Court Records.
Justice Courts.
Litchfield County Superior Court Dockets.
New Haven County Superior Court Dockets
New Haven County Superior Court Files.
New London County Court Records and Files.
New London County Superior Court Records.
New London County Trials and Dockets.
Early Families of Lyme, Connecticut. Record Group 74:36.
East Haddam, Connecticut. Bigelow Collection, 1842.
Connecticut General Assembly Papers.
Lyme Records Town Meeting Book, vol. 2, 1667–1734.
New Haven Vital Records. vol. 1.
Preston, Connecticut Town Papers, 1798.
Probate Records.
Lyme Land Records. vol. 4., 1726, vol. 6, 1736, located in the Lyme town hall.
Lyme Town Papers, 1825.
Old Lyme 1st Congregational Church Records, 1721–1876. Phoebe Noyes Library, Old Lyme, CT.

PRINTED PRIMARY SOURCES

Newspapers

Connecticut Courant (Hartford). 1786.
Connecticut Gazette. 1831.
Hartford Courant. 1853.
Norwich Courier. 1830.

Statutes, Courts Records, and Legal Treatises

Acts and Laws of His Majesties Colony of Connecticut in New England. Boston: Bartholomew Green and John Allen, 1702.

Acts and Laws of His Majesties Colony of Connecticut in New England. New London: Timothy Green, 1715.

Acts and Laws of His Majesties Colony of Connecticut in New England, 1716–1749. Hartford: reissued in facsimile by Albert C. Bates, 1919.

Acts and Laws of the State of Connecticut. Hartford: 1796.

Acts and Laws of the State of Connecticut, 1796–1808.

Connecticut Public Acts, 1849–1854.

Dutton, Henry A. *A Revision of Swift's Digest of the Laws of Connecticut.* New Haven: Henry M. Peck, 1884.

Hoadly, Charles J., et al. *Public Records of the State of Connecticut, 1776–1815.* 15 volumes. Hartford: 1894–1999.

Locke, John. *Second Treatise of Government.* C. B. Macpherson, ed. Indianapolis: Hackett Publishing Company, Inc., 1980.

Manwaring, Charles. *A Digest of Early Connecticut Probate Records.* vol. 1, 1635–1700. Baltimore: Geneological Publishing Company, Inc., 1904.

Public Acts of the State of Connecticut, 1836–1850.

Public Acts of the State of Connecticut, 1839–1843.

Public Statute Laws of the State of Connecticut. Hartford: S. G. Goodrich, 1821.

Public Statutes of the State of Connecticut, 1838.

Records of the Particular Court of Connecticut: 1639–1663. Hartford: Connecticut Historical Society, 1928.

Reeve, Tapping. *The Law of Baron and Femme, of Parent and Child, Guardian and Ward, Master and Servant . . .* New Haven: Oliver Steele, 1816.

Swift, Zephaniah. *A System of the Laws of the State of Connecticut,* vol. 1. Windham, CT: John Byrne, 1795.

Swift, Zephaniah. *A System of the Laws of the State of Connecticut,* vol. 2, Windham, CT: John Byrne, 1796.

The Code of 1650: A Compilation of Some of the First Laws in America. Hartford: Silas Andrus, 1830. reissued 1972.

Trumbull, J. Hammond, and Charles J. Hoadly, editors. *The Public Records of the Colony of Connecticut, 1636–1776.* 15 vols. Hartford: 1850–1890.

Diaries, Correspondence

Butterfield, L. H., editor. *Adams Family Correspondence.* New York: Atheneum, 1965.

Hempsted, Joshua. *The Diary of Joshua Hempsted of New London Connecticut, 1711–1758*. New London: New London County Historical Society, 1901.

Secondary Works

Andrews, Charles M. *The Colonial Period of American History.* Vol. II. New Haven: Yale University Press, 1936.

Aries, Philippe. *Centuries of Childhood: A Social History of Family Life*. New York: Vintage Books, 1962.

Barker, G. Stuart, editor. *Landmarks of Old Lyme*. Old Lyme, CT: Ladies' Library Association, 1968.

Beales, Ross W., Jr. "In Search of the Historical Child: Miniature Adulthood and Youth in Colonial New England." *American Quarterly,* 27. October, 1975.

_____. "The Child in Seventeenth-Century America." In Joseph M. Hawes and N. Ray Hiner, editors. *American Childhood: A Research Guide and Historical Handbook*. Westport, CT: Greenwood Press, 1985.

Beecher, Catharine E. and Harriet Beecher Stowe. *The American Woman's Home*. Boston: H. A. Brown, 1869.

Black, Hugh Campbell. *Black's Law Dictionary,* 6th edition. St. Paul, MN: West Publishing Company, 1990.

Bremer, Robert H., editor. *Children and Youth in America: A Documentary History.* Cambridge, MA: Harvard University Press, 1970–1974.

Brewer, Holly. "Age of Consent? Children, Testimony, and Consent in Early America." In Christopher Tomlins and Bruce H. Mann, editors, *The Many Legalities of Early America.* Chapel Hill, NC: University of North Carolina Press, 2001.

Brown, Barbara W., and James M. Rose. *Black Roots in Southeastern Connecticut.* Detroit, MI: Gail Research Company, 1980.

Calhoun, Arthur W. *A Social History of the American Family.* vol. 1. New York: Barnes & Noble, Inc., 1945.

Caulkins, Frances M. *A History of New London Connecticut.* Hartford, CT: The Press of Case, Tiffany, & Company, 1852.

Caulkins, Frances M. *A History of New London Connecticut.* New London, CT: H. D.Utley, 1895.

Child, Lydia Maria. *The Mother's Book*. New York: Arno Press, 1972. c1831.

Clarke, George Kuhn. *The History of Needham, Massachusetts, 1711–1922.* Cambridge, MA: Privately printed at University Press, 1912.

Cohen, Daniel. *Pillars of Salt, Monuments of Grace.* Oxford: Oxford University Press, 1993.

Cohen, Howard. *Equal Rights for Children.* Totowa, NY: Littlefield, Adams, & Company, 1980.

Dayton, Cornelia Hughes. *Women Before the Law: Gender, Law and Society in Connecticut: 1639–1789*. Chapel Hill, NC: University of North Carolina Press, 1995.

DeMause, Lloyd, editor. *The History of Childhood.* New York: Psychohistory Press, 1974.

Deming, Judson Keith. *Genealogy of John Deming*. Dubuque, IA: The Press of Mathis-Mets Co., 1904.

Demos, John P. "Developmental Perspectives on the History of Childhood," *Journal of Interdisciplinary History,* 2, no. 2. Autumn, 1971.

_____. *A Little Commonwealth: Family Life in Plymouth Colony.* New York: Oxford University Press, 1970.

Dexter, Franklin Bowditch. *Biographical Sketches of Yale College,* vol. 1, 1701–1745. New York: Henry Holt & Company, 1885.

Faber, Bernard. *Guardians of Virtue: Salem Families in 1800.* New York: Basic Books, 1972.

Forer, Lois. "Rights of Children: The Legal Vacuum." In Albert E. Wilkerson, Ed. *The Rights of Children: Emergent Concepts in Law and Society.* Philadelphia: Temple University Press, 1973.

Frost, William J. *Connecticut Education in the Revolutionary Era.* Chester, CT: Pequot Press, 1974.

Goodwin, Everett C. *The Magistracy Rediscovered: Connecticut, 1636–1818.* Ann Arbor, MI: UMI Research Press, 1981.

Greven, Philip J., Jr. *Child-Rearing Concepts, 1628–1861: Historical Sources.* Itasca, NY: F. E. Peacock Publishers, Inc., 1973.

Grossberg, Michael. *Governing the Hearth: Law and Family in Nineteenth-Century America.* Chapel Hill, NC: University of North Carolina Press, 1985.

Haskins, George Lee. *Law and Authority in Early Massachusetts: A Study in Tradition and Design.* New York: The Macmillan Company, 1960.

Hawes, Joseph M. *The Children's Rights Movement: A History of Advocacy and Protection.* Boston: Twayne Publishers, 1991.

Hay, Douglas et al. *Albion's Fatal Tree: Crime and Society in Eighteenth-Century England.* London: Pantheon Books, 1975.

Hirsch, Adam J. *The Rise of the Penitentiary: Prisons and Punishment in Early America.* Chelsea, MI: Bookcrafters, Inc., 1992.

n. a. *History of Middlesex, Connecticut.* New York: J. B. Beers & Company, 1884.

Jameson, Rev. E. O., editor. *History of Medway, Massachusetts, 1715–1885.* Medway, MA: J. A. Reed Publishers, 1886.

Keifer, Monica. *American Children Through Their Books, 1700–1835.* Philadelphia: University of Pennsylvania Press, 1970.

Kett, Joseph F. *Rites of Passage: Adolescence in America 1790 to the Present.* New York: Basic Books, 1977.

Loomis, Dwight and J. Gilbert Calhoun. *The Judicial and Civil History of Connecticut.* Boston: The Boston History Company, 1895.

Main, Jackson Turner. *Society and Economy in Colonial Connecticut.* Princeton, NJ: Princeton University Press, 1985.

Mann, Bruce H. *Neighbors and Strangers: Law and Community in Early Connecticut.* Chapel Hill, NC: University of North Carolina Press, 1987.

Miller, Perry, editor. *American Puritans: Their Prose and Poetry.* Garden City, NY: Anchor Books, 1965

Monroe, Will S. *The History of the Pestalozzian Movement in the United States.* Syracuse, NY: Arno Press, 1969. c1907.

Morgan, Edmund. *The Puritan Family: Religion and Domestic Relations in Seventeenth-Century New England.* New York: Harper & Row Publisher, Inc., 1966.

Morris, R. B. *Studies in the History of American Law*. New York: Octagon, 1974. c1930.

Mumford, Lewis. *The Culture of the Cities*. New York: Harcourt, Brace, and Company, 1938.

Phelps, Richard H. *Newgate of Connecticut*. Camden, ME: Picton Press, 1996.

Pollack, Linda. *Forgotten Children: Parent-Child Relations from 1500–1900*. Cambridge: Cambridge University Press, 1983.

Rothman, David J. *The Discovery of the Asylum: Social Order and Disorder in the New Republic*. Boston: Little, Brown, 1971.

______. "Documents in Search of a Historian: Toward a History of Childhood and Youth in America." *Journal of Interdisciplinary History, 2, no. 2*. Autumn 1971.

Rousseau, Jean Jacques. *Emile*. New York: Dutton, 1961.

Schulz, Constance B. "Children and Childhood in the Eighteenth Century." In *American Childhood: A Research Guide and Historical Handbook*. Westport, CT: Greenwood Press, 1985.

Silber, Kate. *Pestalozzi: The Man and His Work*. London: Routledge, 1960.

Slater, Peter Gregg. *Children in the New England Mind in Death and in Life*. Hamden, CT: Archon Books, 1977.

Smith, Joseph and Thomas G. Barnes. *The English Legal System: Carryover to the Colonies*. Los Angeles: W. A. Clark Memorial Library, University of California, 1973.

Squire, Walter William Thomas. *Charities and Correction In Connecticut*. New Haven, CT: Yale University Press, 1936.

Stansell, Christine. *City of Women: Sex and Class in New York*. New York: Alfred A. Knopf, 1986.

Stark, Bruce P. *Lyme, Connecticut: From Founding to Independence*. Self-published, 1976.

Sunley, Robert. "Early Nineteenth-Century American Literature on Child Rearing." In Margaret Mead and Martha Wolfenstein, editors. *Childhood in Contemporary Cultures*. Chicago: University of Chicago Press, 1955.

Trowbridge, Frances Bacon. *The Champion Genealogy*. New Haven, CT: printed for the author, 1891.

Van Dusen, Albert E. *Connecticut*. New York: Random House, 1961.

Weis, Frederick Lewis. *The Colonial Clergy and the Colonial Churches of New England*. Baltimore, MD: Genealogical Publishing, Inc., 1977, c1936.

Wishy, Bernard. *The Child and the Republic: The Dawn of Modern American Child Nurture*. Philadelphia: University of Pennsylvania Press, 1968.

Zuckerman, Michael. *Peaceable Kingdoms: New England Towns in the 18th Century*. New York: Alfred A. Knopf, 1970.

Unpublished Works

Butler, Eva. "Transcripts of New London Town Meetings," vol. I-X. 1662–1779.

Farrell, John Thomas. "The Administration of Justice in Connecticut." Ph.D. diss., Yale University, 1937.

James, May Hall. "Education and Schooling in Old Lyme, Connecticut." Ph.D. diss., Yale University, 1939.

Index

J

R

Y

Z

For Product Safety Concerns and Information please contact our EU
representative GPSR@taylorandfrancis.com
Taylor & Francis Verlag GmbH, Kaufingerstraße 24, 80331 München, Germany

www.ingramcontent.com/pod-product-compliance
Ingram Content Group UK Ltd.
Pitfield, Milton Keynes, MK11 3LW, UK
UKHW040623240926
475702UK00022B/8
9780415971805